D1600201

Japanese Carriers and Victory in the Pacific

Japanese Carriers and Victory in the Pacific

The Yamamoto Option

Martin Stansfeld

Pen & Sword

MARITIME

First published in Great Britain in 2021 by
Pen & Sword Maritime
An imprint of
Pen & Sword Books Ltd
Yorkshire – Philadelphia

ISBN 978 1 39901 011 5

Typeset by Mac Style
Printed and bound in the UK by CPI Group (UK) Ltd, Croydon,
CRO 4YY

Pen & Sword Books Limited incorporates the imprints of Atlas,
Archaeology, Aviation, Discovery, Family History, Fiction, History,
Maritime, Military, Military Classics, Politics, Select, Transport,
True Crime, Air World, Frontline Publishing, Leo Cooper, Remember
When, Seaforth Publishing, The Praetorian Press, Wharncliffe
Local History, Wharncliffe Transport, Wharncliffe True Crime
and White Owl.

For a complete list of Pen & Sword titles please contact

PEN & SWORD BOOKS LIMITED
47 Church Street, Barnsley, South Yorkshire, S70 2AS, England
E-mail: enquiries@pen-and-sword.co.uk
Website: www.pen-and-sword.co.uk

Or

PEN AND SWORD BOOKS
1950 Lawrence Rd, Havertown, PA 19083, USA
E-mail: Uspen-and-sword@casematepublishers.com
Website: www.penandswordbooks.com

Contents

Acknowledgements

Inspiration for the book is owed to Alan Clark's Diaries. Therein he reports being seated next to a very interesting American admiral at a dinner party. Among the topics that arose between them was what would be more scary for the world, a revival of the German panzer divisions that spearheaded the conquest of Europe from the Atlantic to the Volga or of the Japanese aircraft carrier fleet that covered their conquest of South East Asia. At the time in 1989 the celebrated diarist and historian was serving UK government as Margaret Thatcher's minister in charge of defence procurement. Essentially the book evolved into a study on the procurement of naval arms and the choices and alternatives available in the countdown to the Pacific War. I decided to explore the Yamamoto option, that of going all out developing naval aviation and consigning big gun ships to the scrapheap.

The reader is asked to excuse this as less a narrative history more a series of essays on aspects of the subject but with the historical progress of the Japanese, British and American carrier fleets in time sequence over the first three chapters. Only with the next four chapters do we depart from history and show what might have been achieved if Japan had succeeded in doubling its carrier fleet by Pearl Harbor time and sustaining that production.

I depended upon excellent secondary sources supplemented by delvings into the Internet. So my chief debt is to Amazon Books and to the Wikipedia. They saved visits to libraries. It would have been nice to have interviewed a few participants but alas by this remove they are barely with us still. The excellent secondary sources have in any case already mined that lode.

On the carriers of the three navies themselves there is a comprehensive source, Norman Polmar who cites Japan's naval aviation genius Minoru Genda as a collaborator. There is also David Brown, *Aircraft Carriers*. The main reference work on the Imperial Japanese Navy, always known as Watts and Gordon, is a great stand-by.

The Prologue relied entirely on internet surfing as I could not find any of the usual sources showing any interest in the *Mutsu* incident, even those websites that have thrown light on various neglected episodes of the Pacific War.

The first chapter of the book has for its theme the diplomacy of the the period between the world wars as it related to naval matters and to warmongerings. Here particularly useful among excellent secondary sources consulted was that excellent biography of Admiral Yamamoto by Hiroyuki Agawa, as it proved throughout the book. The opening chapters of *The Rising Sun, the Decline and Fall of the Japanese Empire* by John Toland whose wife was Japanese aroused my interest in the *gekokujo* phenomenon. And there was the incomparable *Old Friends, New Enemies* by Arthur Marder, a Japanese speaker. In particular Edward S. Miller on the financial siege of Japan gave a fresh perspective most intriguingly. Helpful for taking in a Japanese insight on the final days of peace was *Japan 1941* by Eri Hotta.

As for the second chapter, which traces the development of naval aviation in Japan, *Sunburst, the Rise of Japanese Naval Air Power by* Mark R.Peattie was invaluable as it has proved for so many. Agawa also proved useful. For the vignette on the Sempill Mission the internet told all, as it did sorting out the Japanese and American naval replenishment acts.

As explained in Chapter Three there is no book on the subject of the shadow fleet, just references in the prime secondary sources and these seldom accurate. But Watts and Gordon again came up trumps. An impeccable source on the liner conversions is an article by Hans Lengerer & Rehm-Takahara in the periodical *Warship (No IX)* on the liner conversions. Combined Fleet.Com website invaluably researched from Japanese sources the record of movements for many of these carriers. There is a standard work on escort carriers *Combustible, Vulnerable, Expendable* by David Wragg to which I am indebted.

Chapter Four is the cornerstone of the book as it shows how doubling or more the carrier fleet was possible. I call that 'phantom fleet', in contradistinction to shadow fleet which had been a historical reality. The measure of it was what the available launch facilities did historically produce, against what they could have done better! At first I considered the long game, that being to scour the official history of Japanese shipbuilding except it's written in Japanese and light years long. Following much scratching of the head I pinned down how a final answer depended upon Mitsubishi production at Nagasaki. I was about to persuade my Japanese-speaking nephew to visit Nagasaki duly briefed with contacts weaned from the internet, when inspiration struck that it did not matter. There was an entirely good enough answer in what Nagasaki did produce as is recorded in Watts and Gordon and other sources. They show all these liners that were converted into carriers. So you do not need to measure the actual length of the slipways, only go by what the yard historically launched as recorded in Watts and Gordon and earlier in Janes, as are the lengths of the warships, liners, or otherwise constructed there. Length is all. But it could be asked were these the only launch facilities long enough in Japan ? There I consulted the rival reference work (Jentschura et Al, *Warships of the Imperial Japanese Navy, 1869-1945*). Unlike Watts and Gordon they list many more naval auxiliaries and large ships taken out of trade. Anything shown over 10,000 tons displacement originated prior to the countdown years to war when yards were yet to be occupied with naval production. Vital for composing the outfitting tables was *Japanese Heavy Cruisers of the Pacific War* by Eric Lacroix and Linton Wells II. It shows when outfitting facilities became available for new construction following the modernisation of existing vessels.

Chapter Five returns to historical reality by examining the dimension of naval intelligence through a multiplicity of sources, a favourite having been *I Was There* (e.g. at Pearl Harbor when the raid happened), the story of the Pacific fleet's intelligence officer, Eddy Layton. Internet dredging played a big part, often trying to back hunches. Useful in this chapter as in many was *Kaigun: Strategy, Tactics, and Technology in the Imperial Japanese Navy, 1887-1941* by Mark Peattie and the late David Evans. Japanese speaker Arthur Marder provided gems again. I bought second hand editions of *Jane's Fighting Ships* from 1940 to 1945 to help chase the phoney paper record on so-called IJN pocket battleships. Willard Price's forgotten *Islands of Mystery* I found as a ten-year old in the library of my Scottish family home, a wartime purchase by my much travelled grandmother presumably. And talking of family, not to forget my mother's memory of partying on flagship *Nelson* at the 1937 Coronation naval review and meeting officers there from Japanese heavy cruiser *Ashigara*.

The two chapters that close the book give the strategic and tactical take on the altered circumstances of a jumbo-size IJN carrier fleet, where strategical factors alter history radically, but I adhere more or less to tactical outcomes, just their venue transposed by strategical realities. Here my mentor on strategy has been H.P.Wilmott's three volumes on the Pacific War and Churchill for the wider strategic picture. Unexpected sources are credited in the text, particularly in the matter of Hawaii invasion. Samuel Eliot Morison's *History of US Naval Operations in World War* II is the best read on actual battle history. Little has changed since to alter his story of the Guadalcanal campaign inclusive of the great Battle of Santa Cruz nor has his well told saga on the Battle of the Philippine Sea been overthrown only added to by later writers. Midway was a different matter. Here the new standard has been *Shattered Sword, the Untold Story of the Battle of Midway* by Jonathan Parshall and Anthony Tully and other more recent takes on the famous battle, including the Pen and Sword-published *Dauntless Victory* by Peter C. Smith, who interviewed many survivors in Japan. It includes an interesting take on 'Orient' Option. Rather late in the day for the author came Andrew Boyd's *Royal Navy in Eastern Waters: Lynchpin of Victory, 1935-1942* again published by a Pen and Sword imprint, which effectively has ended the Indian Ocean sphere's long neglect by scholarship. Aptly it is Morison who scores the last word, this time in the final chapter on the last battle. His gem was found lying hidden in a chapter on logistics in his Volume 8, a short passage on how the IJN should maybe have chased after less the carriers more their oil.

My debt has been to so many authors. For mine has been the need to feed an almost lifetime obsession with lost great causes, that of the IJN in particular starting with Christmas 1945 following a brief January appearance aged seven in the Battle of the Atlantic aboard the battleship *Nelson* with my elder brother Johnny and our beloved Nanny in the midst of a vast convoy stretching out to all horizons. The great ship had been repairing mine damage in New York and we were conducted to the captain's own cabin to take berth, he in wartime having to live in a cabin located in the bridge tower. That Christmas we unwrapped a model fleet of warships sent by our American uncle. Asked to make my selections I first chose the only two IJN battleships on offer, these because they had weird pagoda masts, that of the *Fuso* like a pack of cards that had been nudged from two directions. It all began from there, sustained by the birthday gift of the latest annual edition of *Janes*. An IJN model fleet in plasticine followed complete with exquisitely modelled pagoda masts. The interest returned periodically over the years as the books began to come out at long last. Morison's volumes opened the scholarly flood gates, before which journalistic rubbish mostly, like how the US Army Air Force won the Battle of Midway when it was US Navy dive bombers that wreaked all of the damage. It was maybe honourably *LIFE* Magazine in the 1950s that finally put the record straight forever on that score.

Finally my thanks to the two friends who egged me on when I put pen to paper, fans of the book both, namely fellow historian Rupert Katritzky and my wife Monica originally of Ohio. I described to them how us two war babies and our nanny were ferried across from the *Nelson* by a tug boat to Portsmouth naval base to view a scene of desolation, before taking a train to re-join our mother's open arms. Hitler's bombers had rendered the city into a sea of rubble. This had been our homecoming – to view the horrors of war, next the value of family. As it must have been for Japanese re-patriated from overseas garrisons after the war typically from the undying fortress of Rabaul as part transported home on Japan's last big aircraft carrier, *Katsuragi*.

Martin Stansfeld

Prologue: 'The Mutsu Incident'

The explosion came shortly after noon on a foggy June day in 1943 at the fleet anchorage off Hashirajima Island in Japan's Inland Sea. It was heard as a dull thud in communities around Hiroshima Bay. Close by, some thought a volcano had blown its top. Mountains shrouded the boom from nearby Kure Naval Arsenal and the Etajima Naval Academy tucked away in coves by the near end of the bay. Approaching the anchorage surged the battleship *Nagato*, erstwhile flagship of the Combined Fleet. From its bridge was sighted a white flash in the mist. Minutes later, a radio call came in from the anchorage: '*Mutsu* just blew up!'

The transmission came from the captain of the battleship *Fuso*, which was moored to a buoy 1,000 yards away from the incident. *Mutsu* was seen to jack-knife, the front end immediately capsizing to starboard as far as its tall pagoda mast would allow in the shallow water. The shorter rear end bobbed up to the perpendicular before sinking more slowly. The *Fuso*'s captain ordered rescue boats away. Of 1,474 men aboard the *Mutsu*, only 353 survived, and a mere thirteen of the 153 flying cadets and their instructors visiting on a familiarization mission.

Nixed from Japan's order of battle was one of only two battleships with 16-inch guns. They had been the pride of the Japanese Navy in the pre-war years, the mighty sisters *Nagato* and *Mutsu* alternating as flagships of the Combined Fleet. The only other 16-inchers of their day were HMS *Nelson* and *Rodney* of the Royal Navy and the three-ship *Colorado*-class of the US Navy. All seven were built between the last years of the First World War and the 1922 Washington naval disarmament treaty.

Gone with it was a major segment of the next crop of Navy fliers, and also vital instructors who could train future drafts. The battleship was a peek back into the past, the fliers were to become the weather that blew; they were a look into the future.

The irony for those aboard the *Fuso* must have been how *Mutsu* had just returned from war operations in the South Pacific. It alone of the pre-war dreadnoughts had entered a combat zone. The other five spent so much of the war in the Inland Sea that they were disparaged as the 'Hashirajima Fleet'.

What had happened was that the magazine of C-turret (the inner of a stern pair) exploded with such force that the contiguous structure disintegrated and the ship broke in half. There have ensued many post-mortems, the enquiry at the time being conducted most secretively. Was it an Allied submarine, the Japanese asked themselves, or did the new anti-aircraft incendiary projectiles for the big guns somehow manage to cook off inside the magazine?

A more recent investigation has suggested a failure to renew all the original wiring during a massive 'makeover' lasting from September 1934 to January 1935. Much of the original wiring dated from the ship's construction between 1918 and 1921. This theory gained sustenance from eyewitness reports of smoke seen rising from a location just forward of the turret where the aircraft scouts were launched. Could this fire have so heated the interior of the turret as to set off the highly volatile black powder primers, they pondered? On battleships, bags of black powder are used to fire the projectiles. But they are notoriously sensitive and so are invariably stored in a separate magazine, not just left lying around!

The Japanese board of inquiry tried to pass off the incident as an act of sabotage by a suicidal seaman under investigation for theft. His post was inside the turret. That outcome may well have inspired the US Navy to propose a similar verdict following the inquiry into a turret explosion on board USS *Iowa* during peacetime exercises off Puerto Rico in April 1989.

The *Iowa* was the name ship of the class of German *Bismarck*-size battleships that began joining the US fleet in 1943. It included the *Missouri* and the *New Jersey*. The explosion occurred in B-turret, the same location for the blowing up of the *Arizona* at Pearl Harbor. The difference was that compartmentation was far more advanced for these Second World War battleships than it had been for First World War-era dreadnoughts such as *Arizona*. The *Iowa* survived, but the press took poorly to the attempt to blame a disgruntled crewman who could not answer back from the land of the dead. The *Iowa* inquiry began anew, and this subsequent inquest drew attention to lapses in following safety regulations. The US Navy then apologized to the sailor's family.

The *Mutsu* accident happened during wartime on 8 June 1943. There followed an immense cover-up so as not to lower the morale of the fighting forces, particularly as many young crewmen serving on Japanese Navy ships had been the schoolchildren who helped fund the *Mutsu*'s construction as part of a government-led educational programme. Also taken into consideration was what the general public would think of a loss in such ignominious circumstances.

But what if the incident had occurred in early 1936 instead? It could have done. In January of that year, *Mutsu* rejoined the fleet after a rebuild lasting sixteen months. The old wiring was there, the black powder bags came and went, and there could even have been a disgruntled suicidal seaman at large in the turret. More worryingly, there may have been personnel still unsure of safety procedures so soon after the recommissioning. It takes time to 'shake down', the naval expression for bringing a ship to combat operational capability.

Are we stretching credulity here? Far from it. Battleship turret explosions may not have been common, but they occurred in most navies, and no less in peacetime than in wartime, not least with the US Navy. The *Mississippi* twice suffered turret explosions – once on peacetime exercises in 1924 and the other occasion while bombarding the Gilbert Islands in 1943. In both cases, the ship survived, as had the *Iowa*, unlike in the *Mutsu* case where the magazine held a full complement of 240 shells undepleted by firings. Black powder explosions do not always touch off the ordnance in the magazines.

During the course of the First World War, dreadnoughts were lost in port to internal explosions in five cases involving four different navies. Japan itself had lost one of the pair of dreadnoughts to join its navy before the Great War: *Kawachi* underwent a magazine explosion that sank it and killed 600 men exactly one month after *Mutsu*'s keel was laid down on 1 June 1918.

In 1916, the Italians lost the *Leonardo da Vinci*, one of a class of three dreadnoughts (the remaining two were rebuilt to serve in the Second World War, one being sunk in the 1940 raid on Taranto by Royal Navy aircraft carrier HMS *Illustrious*). In the same year, the Russians lost the *Imperatritsa Marya* to an explosion at Sevastopol.

Britain lost HMS *Bulwark* in 1914, and then the *Vanguard* in 1917 at Scapa Flow after what was thought to have been the spontaneous explosion of cordite. Out of a crew of 825 men on HMS *Vanguard*, only three were rescued after a series of magazine explosions. This must have been the worst internal explosion incident of them all. Curiously in view of this horror, *Vanguard* was the name selected for the last British battleship ever to be completed, just after the end of the war.

More dreadnoughts were lost during the First World War to internal explosions in port than in actual combat with the enemy at sea. In combat, the heavily armoured dreadnoughts rather lived up to their name. It was the pre-dreadnoughts, armoured cruisers and battle cruisers that tended to be lost in battle due to being more thin-skinned. The manner of their departure was usually to blow up when a magazine was penetrated.

So why build bigger and better new big-gun ships at ferocious expense if they were going to go 'pop' on the taxpayer everywhere? It was not as if Lloyds was insuring them, though imagine the premiums if they were! More humanly, how could they explain the loss of *Mutsu* to the whole generation of schoolchildren who contributed to its construction?

In early 1936, such an accident would have occurred at a most sensitive moment in naval history, as a whole new generation of battleships were being planned; super-battleships indeed. Arguably, the first political casualty likely to have been impacted would have been the dominant clique in the pre-war Imperial Japanese Navy (IJN), colloquially the 'Teppo Yaya', or big-gun lobby, whose dream it was to build the super-battleships *Yamato* and *Musashi*.

The dream was sustained corporately, institutionally; so many naval careers had been invested in gunnery specialization, because it had become the well-trodden path to the top ranks of the IJN. Very few, in contrast, had gained aviation experience. But what the airmen lacked in status they made up for in lip. One can imagine the gunners expostulating, 'Here are these impudent upstarts of the fancy flier ilk trying to tell us we are all redundant. How dare they, how dare they, how dare they! Anyone know what the Emperor thinks? Let us go to him, in order to have these charlatans put in their place smartly!'

As for Emperor Hirohito, in 1936 he might – under the shock of losing his *Mutsu* – take special pains to seek widely for advice through his councillors. Some might urge, 'If it is new ideas the Emperor wants to hear, then let him meet the new Navy Vice Minister in the Government.' Such was one Isoroku Yamamoto, recently head of the Aeronautical Department and commander of the 1st Carrier Division. This fast-rising star of the fleet much regretted leaving that position; as top navy aviation leader, he felt he had achieved much progress in this field and wanted to take potential world-beating developments further. All these milestones Yamamoto relates in the Imperial presence and predicts all manner of aerial marvels to come.

Yamamoto summarizes to the Emperor the points he has wearied of making in senior circles of the IJN:

First, are not even some of the Teppo Yaya willing to concede how one day, naval aviation may supplant the big-gun battle-line?

It takes over five years to decide blueprints, prepare a navy yard and then lay down, launch and complete a super-battleship. In the interim, naval aviation technology will have advanced to the tipping point and production started of the revolutionary new aircraft models.

Meantime, consider how there are already carrier designs ready to roll, and large carriers only occupy the stocks for two years; less with standardization.

Does the Emperor know how Japan already enjoys carrier equality with the US? Why not aspire to outright, even overwhelming superiority, and keep the peace that way?

While it has to be admitted that carriers are very vulnerable ships, isn't there such a thing as safety in large numbers? Japan had slipways suitable for building simultaneously eleven carriers of assorted sizes, whereas only *two* of the four yards traditionally used to build battleships were presently suited for the super-battleships being proposed.

Building these carriers is therefore submitted as a chance to run ahead of the game, instead of constantly trying to catch up.

Finally, carriers do not blow up spontaneously as battleships have a notorious habit of doing.

(We append a historical reflection on that last point, in that there has never been a case of a fleet carrier being sunk in an accident. Being highly combustible, there were bad fires, such as with the *Bennington* a long time after the war, but repairs were made.)

Down at the Navy Club, usually over-confident voices are stilled in shock at the shame of letting the Emperor down over the '*Mutsu* Incident'.

They are quite put off their stride. Their ears more willingly hark to the rarely heard 'voice of the crane' – a traditional and respectful term for the allusive diction of the Emperor as spoken in a shrill archaic Court dialect in formal audience. It ordains them all please to think afresh and strive hard for the new. The Emperor closes discussion with his plea: 'May there auspiciously flock from the north great autumn migrations of geese over many years to come.'

The poetic symbolism was clear to all. Mutsu is the name of an ancient province of Japan at the extreme northern end of the main home island of Honshu, in sight of Hokkaido, the smaller northern island. The battleship *Mutsu* was now dead, but may the spirit of those who died flock south in the form of aviators as numerous as the autumnal geese.

For this migration, they can look forward to what was already on the drawing boards, such as the Zero fighters, Val dive-bombers and Kate torpedo-bombers, that were the real-time vehicles of the carrier aircrews of 1942 and the nemesis-to-be of Pearl Harbor.

Yamamoto had made his mark. He had killed the *Yamato* and *Musashi* on the eve of their conception. In their place would proliferate great aircraft carriers with names like 'Soaring Crane' and 'Auspicious Crane', in Japanese the *Shokaku* and *Zuikaku*.

* * *

With the *Mutsu* tale now told, we can move on to the chapters in which our theme unfolds. We compare historical reality to what could have been in a series of stories, each a chapter.

First, how the arms race for most of the interwar era was contained by the Washington Treaty in the case of naval armaments until the political pressures caused by the rise of fascism burst the curbs on national ambition. It was quietly during those years that, internationally, aircraft carriers rose to the status of capital ships. Their design developed from conversions of battle cruisers to keel-up designs that aimed to maximize the number of aircraft carried, but with the high ship speed the better to launch them, and not neglecting at least minimal protection.

Secondly, we address how over the same period prior to the Pacific War, naval aircraft were perfected into ship-killing instruments, particularly under the aegis of Admiral Yamamoto in Japan.

Thirdly, we tell the untold and real-time story of what historians have been ready to call Japan's Shadow Fleet; how in an effort to outpace American carrier production, the Imperial Japanese Navy secretly conspired to see built seventeen passenger liners and fast naval auxiliaries specially designed for quick conversion into aircraft carriers.

Fourthly, we present an alternative story: what if Yamamoto had won the great 1936 'Big Guns versus Naval Aviation' debate, and keel-up purpose-built fleet carriers in assorted sizes were laid down on all launch facilities long enough, instead of super-battleships, heavy cruisers and liners. We call this alternative armada the Phantom Fleet. With fleet carriers, speed is all. At 34 knots heading into the wind gives heavily laden torpedo-bombers the lift-off they need without a boost from catapults.

Fifthly, we present the intelligence picture: how Japan 'got away with' its super-battleships, its Shadow Fleet and much else thanks to tight security and disinformation. So why not also with the Phantom Fleet?

Sixthly, we explore denouements: how might our Phantom Fleet have changed Second World War strategies and modified or delayed its outcome?

Finally, we present 'the mother of all naval battles', when a long-delayed confrontation sees the two sides fairly evenly matched at last in a titanic contest in the waters each side of the Marianas chain of islands, whence the atom bombers historically sortied.

Minoru Genda.

Chapter 1

Treaty Fleets

'The American Immigration Act of 1924 excluded Japanese completely from entering the United States. If Japan had been given a quota like other nations, only 150 to 200 persons could have been admitted annually, a mere drop in the bucket; and Japan demanded no more, since that would have placed her on the same basis as "white" nations. But this absolute exclusion, placing Japan in the same category as other orientals, deeply offended her national pride, built up bitter hatred, and discredited the liberal policy of co-operating with the Western Powers.'
(Samuel Eliot Morison, *The Rising Sun in the Pacific*)

Japan's path to great-power status was accomplished within the span of a lifetime. A 10-year old in the shogun's capital in the late 1860s puttered around a city little changed from *The Hundred Views of Edo*, the celebrated series of woodblock prints by Hiroshige that had been executed in his father's day, and showing a Japan little changed since 1600.

His grandfather would have regaled him with stories of a Japan where foreigners had been forbidden for over 200 years and society had been caught in a feudal time warp. That is until the great lords of the south west – those of Choshu, Satsuma and Tosa provinces – conspired to overthrow the shogunate government in the eastern capital and substitute direct rule by a fledgling Emperor hitherto secluded and powerless in the old Imperial capital of Kyoto in western Japan.

Strolling from the subject of one Hiroshige print into another, he might find himself in Kanda district on Boy's Day, entranced by a sky fluttering with gaily coloured kites in the form of carp swimming in the breezes. On his way home, we can imagine him caught in a downpour on the Ohashi bridge, or back home intently enjoying the family album containing *The Fifty-Three Stations of the Tokaido*, the great eastern road portrayed by Hiroshige in as many prints. The road connected Edo (modern Tokyo) with Kyoto, and today has coursing above much of its ancient way the rail ducts of the Shinkansen, the famous bullet train.

As a teenager, he would have found himself in a turbulent, changing world, such as that portrayed in the movie *The Last Samurai*. Westerners were moving in. Railways and telegraph poles had begun to spread. Old Japan reacted unsurely. Equilibrium was in due course to take root and mature as old settled in with new.

Let us say that he was drawn to a career in the new Imperial Navy. His heart would have pounded with pride over the thrill of Japan's victories over continental Goliaths, first over China (1894–1895) and then against mighty Russia (1904–1905), as a result becoming a great power of the world rather than succumbing to the usual fate of the non-European world in the nineteenth century, which was to become a colony of the 'white' imperialists.

At the heart of this unexpected status, and indeed the acclaimed symbol of it, was the 1902 Anglo-Japanese Alliance. This marked the first time since Napoleonic days the British Empire had deigned to ally itself formally with another nation. Japan had indeed signed into the *Pax Britannica* as junior partner. Following on from this, Britain supplied Japan with its battleships and armoured cruisers. These annihilated the Russian fleet at the Battle of Tsushima in 1905, a few months short of the centenary of Nelson's victory over the French and Spanish fleets off Cape Trafalgar, which had been the birth date of the *Pax Britannica*. Britain became godfather to the Imperial Japanese Navy. In turn the IJN revered Nelson as the greatest all-time naval hero and its inspiration, until a living legend grew with their own Admiral Togo after the victory at Tsushima.

Thanks to the Anglo-Japanese Alliance, Japan joined Britain against the Kaiser in the Great War. The windfall was Germany's Pacific empire, consisting of what the Japanese were to call the *Nanyo* (or South Seas territories) but the Americans and British called Micronesia. The League of Nations later granted Japan a mandate over these many archipelagos, after which this Central Pacific constellation became referred to colloquially as 'The Mandates'.

Japan's First World War achievements, however, did not at all suit America, who found the jugular to its Philippines dependency and to trade with China flanked by the *Nanyo*'s westward and northward extensions, and finally bracketed by the north–south chain of the Marianas and the

Yap and Palau island groups to their south. It had not mattered when Germany had the islands, because the Kaiser was at the other end of the world. But now there was a big difference – Japan, with the third largest fleet in the world, was vying for mastery in the western Pacific. 'Tea clipper Yankees' were turning in their graves, as New England's romance with the allure of China, the market of hundreds of millions, had this unwelcome shudder cross the room. Mega-Wasps (White Anglo-Saxon Protestants) confabulating at their country clubs over bourbon and branch water waxed indignant at what they saw as Japan's arrogant groping towards various appendages and orifices of China.

Alarmingly, Japan also ended its participation in the war by occupying the Soviet Far East deep into Siberia. It was the last of the intervening Allied Powers to evacuate after the Reds defeated the Whites in the Russian Civil War that followed the Communist revolution in 1917.

By 1921, there was much in what a Navy man close to retirement had experienced that would make him proud to be Japanese.

Such a man was Tomisaburo Kato. Born in 1861 in Hiroshima, Kato was the son of a samurai. He joined the new Naval Academy, graduating in 1880, and later also the Staff College in 1889. Aged 44, he became Chief of Staff to Admiral Togo. Aboard the flagship *Mikasa*, they led the fleet against the Russians at Tsushima. There followed after the war's end various appointments, first as Navy Vice Minister and from 1915–1922, Navy Minister successively in three governments. As such, he led the Japanese delegation to the Washington Conference on naval disarmament, becoming Prime Minister on his return. By dying in office a week before the cataclysmic Tokyo Earthquake of 1923, the very distinguished old gentleman, by now a viscount of the realm, was spared the irritation of the two decades of vulgar reaction that led to war and then to the shame of conquest following the nuclear bombing of the city of his birth.

A portrait of Kato in full admiral's uniform shows a figure bearing lightly a gravitas that clocked in as a heavyweight in the councils of the great. The face is austere and poise is reserved, but there is the hint of a twinkle in the eyes. As was the British-led tradition of the Naval Academy, he had been groomed to be an 'officer and gentleman' eligible to walk in as a guest at any London club. Asked if gentlemen should sneakily read other gentlemen's mail, one can imagine him disdaining to answer. Unfortunately for his delegation in Washington, theirs was being read by his American hosts, as shall regretfully be revealed.

When the Armistice came in November 1918, the raucous music of war ceased amidst the reeking ruins and everybody sought a big-power chair in shaping the world that was to follow. There were to be no chairs at the Conference of Versailles for the losers – Germany, Austria and indeed, by virtue of its revolution, Russia.

By the yardstick of naval power, Japan had superseded Germany and Russia. Italy no longer found itself competing with an Austrian navy. France and Italy were in balance. The biggest change in fortune was one that amply belaurelled a triumphant America, to whose industry victory had so much been owed. In the course of the conflict and its aftermath, the US Navy began growing to a size matching Britain's in fleet power.

On the other hand, not at all to US liking was how Japan, across the Pacific, had become the third greatest naval power. Washington reacted by doing two things. First, a naval disarmament conference was proposed in Washington to end the arms race in ever-bigger new battleships. Secondly, Britannia was politely nudged – could she please seek divorce from the Mikado?

It was time to gently prod the 'big stick', to use the pre-war expression favoured by President Teddy Roosevelt, who was an advocate of naval expansion as the means to waging gunboat diplomacy.

This put Britain in a pretty spot. Why abandon a successful alliance that had ably patched up the *Pax Britannica* just to please these bumptious ex-Colonies? On the other hand, there were those who argued that for the Royal Navy to be able to continue ruling the waves, the Japanese might not be enough help now that Uncle Sam was clearly destined for that role in due course. So why not join one's fellow Anglo-Saxons? One could not now beat them; the days of fighting them were long over. As for the Japanese, hadn't one politely guided so many little people to the exit before; wasn't one still that 'perfidious Albion' so deplored in Napoleon's famous phrase?

The government mandarins won the day. The Royal Navy lost its great ally. Japanese pride was the loser; the Emperor could no longer aspire to membership of White's Club on Pall Mall. He was back to wherever it was 'the yellow men' clubbed.

Miserably, the jilt coincided with mounting racism. In Australia and on the western seaboard of the United States, there was agitation against Japanese immigration. On the heels of the reaction came demeaning acts of exclusion by contemptible politicians. Things written in the press were innocent of prophesy in terms of late twentieth-century political correctness.

A supremely sensitive nation riding the crest of a tremendous pride had suddenly been thrown into the rubbish bin by this Britannia, the lady who thought she ruled the waves.

Well, the samurai might have to see about that, given half a chance – as happened all too soon. It came with the world-shaking conquest of Malaya and fall of Singapore to General Tomoyuki Yamashita's three divisions twenty years later. He was executed for his alleged sins after the war, but the kittens of the 'Tiger of Malaya' lived to see the sun set on the British Empire.

The legacy of the Washington Conference was that the early-century embrace of Anglo-Saxonry all too soon turned to vicious bile during the 1930s as it fanned a quasi-brand of fascism.

The loss of face particularly poisoning the well of good will in the 1920s had been how Japan had been forced by the Treaty to genuflect to a humiliating ratio in battleships. Britain and America awarded themselves equal status, but insisted the non-European nation accept a 60 per cent battleship fleet size of either Anglo-Saxon power.

Kato accepted the imbalance for sound arguments of the head rather than overly heeding his heart. His central point was geographic. Japan was concerned with repelling an attack on its home islands and some contiguous possessions. America, meanwhile, was well known to have oceans on each side of its 'Lower Forty-Eight' (the US states minus Alaska and Hawaii); to fight Japan effectively, it would be forced to bring the Atlantic Fleet through the Panama Canal into the Pacific in order to reinforce the Pacific Fleet. That would run the risk of leaving its eastern seaboard bereft of naval protection. The combined fleets must next aspire to fight their way across the world's largest ocean. Kato was thus particularly reassured when America and Britain agreed to develop no naval base closer to Japan than Pearl Harbor in America's case and Singapore in Britain's. Japan could now view itself as safe – at least in the age of steam and the big gun.

The British Empire was far more extended than Japan. For London, the Far East lay on the other side of the world. The august Kato felt that a '60 per cent battleship fleet' was more than adequate in these circumstances, and a small price to pay for ending an arms race that could lead to social revolution in Japan if the burden of it continued. This was an elder statesman's style of approach to the problem, and there were many who applauded it, who became known as the 'treaty faction'. They were opposed by a vociferous majority called the 'fleet faction', led by a naval adviser at the negotiations – another Kato, although no relation. This was Kanji Kato. The row between the factions was to rumble on and on. The death of Tomisaburo Kato within a year of the Treaty being signed rather left the floor to Kanji Kato and his confreres. However, the debate became better balanced with the rise in influence of Yamamoto and other stars of the 'treaty faction' in the 1930s.

For the 'fleet faction', it all reached fury point over what was called the Black Chamber Incident a few years later, when a book by America's former cryptology chief revealed that his unit, colloquially 'the Black Chamber', had deciphered the coded diplomatic cables between Kato's delegation and Tokyo. Washington thereby had foreknowledge that Kato was ready to accept 60 per cent in battleships. They could expect to be robust in rejecting demands for a higher rate without risk of the Conference falling apart. No doubt there had been a quiet whisper into the ear of the British delegation chief, thereby making his nation a partner in the humiliation of Japan. The Black Chamber had won a victory comparable to that of Midway twenty years later.

When the likes of the bug-eyed Kanji Kato realized this sneaky betrayal of his nation by its perfidious Anglo-Saxon 'friends', there was thereafter scant respect for the restrictions of the Treaty. Imaginations sought ways to offset the limitations. An iron determination settled in to make sure that in war, America's battle line would be whittled down by 40 per cent or more as it waddled past the island constellations of the *Nanyo* on the southern flank of its advance before encountering the IJN's battleships close to Japanese home waters. If quantitative parity was to be denied the nation, then qualitative superiority and the advantages of a fortuitous geography could instead prove equalizers.

Central to this strategy would be the torpedo, whether delivered by air or by surface ship or submarine: Japan must have the best torpedoes in the world and the best weapon platforms for their delivery. These developments we shall relate in due course.

In the case of battleships, there is a beginning and end to the story, but no middle, as for the fifteen years that Japan abided by the naval disarmament treaties, it laid down no battleships. Nor could anyone else do more than complete those that had been agreed and then make do with them. In contrast, Japan did more than 'make do'; it performed what interior designers call 'makeovers'; it rebuilt and re-engined its battle fleet.

Aspiring to a qualitative edge very much guided IJN thinking even before the Washington Treaty. The *Fuso* was briefly the most powerful battleship in the world when completed in 1915, and was followed by three more bearing twelve 14-inch guns. The five Queen Elizabeth-class dreadnoughts produced by Britain bore eight 15-inch guns and were the first to be oil-fuelled for higher speed. Japan took due note and went to eight 16-inch guns with the *Nagato* and *Mutsu*. The *Nagato* became the first 16-incher in the world. Britain followed suit with HMS *Nelson* and *Rodney*, and America with the USS *Colorado*, *Maryland* and *West Virginia*.

Kato's heart and head had been in what was called the 'Eight-Eight Project', although privately he was latterly of the view that the programme was beyond the resources of Japan. This called for eight battleships (inclusive of the *Nagato* and *Mutsu)* and eight battlecruisers. Inevitably, the Americans reciprocated. Japan's response in its 1922 programme was a plan 'to go 18-inch on them', rather as Churchill at the Admiralty with his Queen Elizabeths had 'gone 15-inch' on the Kaiser. Such a gun had been tested in Japan and not found wanting, but with the signing of the Washington Treaty, Japan's super-gunned super-battleship concept became a daydream deferred.

The Treaty permitted 16-inchers if they were in the works. Work on *Mutsu* was permitted to go ahead; *Nagato* was already kicking about.

There was, however, much excitement in post-war international naval circles about aircraft carriers, and the negotiators sought to limit these too.

The Interwar Years and the Treaty Quota on Carriers

An irony was that in no navy at the time of the Washington Treaty in 1921/1922 did there yet exist any aircraft carrier designed and built from the keel up as such a vessel. The British were very much in the lead in terms of this new dimension to naval warfare. They had converted the light battlecruiser *Furious*, and a liner as the *Argus*, and were converting a battleship they had been building for Chile but requisitioned and called HMS *Eagle*. A small keel-up carrier, *Hermes*, had been laid down, but its completion had been delayed, such that the Japanese *Hosho* became in 1922 the first keel-up carrier in the world shortly after the Treaty was signed. The *Hosho* thus became the much-talked-about darling of the Japanese fleet.

Japan argued hard in Washington for parity in aircraft carriers, but was denied it by Britain and America. The IJN estimated their needs as three large carriers, which was not satisfied with the proposed quota of 48,000 tons, given that they reckoned each carrier at 35,000. They duly scaled back to 27,000 tons for each carrier. Their expressed needs were obliged with a new quota duly set at 81,000 tons (i.e. 27,000 tons x 3) in return for dropping their parity demand, which had the effect of raising Britain and America to 135,000 tons, which both at the time felt was in excess of their needs. There was then a good chance for Japan to anticipate in practice a proportion of carrier strength closer to parity, provided the Anglo-Saxon powers refrained from building up to their quota.

A side aspect of the agreement was that the three main parties became entitled to a pair of carriers at 33,000 tons maximum (but within the overall tonnage quota), if they so wished. This became persuasive economically in the context of what to do with all the taxpayers' money lavished on unfinished super-battleships now impossible to complete as such.

This way, two super-battlecruisers on the stocks in America were recycled into the super-carriers *Saratoga* and *Lexington*. These were for a long time the two most energetically engined ships in the world and capable of carrying a highly mobile air force into war all by themselves. But between the two of them, a little less than half the Treaty displacement tonnage quota had been used up.

In Japan, the same thinking sought to save two of the super-battlecruisers on the stocks, the *Akagi* underway at Kure Navy Arsenal and *Amagi* at Yokosuka Navy Arsenal in Tokyo Bay. The Great Kanto Earthquake of 1923, possibly the most destructive on record in terms of human impact, wrecked the *Amagi*'s keel. The response was to substitute it with the *Kaga*, a super-battleship already launched at the Kawasaki Yard in Kobe. In due course, it was towed to Yokosuka for conversion.

Thereby, consideration for the taxpayer had vaulted the aircraft carrier into *faux* capital ship status, due to the *Saratoga* and *Akagi*.

Hitherto, naval theory had been content to see carriers as a possible substitute for cruisers as the 'eyes of the fleet', projectors of long-range reconnaissance. Hence the cruiser sizes of the *Hermes* and *Hosho*.

Akagi and *Kaga* were declared at about 27,000 tons each, although clearly way over. There was some slight embarrassment over this, it seems, at the IJN, as the next initiative was what can only be described as a pocket carrier, the *Ryujo*.

Two things seem to have occasioned this aberration: first, the scouting role concept; and second, treaty limitation. As laid down, the *Ryujo* was to be below the standard tonnage displacement of 10,000 tons agreed as the downward limit on aircraft carriers (actually devised as the line in the sand between capital ship and any other warship). Before it was completed came the 1930 London naval limitation treaty, which was prompted by an arms race in heavy cruisers. *Ryujo* came out in the washing to find itself in the IJN carrier quota after all.

What had incited its design had been reports that America was at work on 'flight-decked cruisers' and a misunderstanding of what role these would play, which logically would have been providing more versatile patrolling and protecting of trade routes. These Japan had no ambitions to imperil, although an irony in the case of the *Ryujo* is that it was the only carrier that the IJN ever sent on a commerce raid. This was into the Bay of Bengal in April 1942, while the main carrier fleet was raiding naval bases on Ceylon.

The other persuasion favouring pocket carriers as a means of filling the 81,000-ton quota stemmed from the awareness of the carrier as a target vulnerable to attack from hostile air strikes. That argued for safety in numbers; the more flight decks to hit and the more they were dispersed, the better the carrier forces could survive as air umbrella over the battle fleet. It was better that the enemy knock out a light carrier than smash the mighty *Kaga* or *Akagi*.

After *Ryujo*, the IJN found themselves looking at an unused balance on their aircraft carrier quota amounting to 20,100 tons. The vulnerability argument called for building two light carriers out of that rather than one large fleet carrier. Accordingly, the *Soryu* and *Hiryu* were both ordered under the 1934 fleet replacement programme. They were glibly declared officially at 10,050 tons each, and everybody believed it, even long after they were sunk. Each was written off internationally as a light carrier, each another *Ryujo* in effect, and thus 'pocket carriers'. That, however, was not at all the case. It is a theme we return to in Chapter 5, but suffice to say here that the pair were actually medium-size fleet carriers of the same ilk as the American USS *Ranger* and *Wasp*, the *Soryu* at 15,900 tons and the larger *Hiryu* at 17,300 tons. A very high speed helped by cruiser-style lines and minimal protection, and the provision of three elevators to aid in spotting strikes on deck, enabled these carriers to field a large air group despite their medium size. They became the favoured model for subsequent in-war production.

We now turn to how the US and Britain were faring in meeting their carrier quotas.

As already stated, America in the late 1920s could rejoice in the incomparable *Saratoga* and *Lexington*. There was also a light fleet carrier, the *Langley*, which was later demoted to a lesser role not subject to limitations.

There then ensued America's first effort at designing and completing a keel-up aircraft carrier, the *Ranger*. It was not a success, but from the mistakes emerged USS *Yorktown* and *Enterprise* contemporaneously with *Soryu* and *Hiryu* in Japan and HMS *Ark Royal* in Britain. With these three designs, each major naval power came to achieve a model which could confidently be adapted through subsequent classes of carrier.

America found after the *Enterprise* and *Yorktown* that any quota left over was insufficient for a third Yorktown-class but ample for another *Ranger*-size carrier, and accordingly built the *Wasp*.

The Royal Navy in contrast found itself sailing through most of the interwar period with more flight decks and closer to quota than anybody else. Their answer to America's *Saratoga* and Japan's *Akagi* conversions was conversion of three light battlecruisers. The trio aggregated a near equivalent in aircraft strength to the American and Japanese pairs, although of smaller size. HMS *Furious* had already served in the Great War's late stages as a part-way conversion that later 'went all the way'. Her sisters, the *Glorious* and *Courageous*, were converted in the 1920s. Then, contemporaneously with the Japanese *Soryu* and the American *Yorktown*, Britain brought the soon-to-be-famous *Ark Royal* into play by the eve of the European war.

Pre-war, two decisive moves were set afoot in Britain. The first was to sack the Royal Air Force as provider of naval aviation to the Royal Navy. The original naval air service had been dissolved after the Great War in favour of a single air service for all. This ill-fated association with the RAF might well be judged the most disastrous step ever taken by the 'Ruler of the Waves' in the sense that Britannia lost that role from being incapable of fielding a competitive carrier fleet. Prize colonial possessions fell for lack of the means of sustaining them in the fight, and with them there vanished international respect.

The second move was to lay down the four-ship Illustrious-class, which came on stream in 1940 and 1941, or between Dunkirk and Pearl Harbor, very handily for the war against Hitler and Mussolini. These were ideal for operations in the confined waters of the Mediterranean and North Sea, where land-based air attack could be expected. This was because uniquely at that time, they had armoured flight decks. Regrettably, that made them close to useless for fighting the Japanese, as the weight of the armoured flight deck would render them top heavy unless limited to a single hanger deck, thereby halving the number of aircraft carried.

They needed to be teamed with the larger air groups of US carriers, as happened when HMS *Victorious* briefly joined the *Saratoga* in the south-west Pacific in the spring of 1943. The result was a model of Anglo-American cooperation. In no time, the air groups of each carrier were freely interchanging flight decks, the British carrier taking on the defensive role while the vast American carrier took on most of the offensive role. The latter discarded its obsolescent British model aircraft at Pearl Harbor and took on board American aircraft, such as the Wildcat fighter and the Avenger torpedo bomber. Later in the war, British carriers in the Pacific even operated the gull-winged Corsair fighter-bomber.

Originally, six Illustrious-class carriers were ordered, of which four were completed by the end of 1941. The other two were deferred due to material shortages, with priority switching to destroyers and convoy escorts. Consequently, the *Indefatigable* and *Implacable* were delayed by two years from 1942 to 1944. There also followed a class of ten 'utility carriers' of half the size, known as the 'light fleets'. These Colossus-class carriers began reaching the Pacific as the war ended.

The truth is that until then, British carriers became irrelevant in the circumstances of a war in the broad and open spaces of the Pacific, where fleets could distance themselves from enemy land bases and air ranges until it suited them. Then they could throw overwhelming air superiority at the point in question and smother it, as gave coinage late in the war to the expression 'the big blue blanket', when voluminous carrier air numbers and increased proportions of fighters encouraged the tactics of standing off enemy air bases and pummelling them continuously rather than simply raiding and then withdrawing.

That was how the kamikazes were beaten. When the British Pacific Fleet finally arrived, its part in the Okinawa campaign was to blanket the air bases in the archipelago south of Okinawa. Air strips there were being used to stage in kamikazes from Formosa against the US fleet off Okinawa. The British carriers' armoured flight decks came in handy, being impenetrable to the kamikazes. In the meantime, the air groups on the carriers were increased by ingenious deck parking innovations and by using aircraft models with folding wings.

In terms of pre-war planning, the Illustrious-class had been intended to replace four of the early carriers that were small, slow and redundant in order to keep within the tonnage quota.

Japan and Italy might withdraw from the disarmament treaties, but Britain, America and France – until war began in Europe – wanted to continue with the quotas. Britain was hobbled by a limitations agreement of its own with Germany.

None of this inhibited America laying down a third member of the Yorktown-class in September 1939, the very month the European war broke out in Poland. The *Hornet* had been authorized in 1938 in response to Japan's 1937 naval replenishment programme. It took only two years and one month to complete, compared to its sisters having taken four years, a consequence of being able to follow a successful design. The US was not alone in taking advantage of this factor. Contracting the third carrier of the class to the same shipyard as built the first also acted to speed construction and fitting out.

The *Hornet* was completed a month or more ahead of Pearl Harbor, but was not sufficiently worked up to join the Pacific Fleet until April 1942. This was in contrast to Japan's *Shokaku* and *Zuikaku*, completed respectively in August and September 1941 but worked up sufficiently to join the raid on Pearl Harbor on 7 December 1941. The pair took three-and-a-half years to build and were to prove the most successful design to fight in the Pacific War until America's Essex-class came to dominate the stage in late 1943. We will come back to the 'Shockers' in Chapter 4.

There were two further Japanese initiatives in the countdown years to war between 1936 and 1942. First, the *Kaga* and *Akagi* were rebuilt, most expensively and laboriously, at Sasebo. Then, experience of the need to upgrade flight decks to match the increasingly demanding needs of the new aircraft models prompted the idea of building seven large liners that could be converted in short order. Five fast naval auxiliaries had already been authorized under the 1934 Programme with the same idea in mind. The other consideration was the lack of long slipways in Japan. Consequently, endeavouring to 'get hulls in the water' while peace still lasted was the logic. Once the hulls were afloat and could be moved elsewhere, the fitting-out process that followed did not need slipways. Fitting-out facilities could also be modified or expanded more easily than slipways or construction dry-docks.

This early embrace of the notion of conversion carriers on the part of Japan is generally referred to as the 'Shadow Fleet'. Indeed, it was as secret as any other naval construction in the countdown years. It is a story in itself which we expand in the third chapter, 'Shadow Fleet'.

We can best round out the Treaty era with tables (see close of chapter) showing the Japanese, American and British line-ups in relation to the quotas and their pre-Pacific War aftermath. These are introduced with commentary at the close of this chapter. But note our use of an asterisk alongside those carriers sunk in the 1942 battles for seeing at a glance how destructive were those Pacific War carrier-to-carrier battles. So much so had this been during 1942 that on neither side was a fleet carrier to be lost again until June 1944, partly because there were now so few to lose but also as it was important to protect these survivors. The whole war in the Pacific had to slow down for well over a year.

Despite Japan ending up by exceeding its aircraft carrier tonnage quota by close to 40 per cent, this translated poorly in terms of offensive hitting power. This was partly because the US Navy adopted the open-air 'deck park' configuration for aircraft, whereas the IJN (like the Royal Navy) preferred to house their aircraft in the hangars below the flight deck.

In fairness to the Japanese, the huge overrun of the tonnage quota was actually a result of the rebuilds of the early carriers in the period 1934–1938. Such work was interpretable in their case as a post-Treaty development.

As for the *Soryu* and *Hiryu*, the former was not ready to be 'weighed in' at the point of abandonment of the naval treaties by Japan, while *Hiryu* was only laid down after the walk-out. Three seaplane carriers likewise ordered by the 1934 Fleet Replenishment programme also emerged post-Treaty, although as seaplane tenders they were excluded from the carrier quota. We also meet them again in the third chapter, 'Shadow Fleet'.

Nonetheless, it can be argued that both the *Akagi* and *Kaga* weighed a lot more than was declared long before their rebuilds. On the other hand, their US equivalents – USS *Saratoga* and *Lexington* – were actually in excess of 36,000 tons although officially only 33,000.

What was available to both navies in 1942 was more important in the context of the Pacific War than with whatever quotas the treaties had encumbered either side. Here, we see how Japan so ably prepared during the countdown years to war with its back-up strategy of a Shadow Fleet. The argument of this study is to proclaim that the Emperor's loyal naval brains might have prepared it even better by devoting the crucial five countdown years to building a 'phantom fleet' of keel-up, custom-designed fast fleet carriers exploiting Japan's limited launching facilities to the max, instead of cluttering slipways with battleships, cruisers and even liners that might or might not be converted into carriers. That theme we will pursue in the fourth chapter, 'Phantom Fleet'.

Why historically the Emperor was not better served in this way is what we will attempt to explore in our next chapter, 'Raising Eagles'. Our vehicle for this exploration is a familiar figure, whose presence conveniently nudges its spirit into every chapter, Isoroku Yamamoto, here in this chapter as diplomat and politician. His role as apostle of naval aviation inspires the following chapter.

Pipe Aboard the Admirals

Yamamoto and his generation of Imperial Navy officer emerged out of middle level commands in the early interwar years, and by the 1930s had become the flag officers at the very pinnacle of command. As such, the main foreign influence on them had been British, whether in their training at the Etajima Naval Academy or later at staff college. The cream of the crop were given postings overseas, mostly to America as up-and-coming naval power and to Britain, where the Anglo-Japanese Alliance offered much to be readily and welcomely learnt. English overwhelmingly predominated as the language they chose to become proficient in. Thanks to the linguistic access and to the overseas postings, they learnt what Japan would be up against if it challenged the two greatest naval powers. Between them, they appreciated how Britain and America rated at well over half the aggregate combined total of world industrial power and technology. There runs a modern American expression, 'As a car driver you don't pick an argument with a Mack truck'; least of all should you pick an argument with two Mack trucks!

Not surprisingly, all this changed when the Alliance came to an end. The IJN found that in addition, they would be wise to consult other foreign sources of expertise and to consider encouraging more Etajima graduates to master other languages. As a result, the next generation – who occupied middle-level command posts in the turbulent 1930s – gravitated towards Germany and became anti-American. As for the attitude towards the British, the new generation knew not the golden years of the Alliance, emoting only over the 'betrayal' of their fathers and grandfathers. It was a generation gap with a vengeance. The younger the officer, the more he might feel contempt for the 'officers and gentlemen' who were his seniors, as typically when one Anglophile officer returned from a London posting and unconsciously talked of the Royal Navy as 'our navy'. The cries in revulsion were shrill. For one, was not Britannia threatening Japan with its vast new naval base at Singapore? And was the British Empire not in the way of the Greater East Asia Co-Prosperity Sphere? We can also imagine the new generation of officers going on and on about not wanting to hear bletherings about Texan and Californian oil reserves, 'Yankee Can Do' and 'Yankee Know How'. Least of all did they want to be told about what exclusive London clubs the Emperor's priceless gentlemen hob-nobbed in so decorously. Didn't some of these suave and portly gentlemen even sport pin-ups of the 16-inch gun battleship *Nelson* on their noticeboards? Where would be *their* Singapore, where *their Nelson* and its sister ship *Rodney*, when the IJN spawned its super-secret 20-inch gunned 'meganauts'? As for how big and how fast might be HMS *Hood*, that was another of yesterday's questions.

Sheltering this cast of opinion spread a seniority umbrella in the form of the adherents of Kanji Kato and his successor as leader of the Fleet Faction, the pouchy-eyed Admiral Nobumasa Suetsugu. Thereby, the zealots' insidious and unrelenting pressure increasingly came to be rewarded with promotions to key committees and departments by the late 1930s, and hence to the policy fonts of the IJN. During the countdown years to the Pacific War, these war hawks were sedulously groomed by the German Naval Attaché, Vice-Admiral Paul Wenneker. The Nazis were desperate for Japan's agreement to a Tripartite Pact of Germany, Italy and Japan.

The Germans had jockeyed a more-than-willing Japanese Army to agree to that, but nothing could be signed until the Navy agreed – a log stemming the propaganda-driven flow. Top of the heap in the IJN at that time were leading admirals adamantly against a Tripartite Pact, for fear it would draw Japan into a war with America.

For the quasi-fascist circles increasingly infecting and perverting the Imperial ideal of a heaven-driven state of humanity, the big question was how the relic colonial possessions of the European powers could be brought into a state of submission.

In contrast, traditional IJN circles prided themselves on being cosmopolitan, and realistic enough to recognize Japan's dependence upon the United States for oil and steel. They appreciated how there only existed two ways of ensuring a continued supply for the Navy: either giving into American demands by ending the Army's China war, or grabbing the Dutch oil fields in Indonesia and the British oil fields in Borneo and Burma along with their tin and rubber in Malaya. Surely America would come in on the side of the British and Dutch, they agonized. That was fine and perfectly possible in a short-war context, they could acknowledge. But as for taking on the industrial giants of the world in any long-term war, then forget it. They argued that Japan in all circumstances must avoid a drawn-out war against America.

Those standing in the way of the Japanese Army and of the pro-war elements in the Navy were a 'big four' of senior admirals controlling the Navy in the late 1930s. These were Navy Minister Mitsumasa Yonai, his Vice-Minister Isoroku Yamamoto, Zengo Yoshida – who was Commander-in Chief of the Combined Fleet – and Shigeyoshi Inouye, who more or less concurrently served as chief of the influential Bureau of Naval Affairs. Yamamoto followed Yoshida as Combined Fleet Commander, while Yoshida followed Yonai as Navy Minister. Things looked even more secure for peace when Yonai became the Emperor's

Prime Minister in January 1940, with Yoshida continuing as Navy Minister. These were men of big minds and resolute leadership powers, internationally and nationally highly respected. Not the least confident in them was the Emperor himself, who was a long-term admirer of Yonai's moral integrity. There was little the fascist-minded infiltrators to the middle echelon heights could do without big events unexpectedly aiding their cause. Events were needed.

The Fall of France that summer of 1940 was the event that made Yonai's task of opposing the Tripartite Pact, in his own expression, like having to row a boat upstream from the lip of Niagara Falls.

Suddenly, here was the temptation to the militarists of a fruit ripe for the picking – French Indochina's great bulge into the South China Sea, the perfect jump-off position for an invasion of Malaya and the Borneo and Sumatra oil fields. The strategic fortress and naval base of Singapore had come inside bomber range, a mere hop across the Gulf of Siam from Saigon.

The proposed Tripartite Pact provided for German and Italian support in the event of Britain or America thwarting any Japanese 'Drive South' by declaring war against Japan, or threatening to do so. The logic was that America might flinch from a war simultaneously with Germany and Japan.

By the autumn of 1940, the Japanese Army had won the fight. Late that summer, they forced the collapse of the Yonai Government and the return as premier of Prince Fumimaro Konoye. Under accumulating pressure that summer, Navy Minister Yoshida collapsed – from nervous breakdown in some accounts – his unrelenting opposition to the Pact having left him increasingly isolated in Navy circles.

His successor, Oikawa, proved a weak reed by giving in to the pressure, not least from the fear of an Army-sanctioned *coup d'etat*. There was every reason to fear one. To explain why this was a realistic apprehension, we need to look back to the defining event in Japan's 1930s march to war.

The Rise of *Gekokujo*

Back in early 1936, junior Army officers had led a revolt in Tokyo known to history as the 'February 26 Incident'. Their seniors behaved for many days as if in sympathy, or indeed testing the nerve of the government to see which way it might turn. Admiral Inouye was at that time stationed in nearby Yokosuka. With the encouragement of Admiral Yonai, he organized a navy intervention force in the hope that naval support for the government might stay the establishment's hand. In the end, nerve failed in Army circles, despite deep sympathy with the ideals of the rebels and disgust at politicians.

Invoked by its defenders was a notion called *gekokujo*, the essence of which is as untranslatable as its meaning is preposterous to Western ears inured to the notion of the rule of law. *Gekokujo* was an honoured, even romantic, tradition of insubordination dating back to the turbulent fourteenth century. An example was the abiding popularity of *The Tale of the 47 Ronin*, these having been rogue samurai whose lord had been treacherously killed by a government leader. They mustered in due course to storm the politician's lair and assassinate him. Then, in deference to the Emperor, they committed mass *hara kiri*. It was much noted at the time how both the 47 Ronin and the 26 February rebels had struck in a snowstorm. The atmospherics on any given day are of great importance to the Japanese soul, not least to any writer of *haiku* poems. But rather than the ringleaders bowing out like the 47 Ronin, they preferred to be executed after standing trial in a public courtroom, because at least that way they could be heard.

While in Japan there was no growing fascist political party like the Nazis in Germany, Mussolini's Fascist Party in Italy, the Iron Guard in Rumania, nor even Sir Oswald Mosley's British Fascist Party, there were always ultra-nationalist and anti-communist secret societies in the background, powerful in propaganda and adept at assassinations.

Any national-socialist sympathies could be found more among young Army officers appalled at the impoverished condition of Japan's peasants, who were largely the enlisted men they led. The beacon for them was Manchuria, a thinly populated *lebensraum* rich in natural resources. The way they dreamed, nothing should stand in the way of Japan's manifest destiny in mainland Asia.

Manchuria was to the Imperial Japanese Army what Texas had been to the United States in the 1800s, its high-handed seizure by them in 1930 a monstrous act of *gekokujo* in itself. In defence, voices reproached, had not Hitler seized the Rhineland and Austria, and Mussolini much of East Africa? Meanwhile, the *zaibatsu*, Japan's business conglomerates, had moved into the new lands.

In high places, many older men's ears cocked to the song of apologist tongues. Had not the Army, for instance, its young 'corporate pets', like any other large business? These had started to get dangerously out of hand by rocking the good ship of state. But the generals had brought them back to the parade grounds, although it was regrettable that these 'pets' of theirs had sliced up half the cabinet in their own homes, and in front of their families. It had been felt necessary in ruling circles to execute a token handful or two. Yet might not their heroism encourage the survivors in the cabinet to act more patriotically towards the new frontiers of Nippon? Didn't most of them in one way or another now have a stake in Manchuria?

At this point one should introduce a figure of that time who encapsulated the contradictions seething inside the exploding plot that for Japan measured the countdown years to the war that killed the Japanese Empire: Yosuke Matsuoka. Matsuoka was a man of very diminutive stature with a Hitler moustache who could talk nineteen to the dozen. As a child he had been brought up in Oregon by American foster parents and spoke perfect American English. He converted to Christianity, taking the name 'Frank Matsuoka'. Returning as a young adult to Japan, he became distinguished for the efficient running of the Manchurian railways, which endeared him to the military control cliques in the Japanese government, for whoever ran the railways strategically controlled Manchuria. As for his Christianity, he is reported as having on his return to Japan spent equal time at Shinto and Buddhist shrines.

Matsuoka, twice Foreign Minister of Japan, was awarded the honour of strutting the world stage as a cynosure of global attention at two great moments in history. The first was when, as Japan's delegate, he walked out of the League of Nations over the Manchuria issue in 1933, from which day has generally been dated the eclipse of the influence of that august body. The second was in 1941, when as Foreign Minister he journeyed across Siberia by rail to meet Hitler, Mussolini and Stalin. In the interim, he had been the main driver in Japan's final long drawn-out decision to join the infamous Tripartite Pact in the autumn of 1940. He wanted that now to become 'Quadripartite' by binding in Russia, so that America would no longer dare to oppose Japan's destiny in Asia – any more than Japan would presume to question America's Monroe Doctrine.

Across the Anglo-Saxon world came the arrogant question, 'what in his Oregon childhood could have so turned Matsuoka against us all?' How had he been insulted? The answer may have been that in his American childhood he endured racial slurs, but far more important to a man of ideas and of cosmopolitan sophistication, Matsuoka had something else as his driver. He had been brought up on the edge of America's Wild West, and now he had helped develop Japan's newly acquired equivalent: Manchuria.

The man was above all else the eternal optimist; he reached too far for everybody, as we shall shortly see. Churchill, in his six-volume history of the Second World War, devotes a whole brilliant chapter to the suspense of Matsuoka's 1941 odyssey across Asia to meet Hitler in Berlin, Mussolini in Rome and then Stalin on the way home. Rumbling across Siberia on the rails that took his delegation, there also thundered in the chancelleries of the world the dread of some fateful thread of history in the making. It marked what Churchill called 'doom-balance time for the great dictators'.

Despite all the hoopla and angst that it caused worldwide, nothing much came of the Japanese envoy's trip. To the total surprise of Stalin, Hitler invaded Russia without warning his ally Japan. Matsuoka lost face as a result, and was replaced as Foreign Minister in a cabinet reshuffle.

Matsuoka had, however, already succeeded in consummating the Tripartite Pact.

The Pact was a defensive instrument for Japan, not an offensive one, Matsuoka had argued. If America made war on Germany, it did not oblige Japan to declare war on America. However, Article 3 provided for Japan, Germany and Italy 'to assist one another with all political, economic and military means if one of them is attacked by a power not involved in the European war or in the China conflict' – for example, America. The Pact was, for those who wished to see, a means to an offensive end – the drive south to seize Dutch oil in Indonesia.

The admirals who reluctantly acceded to his arguments tried to convince each other that the 'drive south' could be accomplished incrementally without hostilities necessarily breaking out, or not at least with America. The Japanese Navy was the impulse behind the move into French Indochina. It was disagreeably surprised when this triggered the US dollar freeze of Japanese assets, which created a *de facto* oil embargo, quickly reciprocated by Britain's pound sterling bloc which denied the Middle East as an alternative source, and by the Dutch East Indies who required payment in dollars. Suddenly, there was no oil anywhere to buy. Japan had only its reserves, albeit substantial, but these had no expectation of replenishment except by means of conquest of oil reserves belonging to other people.

The dollar freeze was a riposte as close to war as one could dare, for it was a garrotte to the IJN's jugular. Japan could itself only supply a tiny proportion of its oil needs. For the rest, it depended on imports from America or the Dutch. While Japan had been stockpiling oil for years, there were only enough reserves to fuel IJN operations for two years at the very most. The only reserves sufficient to fuel the Navy and within reach of it to seize were the Dutch oil fields in Borneo and Sumatra – and if a pinch more were needed, Burma was in reach.

The Navy as a result became instigators of the 'drive south'. They calculated that the Dutch East Indies would surely offer no contest. How to overrun them without provoking Britain and America became the big question.

With the Dutch being found recalcitrant in negotiations, this begged a question: could they have been given pledges from Britain and America? If Japan went all out to conquer Malaya and Singapore, as the Army wished for a first move, would America come to Britain's assistance? In that case, there entered the danger that the Americans would attack the flank of the Japanese advance and its support lines from their bases in the Philippines, and that Japan would be dragged into a long war it could not negotiate an end to without total defeat and loss of empire.

As a supreme irony, there actually existed no useful American guarantees to the British, Dutch and Australians. For explanation of how that came about, we need to move not to Washington but to Chicago, of all places, to the offices of the *Chicago Tribune* no less. There reigned Colonel Robert R. McCormick, owner and publisher of the most successful broadsheet newspaper in America and bandleader to the isolationist cause. McCormick abhorred Roosevelt and regarded his New Deal administration as Communists. He was adamant that America could never go to war to save the colonial empires of the British, French and Dutch, and was convinced that Roosevelt was scheming to join Britain against Hitler. Consequently, Roosevelt flinched from making good whatever vague promises he had made to Churchill at the Atlantic Conference, which had been convened principally in order to devise a joint front in the face of the Japanese threat.

There was therefore no need for Japan to raid Pearl Harbor or attack the Philippines. The Dutch oil wells were up for grabs; the Dutch and the British were too weak on their own to prevent it.

Yamamoto and his ilk refused to believe that was possible, and so added to their target list the Pacific Fleet at Pearl Harbor and MacArthur's fleet of Flying Fortresses in the Philippines. The figure to have skipped their screens was that tall aristocrat and far-right demagogue, Colonel McCormick. Either that, or Tokyo had dismissed the *Chicago Tribune* owner as an eccentric and the Windy City as not exactly on the diplomatic cocktail party circuit. The colonel, after all, was widely celebrated for having 'the best mind of the fourteenth century', as one opponent put it.

Even as the code books were being burned in consulates and embassies all over the Far East, the British, Dutch and Australians were desperately seeking a commitment from President Roosevelt. But the *Tribune* struck again in the final days before Pearl Harbor with the publication of an article headlined '(ROOSEVELT'S) WAR PLANS', occasioned by the leak of US Army planning to one of the leading champions of the isolationist cause on Capitol Hill.

On the heels of the media storm, the British ambassador, Lord Halifax, visited Roosevelt but was fobbed off once again. He was to describe the conduct of US foreign policy at that time as 'resembling a disorderly day's rabbit shooting'. As an example of presidential-inspired initiative, the Asiatic Fleet commander's yacht in Manila was purloined, armed and kitted up. It was crewed with an American officer or two and some Filipino seamen, and ordered to loiter in Japanese-controlled waters, making a nuisance of itself in the hope of it being sunk and therefore providing a *casus belli*. The precedent that had sprung to mind had been the 1898 sinking of the battleship *Maine*, allegedly by the Spaniards, which had set off the Spanish-American War (that incidentally had delivered the Philippines into American hands).

The more serious side of things was that this had become a bed of the president's own making. Here the good Dr Jekyll was doing everything possible to put off war with Japan, yet the naughty Mr Hyde was doing everything to shorten the fuse.

There was an over optimistic US military strategy to stock up the Philippines over the next four months with a vast armada of Flying Fortress long-range bombers as a deterrent to the Japanese. Meanwhile, a whole US Army division was about to set sail from the West Coast to reinforce General MacArthur. How it could reach Manila Bay before the Japanese Navy struck was the great anxiety. Only in peace could the convoy stand a chance of reaching the islands intact.

Yet in an act of near-insane political misjudgement for a country so ill-prepared to meet the Japanese in battle, Roosevelt had cut off their oil and their iron. And time was running out.

It seemed that all anyone could do was lurch around and pray that 'the Japs' would magically grant everyone a break, and hope that 'the colonialists' in their pin-stripe suits and wing collars might forebear from embarrassing the White House again anytime soon. Alternatively, maybe Colonel McCormick could quietly go and die somewhere. It was 'head in the sand' time.

Public opinion was mostly isolationist then, in many cases very strongly so. It has to be remembered of America that in 1941, it was ethnically very much a German and an Irish country, and neither race had much love for the Brits, or at least not then. Indeed, it might be said of pre-war America that it was the colonel's country, and that meantime Roosevelt was merely its president.

Overlooked in most accounts, or only awarded passing mention, was how the dollar freeze did far more damage to Japan than merely forcing the IJN to use up its stockpile of oil. Its effect was to promise bankruptcy for Japan and threaten rural revolution; Japan was facing a black hole. There were only two ways out of the swirling magnetic pull of a socio-economic abyss. One was to march to war, and thereby snip the Allied garrotte and seize their oil. The other was to give in to the Anglo-Saxons and withdraw from China.

We will come back to that choice in due course, but meanwhile the economics of the dollar freeze are bizarre enough to invite a quixotic money diversion. It came about after the Japanese moved into southern French Indochina (South Vietnam), thereby gaining a strategic leg-up on British Malaya and the Dutch East Indies.

Round and Round the Mulberry Bush

Preposterous as it might seem, the economic Achilles heel of the pre-war Japanese economy was worms, specifically silk worms. They fed on mulberry leaves and were tended by peasant womenfolk on a million small farms.

As a commodity, the product of the worms when processed into silk fabric at filature factories represented two-thirds of the value of Japanese exports to the United States, for which Japanese silk was 100 per cent of American supply and raw silk 25 per cent of all Japanese exports outside the yen bloc. Better than that, raw silk was wholly Japanese as it included no imported products, as did for example finished fabrics such as those in the warp and weft of Philippine hemp and Indian jute, or cotton products dependent for their manufacture on imported cotton. Raw silk was close to 60 per cent of Japan's US dollar earnings from the American hemisphere. These paid for most of the oil and other war materials.

Whereas demand for broad silk as a luxury fabric was devastated by the Great Depression, Japanese revenues were largely balanced by demand from the American hosiery trade, of which more fascinatingly anon. But first let us look at how that demand was killed off and then examine the consequences upon everything from simple rural peasant girls to super-battleships in the works. The killer was a paragraph or two in a forgotten piece of legislation.

America's closet trade-busting weapon was an obscure section of the 1917 wartime Trading with the Enemy Act (TWEA), which harboured the recourse of financially restricting the trade of neutral powers – albeit in 'merited' particulars. In brutal practice, it meant the president could tweak pretty much what he damned well liked, any particulars 'merited' or not. This Section 5(b) of the TWEA was rediscovered when Secretary of the Treasury Morgenthau set his general counsel on the job of seeing what could be done about Japanese aggression without daring anything so crass as an actual embargo, such as might precipitate armed conflict. Could there be something cute they could try?

Section 5(b) was invoked outright when, in July 1941, the Japanese moved on Saigon. It became the instrument for the dollar freeze that acted as good as an oil embargo. US officials, encouraged by the president, proclaimed this use of the TWEA as a gentle squeeze intended 'to bring Japan to its senses, not its knees'. In the hands of unscrupulous officials, it became less a case of 'gently gently catchee monkey' and more one of *gekokujo*. Officials nudged each other in the ribs; they laughed, they hooted – let the Japs flounder around with all their clever proposals, the

US would first egg them on and then waste their time in delay. Meantime, the US would fish around for a half-credible reason for turning down each and every proposal. Through the late summer and into the early autumn, with the greatest personal courtesy, the garrotte relentlessly tightened.

The whole story was vividly unearthed and unfolded by Edward S. Miller's *Bankrupting the Enemy; the US financial siege of Japan before Pearl Harbor*, to which we are indebted. The story is incredible, outrageous and never before properly told.

To remind the reader, Japan had very little iron, let alone oil, even in Manchuria. Almost all of the scrap iron for forging the steel had to be imported, and that mostly from America. Japanese raw silk exports earned the dollars to pay for the American scrap iron that Japan imported to help expand its navy in the timeframe 1937–1941, just as it came to be expected to pay for the Californian oil that allowed the IJN to train hard and the IJA (Imperial Japanese Army) to beat up folk in China.

The irony was that the IJN was dependent in the 1930s for its near-time future upon the whim of American fashion, namely hemlines. When hemlines were down around the ankles, American women had no cause to worry about the look of their legs. No longer so in the era of the Flapper and the Gibson Girl, as you could not dance the Charleston in Gatsby's ballroom without silk stockings, for hemlines were now way up to here. The alternative was unsightly and sagging cotton stockings that made one look like a complete frump.

Silk stockings clung to the curves. They even created a class distinction, with the expensive women who wore them said to live in 'silk stocking districts'. Alas, your ordinary factory or office worker or housewife could not afford silk stockings.

The rise of the silk hosiery market in America offset the broad decline in silk as a fabric for dresswear due to tightened budgets during the Depression. It became the most exciting example of a niche market volume-wise there ever was. The major beneficiary of Japanese earnings from the silk stocking hosiery boom in America were the two Japanese super-battleships, *Yamato* and *Musashi*, not to speak of the two heroes of our story, the fast fleet carriers *Shokaku* and *Zuikaku*; all four of them great feats of naval architecture and engineering ordered in the great 1937 Naval Replenishment Order, but mostly built from recycled American scrap iron imports. Their story began in the typical peasant's home, in thousands of rural villages humming at night with the sound of silk worms crunching on mulberry leaves. The mulberry bush was key to the story. Japan had millions of them, while America had near none at all.

The costs of the 1937 Naval Replenishment Order included over 800 million Yen for sixty-three warships, requiring enough steel for these vessels to displace close to 300,000 tons of water. Just two ships cost 45 per cent of this figure (but actually a lot more given massive use of highly expensive special steels for armour plating). No awards for guessing which two these were. Next in cost, at a mere 18 per cent, were the two large aircraft carriers. The other fifty-nine vessels were minnows in comparison – destroyers, submarines, patrol craft and fleet auxiliaries.

The Fourth Naval Armaments Supplement Programme in 1939 listed a second pair of Yamato-class super-battleships and a third large carrier. This was in its legislative phase on 15 May when 'Nylon Day' was proclaimed at the New York World's Fair. Within a year, nylon accounted for 7 per cent of sales to the American hosiery trade. Its manufacturer, Du Pont, allocated its entire production to hosiery. Nylon was to become for the silkworm what myxomatosis became for rabbits.

By the war's end, a pair of nylon stockings had become the best-known staple of black markets everywhere the Allied flags flew. There were now no silk stockings, thanks first to the dollar freeze and secondly to the war. Nylons clung to the curves better, and they got cheaper and cheaper. A young gal simply had to have nylons … or look like a frump!

Pathetically, there came a query from the Japanese Embassy: might not the American military be in need of the humble Japanese peasant woman's superb raw silk for manufacturing parachutes? 'No, we are looking into nylon for parachutes,' came the rebuff. Finally, all hopes rested on an elaborate barter proposal – raw silk could be exchanged for mostly oil and other US exports (the list was careful to omit products of military use, these being mere window dressing for the oil). News that this, too, had been thrown back in their faces broke on the eve of a conference in Tokyo convened to decide on war or peace. It was to be an end to wishful thinking. The dollar freeze was now perceived as a one-way street to national bankruptcy.

There was enough steel stockpiled to complete the 1937 programme and most of the 1939 naval programme. But the 1941 programme was to partly founder from shortages. Meanwhile, there was barely enough oil stockpiled to last out a determined attempt to seize the Dutch East Indies and consolidate a front afterwards. The Japanese must seize the Indonesian oilfields if the war was to be sustained.

We move on now to Washington and Tokyo.

In Tokyo in early October 1941, the magma was rising up the conduits and political emotions were quaking. It seemed inevitable that the political volcano would blow its top and explode into war.

It had been decided a month before that by early October, the decision for a 'drive south' must be made one way or the other, or the Japanese would lose the military advantage and see the dwindling oil supply further depleted. Since then, negotiations with the US had got nowhere. Ambassador Nomura had appealed to Tokyo for help. For moral support and to provide more advanced linguistic skills, they sent Saburo Kurusu as Special Envoy. Kurusu had an American wife, but on the flip side was the fact that as Ambassador in Berlin a year or so before, he had signed the Tripartite Pact on behalf of Japan.

The pudgy pair perfected their social grins, but found these withering when confronted by the bleak puritanical stare of US Secretary of State Cordell Hull.

Hull found himself rather in a quandary working with the two diplomats. Behind Hull's back, Dean Acheson and his legal eagle and economist minions were strangling the Imperial Japanese Empire – well-tailored bureaucrats incongruously and joyfully playing at hawks. Hard in his ear were the stern pleas of the military, contrary to popular tradition playing at doves. They pleaded that they were not ready for war, needing another six months to beef up forces in the Philippines.

Where the president stood was never too clear. Was he aware of the ruthlessness of the brutal Acheson and his eager young flock of lawyers and economists, or was he quietly winking at it – was this *gekokujo* Georgetown-style? Like Yamamoto, Roosevelt did not survive the war, so no-one was ever able to ask.

On both sides, late 1941 saw open season for the hawks against the doves of peace.

Unaware of this conflict, the Japanese diplomatic pair equated US intransigence with the increasingly apparent bankrupting strategy. Was not the first an omen for the other? They advised Tokyo by cable, unaware that America had broken their diplomatic code, that the peace mission could expect to go no further without a China deal.

For the Imperial Japanese Navy, the practical answer seemed absurdly simple. The IJN could not expect to win a war against the British, Americans and Dutch combined, particularly with the Japanese Army bogged down in China. If the IJN wanted to see its oil supply restored, someone would have to persuade Army Minister Tojo to begin throwing Army boots out of China. After all, wasn't it a 'no-win' situation there?

The abiding message was that someone needed to do something fast in order to bring Tojo to heel.

If this someone who was expected to do something was the Prime Minister, Prince Konoye, then that effete aristocrat proved 'too weak-kneed to control the armed services', in the words of Navy Minister Oikawa. Worse could be accused of Oikawa, who by resigning would have brought down the cabinet and thereby helped the emperor to preserve the peace. Instead, he passed the IJN's buck to Konoye, claiming this might 'encourage' the prime minister to exercise strong leadership. Prince Konoye, however, failed to make any headway with Tojo, who threatened to resign as army minister, whereupon Prince Konoye resigned himself. In Japanese custom, the resignation of any of the three – prime minister, army minister or navy minister – was fatal to any government.

The *Jushin*, a council of seven elder statesmen – mostly ex-prime ministers like Yonai – could not agree on a replacement prime minister, whereupon the much respected Marquess Kido, Lord Keeper of the Privy Seal, who was Emperor Hirohito's political confidant, proposed the man who had caused all the trouble. Kido was hopeful that the emperor's will for peace might overcome in General Tojo's heart and head his dreams of continental conquest.

At first it looked like a sound bet. Tojo supported those who wanted the negotiations with Washington to continue, and for these to be given more time even if preparations for war continued. He genuinely preferred to win the peace. But there was no accounting for the actions of the Americans. Just as a *modus vivendi* was beginning to be worked out, America raised its terms with an insulting degree of severity in late November. It did so because the 'move south' was by now in sight as the troop convoys headed out to sea bound by tight schedules.

A brief word about the China war comes in as useful perspective here.

From the Incident at the Marco Polo Bridge to the 'Army of Ghosts'

During the eight years it was waged, the war in China cost the Japanese over two million casualties, of which half a million were dead once the war's Allied-encouraged extension into Burma is included. Yet to the spin doctors, it had begun as the 'China Incident'. The dead garnered political influence, being termed the 'army of ghosts'.

The war started with a genuine incident at the Marco Polo Bridge north of Peking, expanding in September 1937 into invasion of northern China. Chiang Kai-shek retaliated by sending his best German-trained divisions to attack the Japanese civilian community and its garrison of 6,000 naval troops in Shanghai. An IJN rescue mission poured Japanese Army divisions into the port by sea. The media in Tokyo boasted that Shanghai could be won in three days and China defeated in three months. In the event, it took three months to win Shanghai, a Pyrrhic victory indeed, given the forbidding casualties.

Now reinforced and with Navy air cover, the IJA raced up both banks of the Yangtse to the Nationalists capital at Nanking and ran amok in an orgy of atrocities. For example, two army officers became media stars for their competition to see who could behead with samurai swords the most Chinese prisoners. Their enthusiasm took them well into three figures each.

Nanking duly fell. It was left to the foreign community, led by of all people an avowed Nazi, the German consul, to witness for posterity and to protest at what became called the 'Rape of Nanking'. The slaughter of Chinese, both civilians and prisoners, and the rape of women went on unchecked for weeks on end. Deaths are reckoned in some accounts to have approached the scale of those killed at Hiroshima. The world reeled aghast, as indeed it might, for the true start to the Second World War had begun. The 'Rape' was an ominous sign of a compounding evil that was to unfold in Europe. Nanking was a case of *gekokujo* finally going viral, opening the door to genocide and to hell on earth.

The Chinese retreated up the Yangtse, determined to hold Wuhan, the city that after Shanghai was the heart of the economy. It fell in October 1938 after a hard fight, notable for at least one Chinese victory. From here, the Chinese forces traded space for time by resisting further Japanese advances up the Yangtse to Chungking, while their guerrillas closed in all along the roads and railways sustaining the Japanese advance. The flood tide of conquest was now spent.

A symbol of that struggle was a city called Changsha, for which four major battles were fought. The Chinese won all but the last, but that came too late to help the Japanese Army with the war then about to end.

The IJN despised the Army. Admirals were wont to describe them as 'horse dung'. This was not inapt in a way, because in spite of the global advance of mechanization, the Imperial Japanese Army was primarily horse- and donkey-driven (as for that matter were most of Hitler's infantry divisions in the war against Russia).

Yamamoto, for example, had no time for the verbosity of the emperor's generals. His biographer amuses us with examples. A warmongering general seated at a meeting beside him had risen to his feet to rant on emotionally and arrogantly for such a length of time that Yamamoto, with his foot, eased the general's chair back so that when he sat down, his backside hit the floor. The admiral's customary poker face did not change throughout, but nor did that of the general, to offer him his due. On another occasion, Navy Vice Minister Yamamoto sat through an ecstatic presentation by Army Vice Minister Tojo of the Army's progress in aircraft design. Yamamoto congratulated his colleague that 'there were now Army aircraft that could actually fly'.

Yamamoto had a good point. Once the Army's 'China Incident' provided the arena to test aircraft models in combat, it was naval aircraft that performed prodigies, whereas the Army became reliant on the IJN, due to the shortcomings of Army models and aircrew training. As with the US at that time, there was no independent air force as such, only a naval air arm and an army air arm, unlike in Britain where there was the Royal Air Force and in Germany its Luftwaffe.

There were deep cultural divisions between the Japanese Army and the Navy. Here was a nation advanced in its industrialization and technical self-reliance, yet Japan was still largely a country of peasants and fishermen. The fishermen flocked to the Navy, the peasants to the Army. As for the officers, their horizon was continental in the case of the Army and trans-oceanic in the case of the Navy. The IJN elite was cosmopolitan and technical, much of it English-speaking. Navy men saw their opposite numbers in the IJA as a bunch of hicks and thugs.

But one thing could be said of the Army: they had a sympathetic hand on the pulse of the nation. The enormity of the loss of the silk market sank in. The peasantry would be ruined and the spectre of social revolution haunted their imaginations. The generals' nightmare was that even the Army itself might become subverted. For instance, had it not been the defection of the common soldiers in the Czar's armies to the Bolsheviks that secured the Russian Revolution? They agonized accordingly. In the short term, they comforted themselves that the ardour of the enlisted man could be whipped up with propaganda about the wicked Yankee capitalists throwing the poor peasants' precious hard-worked silk back in their earnest faces. Once in the fight, the men would know what to do. After all, was it not their womenfolk who had been so slighted? While the menfolk on the farms laboured on the rice crop, it was their women who, night and day, fed the mulberry leaves to the silkworms. And it was the daughters of peasants who flocked to the cities to work in the filature factories processing silk from the cocoons.

There was already a vast blood bill to pay: the Army was morally deeply in debt to hundreds of thousands of countryside families who had lost sons or husbands in Chinese fields. Such was the national pride in the IJA that this sacrifice could be borne. But why go on and risk all?

Many have put it to the writer that there is a Vietnam analogy somewhere here. Japan was totally bogged down in its China war with no hope ever of winning against a most populous and talented nation. In rather similar circumstances, had not the US withdrawn from Vietnam?

Why could Japan not retreat to a northern redoubt and withdraw from Shanghai and the Yangtse watershed? After the great victories of 1937, this had indeed been Tokyo's policy, except that rampant *gekokujo* mocked central government control; the lust for conquest had moved on up the Yangtse and mopped up enclaves along the coast.

For Tojo, there was no parallel. While America could accept losing face by withdrawing from Vietnam in the 1970s, Japan was an oriental country; and orientals do not lose face lightly. There was a practical difference too. In 1941, Japan still had hope of winning in China. It had, after all, cornered Chiang Kai-shek's Chinese Nationalist forces in the upper watershed of the Yangtse, and the Mao Tse Tung Communists then in Yenan were not a particularly serious threat.

In contrast, the American problem in Vietnam in the early 1970s was that they had become transparent losers – albeit politically rather than militarily.

For Tojo, whether party to it or not, much had been ventured by *gekokujo*, and much could still be consolidated from it. The fear of *gekokujo* might suffice to suborn the Tokyo establishment into submission to the Army's will – this was the dread it had sought to cast increasingly since the 'February 26 Incident' of 1936.

But nothing is ever that simple with leadership in Japan. There is the public voice (*tatemae*) and the true voice (*honne*), the latter most often spoken discreetly in private. It was this convoluted trait that allowed the country to fumblingly monger itself into a war it could not win.

Prime Minister Prince Konoye, by October 1941, had no wish to risk a Pacific war with America. He had ridden the tiger of militarism during the China Incident, the better, he thought, to try and control it. It could wryly amuse him to dress up as Hitler at a fancy-dress party. Heartfelt had been his antipathy to what he saw as the worldwide Anglo-American hegemony. Here were Hitler and Mussolini proclaiming a 'new order' in Europe, so why not a 'new order' in East Asia, or the Greater East Asia Co-Prosperity Sphere as it came to be hailed? Meanwhile, the China war was increasingly becoming an embarrassment; it needed some political window dressing, and the Greater East Asia Co-Prosperity Scheme fitted the bill.

The Prince had lost his taste for war, but how now to shimmy out of another one?

He perceived his first need was to persuade Navy Minister Koshiro Oikawa to state outright to the cabinet that the Navy could not expect to win a war against the Americans, British and Dutch combined, hopefully even to the point of making it a resignation matter. It would be the Navy that would principally fight such a war, and if they did not feel they could win it, then the Army could do no less than desist. It just needed Oikawa to be honest and admit the IJN could not beat America.

For sensitive discussions, Prince Konoye preferred to use his Tekigaiso villa, with its spectacular view of Mount Fuji and eclectic interior blending Chinese antique furniture with the Art Deco designs that were so fashionable in 1930s Fascist Europe. Here, one-to-one with him, Oikawa felt able to speak *honne*, but demurred from doing so in front of the cabinet, using the excuse that going to war was a political matter that only the prime minister could decide. Did the prime minister already know the doubts of the admirals? Oikawa shared these doubts, as Prince Konoye well knew. The 'go to war or not go to war' buck was to be passed back and forth.

Konoye's next ploy was to assemble key cabinet members at Tekigaiso, including the army and navy ministers. However, impasse occurred when the former proved obdurate. The last chance was to confront Tojo one-on-one, in order to tease out his *honne*. There, before the view of Fuji, it finally poured out. Tojo had his doubts too. He admitted to his temptation to disengage from China in order to avoid a Pacific war with America. Hundreds of thousands of Japanese soldiers had already died in China. At least as many again could die in a war against America. But, he asked, how could the Army forgive them all if they dishonoured this 'army of the dead' by copping out?

Tojo would have known that the general commanding the armies in China was urgently advising not to get into a war with America. This was Shunroku Hata, who had been army minister in the Yonai cabinet and had been prevailed upon by the Army to resign in order to bring that cabinet down and enable Konoye to form a government. Tojo admitted to being torn both ways. He told Konoye that sometimes he felt like mounting the platform of the Kiyomizu Temple in Kyoto and jumping into the abyss, to which Konoye asked whether it was fair to drag Japan with him. Some who jumped from the Kiyomizu traditionally survived, but many died. It was a metaphor for risk taking.

*   *   *

The six big fast fleet carriers of the First Air Fleet discreetly gathered in the wintry mists of Tankan Bay in the desolate Kuriles, a volcanic string of islands linking Hokkaido, the northern home island, with the Soviets' Kamchatka peninsula.

Last to arrive came the *Kaga*, bearing the forty aerial torpedoes specially modified so as not to sink into the mud of the shallow Pearl Harbor. These were duly redistributed to other flight decks. Then, on 26 November, Admiral Chuichi Nagumo, flying his flag on *Akagi*, led the fleet out into the storms of the lonely North Pacific. Radio sets were sealed against use, so the carrier division call signs would vanish from the ether and the carrier force would become untraceable; destination Pearl Harbor.

The Pacific War ensued. There came retribution for the losers and celebration for the victors with the end of it forty-five months later with unconditional surrender. War crime trials ensued. Tojo was to mount a different platform to that of the Kiyomizu, in this case for an involuntary drop into the abyss.

At Sugamo Jail, on 23 December 1948, they were marched out in the chill of dawn in two batches, there being gallows enough for only so many at a time. First, there had been laid on a communal breakfast, at which there were farewell toasts. Among the first batch condemned to be hanged as war criminals was General Tojo. Prior to his arrest, he had attempted suicide but failed. In contrast, Prince Konoye succeeded. He had anticipated a trial, probably for warmongering in China. Disappointingly for the American media, Yamamoto was already dead, as was Admiral Nagumo, both killed in the war.

In Washington, Dean Acheson had become President Truman's Secretary of State. In contrast to his enemies, the most Acheson could expect to suffer that day was possibly a rough afternoon following a three-Martini lunch. 'It is the manner of enduring that is more important than what it is that is to be endured' has remained Dean Acheson's best-known quote.

It rested ironically with General Douglas MacArthur to become the unwitting early godfather to Prince Konoye's vision of the Greater East Asia Co-Prosperity Sphere. One of the greatest political generals of all time, 'Big Mac' became the peacemaker, the brief shogun of post-war Japan. He was the lead figure at the onset of the American century, the great conciliator of the defeated but also for them the champion of east Asia against Stalin and Mao.

When his sacking by President Truman shocked Japan, some even mourned. One might not be loved in life, but surely the greater privilege is to be respected.

Thus ends this brief round-up of the political march to a war which at least in its aftermath redeemed its inception.

We can now return to how the Pacific War was won. The winner was the aircraft carrier. Indeed, even today it is carriers that police the oceans of the world.

We round off the chapter on the Treaty fleets of the three major naval powers with a chart showing first the carriers built in the interwar years to Treaty limitation, and then additional carriers that became operational during 1942 in the Pacific or up to the conclusion of the Guadalcanal campaign, excluding auxiliary carriers too slow for fleet or support roles, such as the Japanese *Taiyo*, *Unyo* and *Chuyo*, and the American *Long Island*, *Sangamon*, *Suwanee* and *Chenango*.

Those ships sunk during the course of 1942 are asterisked in order to show the high rate of loss on all sides.

The *Ranger*'s air group is excluded from the US total as it remained in the Atlantic theatre throughout 1942 and 1943. At the outbreak of the war, USS *Lexington*, *Enterprise* and *Saratoga* were stationed in the Pacific. Switched from the Atlantic were the *Yorktown*, *Hornet* and finally the *Wasp*, the latter after Midway. USS *Saratoga* also missed Midway, just. It had been torpedoed by a Japanese submarine early in the year and took five vital months to repair.

It can be seen from the air group totals how post-Treaty, the IJN began the war with close to parity, thanks to making the two 'Shockers' ready in time. But their actual superiority was owed to the USN's 'two-ocean' problem. As the year went on, however, more Shadow Fleet units began kicking in, notably the *Junyo* and *Hiyo*. The Yamamoto vision had beaten the Treaty disparity in what were now the true capital ships.

We show first the official displacement tonnages for the Japanese carriers as declared for Treaty purposes (or otherwise), with the actual tonnage alongside. American and British carriers actuated close to official declarations, with the exception of the *Saratoga* and *Lexington* each at 3,000 tons in excess.

Secondly, we show any subsequent production capable of fighting in the first year or so of conflict.

Top speed is shown in knots, and finally there is the operational size of the air group, less reserve aircraft, which were up to twelve as stored in the IJN carriers.

1. INTERWAR YEARS AS LIMITED BY TREATY (Fast fleet carriers in upper case, light carriers in lower case)

JAPAN	Tons Declared	Actual	Speed	Aircraft	UNITED STATES	Tons	Speed	Aircraft
Hosho	–	–	25	11	Langley* converted to seaplane tender			
AKAGI*	26,900	36,500	31.2	63	SARATOGA	33,000	33.91	78
KAGA*	26,900	38,200	28.34	72	LEXINGTON*	33,000	34.24	78
Ryujo*	7,100	10,600	29	36	RANGER	14,500	29.5	
SORYU*	10,050	15,900	34.5	54	YORKTOWN*	19,800	32.33	79
HIRYU*	10,050	17,300	34.3	54	ENTERPRISE	19,800	32.33	79
					WASP*	14,700	29.5	72
TOTALS	81,000	118,500	290			134,800	386	

2. ADDITIONS TO END OF 1942 (post withdrawal from treaties by Japan)

JAPAN	Tons Declared	Actual	Speed	Aircraft	UNITED STATES	Tons	Speed	Aircraft
Zuiho	–	11,262	28.2	27				
SHOKAKU	14,000	25,675	34.2	72				
ZUIKAKU	14,000	25,675	34.2	72				
Shobo*	–	11,262	28.2	27	HORNET*	19,800	32/33	79
JUNYO	–	24,140	22.5	48				
HIYO	–	24,140	22.5	48				
Ryuho	–	13,360	26.5	27				
TOTAL		252,000	321			154,500		
AIRCRAFT TOTAL (groups 1 & 2)				611		463		393

BRITISH EMPIRE

1. TREATY-CLASSED CONSTRUCTION

Argus	14,000 tons	18 knots	15 aircraft
EAGLE*	22,600	24	22
Hermes*	10,850	26.2	12
FURIOUS	22,450	30	33
COURAGEOUS*	22,500	30.5	42
GLORIOUS*	22,500	29.47	42
ARK ROYAL*	22,000	31.75	54
TOTAL	136,900		220

2. EARLY WAR COMPLETIONS

ILLUSTRIOUS	23,000 tons	30.5 knots	33 aircraft
FORMIDABLE	23,000	30.6	33
VICTORIOUS	23,000	31	33
INDOMITABLE	23,000	30.5	45
Note. The air groups were later increased substantially thanks to folding-wing aircraft models and to ingenious deck parking gambits.			
TOTAL		144	
AIRCRAFT TOTAL (groups 1 & 2)		364	

Chapter 2

Rearing Eagles

'The modern development of aircraft has demonstrated conclusively that the backbone of the Navy is the aircraft carrier. The carrier, with destroyers, cruisers and submarines grouped around it, is the spearhead of all modern naval task forces.'

(Carl Vinson, the Father of the Two-Ocean Navy Act, so-called in Congress, July 1940)

Representative Carl Vinson of Georgia was primarily responsible for a series of naval expansionary Acts of Congress, namely those of 1934, 1938 and the Third Vinson Act of early 1940, which was shortly followed by the epochal Two-Ocean Navy Act that followed the Fall of France and start of the Battle of Britain. The latter's aim was to make the US Navy dominant in each of the major oceans – the Pacific and Atlantic – and eventually all oceans, whereas the 1934 Act merely sought to bring the US up to the Treaty quota, and the 1938 Act was motivated by concerns after Japan abandoned the Treaties.

The Two-Ocean Act marks the birth of the maritime worldwide super-state that the US became, thereby heralding the 'American Century'. Its instrument *par excellence* was less nuclear weapons, more the peacekeeping and war limitation skills exercised in action by aircraft carrier fleet second to none. That is how the *Pax Americana* is still being played, not that it has been flash free, but then nor had the *Pax Britannica*.

Vinson's vision of the carrier-centred task force in 1940 was way ahead of his naval contemporaries internationally, with the exception in Japan of Yamamoto and his confreres, who were so prescient of the fast pace of aircraft design on which, as we shall see, he acted as main driver. The closeness of the moment when the aircraft carrier would replace the battleship as capital ship depended on the progress of naval aircraft design and performance, and of course on having a reasonably decisive number of aircraft carriers to fly them off, which is the theme of this chapter.

To what might Carl Vinson have owed his foresight?

In 1940, there was no need to visit the Louvre Museum in Paris in order to admire its Ancient Greek marble masterpiece, the famous Winged Victory of Samothrace. A home-grown American winged victory-to-be called the Douglas Dauntless ship-borne dive bomber (SBD) was open to view and it was no museum piece, as already were the biplanes that preceded it.

Dauntlesses were to act as the avenging angels for Pearl Harbor when, at the Battle of Midway, they torched four of the six Japanese carriers that perpetrated the deed, having so damaged the other two beforehand at the Battle of the Coral Sea that the pair missed Midway. The attributes of the Dauntless were known in 1940, having been tested and modified in May. Deliveries of the US Navy's new wonder plane began reaching the fleet later that year.

The Grumman Wildcat fighter was likewise as advanced. The Devastator torpedo bomber was already in service, while its successor, the Avenger, was far enough advanced in 1940 that it was ready to begin replacing the Devastator at the time of Midway; the US Navy was as yet not to know that American torpedoes were defective and too slow.

What proved a great unknown was the Japanese state of progress in naval aviation. It came as a devastating shock for the US to find at the outset of the Pacific War that the IJN was the world leader in naval aviation, its planes outmatching the US Navy's in every department except ship-borne dive bombers, although even the Dauntless was only marginally more effective than the Japanese Val.

This surprise progress by the IJN was very much due to the forethought of Yamamoto. The kind of carrier-based high-speed task force that comprised the Vinsonian prophesy became an IJN reality less than a year later with the creation of the First Air Fleet, or *Kido Butai* (the usual translation being 'striking force' or as later preferred, 'mobile fleet'), which grouped Japan's large high-speed carriers together in the world's first 'shock and awe' air-sea armada. The old fuel-guzzling, ploddingly slow battleships were out of date. They could not keep up, except for the Kongo-class former battlecruisers which had been strengthened and re-engined for the high speed necessary to beef up the *Kido Butai*'s escorting contingent.

But first, some perspectives and ironies need airing.

In its day, the English longbow was a game-changing weapon, so long as it had enough arrows to shoot and well-trained bowmen. Effective as the superbly trained English archers were in mowing down the armoured cavalry of the French kings, this did not mean the absence of horse-mounted English knights in armour on the battlefields of Crecy and Agincourt.

Likewise, the battleship could and would remain on the ocean's battlescapes in 1942.

Indeed, even as Carl Vinson spoke before Congress, rivetters and welders were hard at work around the world constructing the hulls of a whole new generation of battleships, and not least in the United States. In comparison, any progress in building new aircraft carriers looked more of an afterthought in the countdown years prior to the Pacific War. It was as if Vinson had never spoken and Yamamoto never dreamt.

Hitler had already launched the *Bismarck* and the *Tirpitz*. In France, Admiral Darlan had answered with the superb *Richelieu* and *Jean Bart*. Mussolini's Italians were intent on making the Mediterranian a new Roman lake with their three-ship Littorio-class and four rebuilt older battleships. None of these three continental European nations ever got to the point of having a new keel-up aircraft carrier in operation, due partly to the priority given to battleships.

Churchill, meanwhile, was worrying that the up-and-coming five-strong King George V-class was under-gunned compared to what everyone else was launching on the waters of the world. There were soon to be three such KGVs ready for war, and a further pair down the road. Churchill's worries would have come close to panic if he knew that in any contest with Japan's *Yamato* and *Musashi* (and prospectively by the late-war *Shinano*), the British KGV's ten 14-inch guns would be overwhelmed by the super-battleships with their nine 18.1-inch armament. In displacement tonnage, the Japanese trio were to be almost double their size.

Vinson's earlier naval appropriation Acts conceived for the US Navy no less than six battleships of about the same size as the KGVs, but armed with nine 16-inch guns. The *North Carolina, Washington, South Dakota, Massachusetts, Indiana* and *Alabama* were to join the fleet inside 1942. A further class of US battleships of *Bismarck* size were to be larger, faster and better protected, if similarly armed, the *Iowa, New Jersey, Missouri* and *Wisconsin* joining the Pacific Fleet from mid-war onwards.

So, let us now turn to aircraft carriers.

Carrier Production in the Post-Treaty Countdown Years to the Pacific War

Progress on carriers seemed somewhat hesitant by way of comparison. In the lead were the British, with four armoured deck carriers of the Illustrious-class, except they were intended only to replace the Treaty tonnage of four or five older, slower and inadequate flight decks. However, when war broke out, the latter were retained in order to spare the new carriers from endangering themselves in the course of performing humdrum roles such as commerce protection and aircraft ferrying. With war now rampant, the Treaties' tonnage limitations had become redundant.

An irony is that while it was the British in the build-up to war who ordered four large fleet carriers, they of the three leading naval powers were least able to make good use of them due to the hopelessness of the aircraft designed to fly off them (of which more anon). America and Japan, both far more advanced in their naval aircraft development, paralleled matters with just two new fleet carriers each.

America had commissioned the *Wasp* in April 1940 in response to the 1934 Vinson Act requiring the US to build up to its quotas. But in the next two years, America was only belatedly able to add one more fleet carrier, the *Hornet*. Meantime, Japan had beaten them to it with the two best carriers of any navy up to that point, the *Shokaku* and *Zuikaku* (which will feature over and again in these pages). Japan could not match Britain with a class of four new fleet carriers because their commitment to super-battleships permitted only the low-quality further recourse of building a fleet of liners that could be converted into carriers on the outbreak of war, as indeed they began to be after the start of the European conflict. This was due to the shortage of slipways and construction dry-docks long enough for keel-up warships in battleship, carrier or heavy cruiser lengths. We proceed to the conversions story in detail in the next chapter. Suffice to say here that the Shadow Fleet, as it has been called, was a response to the Second Vinson Act, that of May 1938, to which the IJN's reaction was to order liners that would be convertible. Then, in 1940, the Two-Ocean Navy Act ensured they were put on the conversion list.

In America, the 1938 Vinson Act permitted a 40,000 rise in carrier tonnage, in effect permitting two new fast fleet carriers; *Hornet* as a third vessel of the *Yorktown* class was first. The second was to become the lead ship to a new class-to-be of fast fleet carriers, this time to a post-Treaty design. This was the *Essex*.

The *Hornet* was laid down in September 1939 at the Newport News Shipbuilding Company in Virginia. It was completed two years and one month later. The *Essex* was not formally ordered until February 1940 and, due to it having to be designed first, not actually laid down at Newport News until April 1941. It then took two years and eight months to complete. That slowness was due to the Vinsonian vision not having supplanted the lingering faith in battleships on the part of an entrenched naval bureaucracy – the vision percolating but the coffee not yet ready to pour.

One factor was that naval intelligence proved insufficiently aware of Japan's desperate efforts to retain parity in carriers. Meanwhile, progress on the new battleships was rocketing along.

Another factor was how USS *Hornet* was built to an existing design at Newport News Shipbuilding, which had already built its sisters the *Yorktown* and *Enterprise*, whereas *Essex* was to a new design, although also a product of that same yard. So also would be two sisters ordered under the Two-Ocean Navy Act of July 1940 in reaction to the fall of France. That the *Essex* was down on paper that early proved a major advantage to the dramatic subsequent surge in production of the model.

With the Battle of Britain at its height two months later, a further eight Essex-class carriers were ordered, four from Newport News in Virginia again and four from Bethlehem Steel's Fore River Shipyard in Massachusetts. The latter four proceeded rather faster than at the Virginia yard. Two more Essex carriers were ordered within days of Pearl Harbor, and in due course a staggering nineteen more. Those completed and not cancelled amounted to twenty-four, inclusive of post-war completions.

During the war itself, there were rarely more than a dozen Essex-class carriers operational at any one time due to overhauls and battle damage. New construction and the arrival of the British Pacific Fleet helped replenish numbers badly diminished by the suicide storms of the kamikazes. None of the famous class of carrier, however, was actually sunk.

This air-sea armada became the relentless force that brought about the fall of the Japanese Empire, not atom bombs, as the American shogun of post-war Japan, General MacArthur, himself recognized. Thousand-plane raids from the massed flight decks wrecked communications, making the home islands non-functional, almost paralyzed, as well as wasting away the military's remaining air assets. There was virtually no oil left, so the IJN's last surviving major surface units were immobilized at their anchor chains, sitting ducks to be ruthlessly destroyed by Admiral Halsey's victory-winged harpies of vengeance. The man who nudged the carrier he skippered into the smoking ruins of Pearl Harbor in the wake of the 'Day of Infamy' vowed to make the Japanese language spoken only in hell.

Whereas it was the sum of Carl Vinson's Navy Acts that provided the means for beating Japan, his Two-Ocean Navy Act created the world's superpower, king of all the oceans. He was honoured in 1979, at the age of 96, when invited to attend the launch of the nuclear-powered carrier *Carl Vinson* – the only case of the US Navy naming a major warship after one of its heroes in his own lifetime.

Ironically, the Act was also one major cause of the Pacific War, as few of the larger vessels included in the programme could be completed by 1946, or indeed until 1947 (on the basis at least of peacetime construction progress). There thus gaped a never-again window of opportunity for Japan's well-trained 'Treaty Fleet' (and its Shadow Fleet in the works), as all would be operational in 1942. Before that could ensue, Japan would run out of oil reserves unless Dutch oil was seized in Indonesia. In the meantime, Japan had achieved parity in pre-war fleet carriers, and the Shadow Fleet conversions presaged superiority. Add to all that the fact that America did not yet have a 'two-ocean' navy. Some of its carriers could be expected to remain in the Atlantic, thereby increasing the margin of superiority for the IJN in the Pacific. This was the political window through which Japan's harpies of war enthusiastically surged.

As we shall now see, the Japanese carriers would be armed with the best naval aircraft in the world at that time. Meanwhile, the width of the window of opportunity was diminishing by the day due to a *de facto* Allied oil embargo and the completion of new constructions ordered under the earlier Vinson Acts.

We shall now go back to the beginning of Japanese naval aviation and explore how these famous models and their revolutionary predecessors emerged in the 1930s, before proceeding to Pearl Harbor, where that window was opened as if to thunderbolts.

How this started has us introduce an improbable and eccentric 'midwife'.

The Scottish Aristocrat

Japan took a very early interest in the possibilities of flying aircraft off ships. As Britain's ally in the First World War, their official observers were often witness to the progress in ship-borne aviation being made by the Royal Navy in the North Sea against the German Kriegsmarine. Earlier, enthusiasm for naval aviation had preceded the influence of the founder of aircraft manufacturer Nakajima, whose enthusiasm for the new development as a commander in the IJN became so intense that he left the navy to build aeroplanes. With the end of the war, the interest in the new aerial dimension to warfare on the part of the IJN did not wane.

And so it was that the Japanese ambassador in London was instructed to ask the British Government for a naval aviation mission to visit Japan in order to pass on the Royal Navy's experience gained during the war with Germany. The Admiralty firmly declined several times. They were not ready to yield their secrets.

The Foreign Office and the Board of Trade, however, were. They remonstrated how the two countries were partners in the Anglo-Japanese Alliance and that Japan had given much help during the First World War. The Admiralty reply was that Britain was so far ahead of everyone else with the new art and technology of flying aircraft off naval vessels that they should not give away this edge, even to an ally. They were overruled. Britain was impoverished after the war and debts were owed. Aircraft could be sold to the Japanese; aircraft carriers could even be built for them. There was some fancy footing around what to call the mission. The form of words devised for it emphasized that this was to be an 'unofficial mission', while a colourful gentleman was chosen to lead it. His name was Colonel William Forbes-Sempill, who bore the Scottish courtesy title Master of Sempill as heir to Lord Sempill, which he became in 1934 with the death of his father, who had served as naval aide to King George V.

Sempill ran away from Eton aged 16 and joined Rolls-Royce as an apprentice. He enrolled in the Royal Flying Corps during the First World War and progressed quickly thanks to his technical background. In 1921, he was voted the perfect leader for the mission for that reason, and no less for his personality and aplomb. He chose a team of thirty technicians and instructors, and arranged for the latest planes to be shipped over. Upon arriving in Japan, he was inducted as an acting captain of the Imperial Japanese Navy.

Sempill's mission enjoyed huge success. Admiral Togo himself, the world-renowned victor over the Russian Fleet at the Battle of Tsushima, came to admire the aircraft and to be charmed by the Master of Sempill. Prime Minister Kato personally wrote Sempill a thank-you letter at the visit's conclusion, praising the mission's work as 'epochal'. Sempill was invited to state whatever reward he might want, and settled for a traditional Japanese house to be sent for reassembly in Britain. The young Japanese pilots under his instruction, in their enthusiasm for the Anglo-Japanese Alliance and in gratitude for the gift of the mission, staged an 'official' fly past over the battlecruiser *Renown* when it visited Japan with the Prince of Wales and his aide, Lord Louis Mountbatten, on board, to the further embarrassment of Whitehall.

Twenty years later, pilots of an age to be their sons sank the *Renown*'s sister ship, HMS *Repulse*, and the brand-new battleship *Prince of Wales* off the coast of Malaya, an event that shocked the world and broke an empire. And that was just the trouble. At the Admiralty and the Foreign Office, people could see ahead. In dispatching the Sempill mission, the Establishment began to fear they may have swallowed a mouse. Meanwhile, America was vociferously demanding an end to the Alliance. Upon the Washington Treaty being signed in 1922, the Anglo-Japanese Alliance ceased to be and the 'unofficial mission' was officially withdrawn. That should have been an end to the matter.

However, it wasn't for Lord Sempill. He had never been official, so he went on being 'unofficial'. Much in love with Japan and its people, there were upon his return to his native country material matters to consider, such as rather heavy debts incurred as a result of trying to prove that all anyone needed to fly everywhere was a pair of motorcycle engines and a suitable frame. After an accident in America, he had incurred very heavy medical expenses. Then there was the dream-like fairy-tale chateau in Highland Aberdeenshire, Craigievar, to maintain. As a peer of the realm with a seat in the House of Lords, there were appearances to keep up, such as expensive memberships at clubs, the Atheneum a favourite in his case. One could bring one's very affable chums from Mitsubishi and the Japanese Embassy there, and when alone in a large leather chair with a freshly ironed copy of *The Times* newspaper in hand, the Atheneum was at least the sort of place one could munch raw garlic when bores approached through the smog of the smoking room – a recourse deplored by his family but all part of his eccentric nature. As chairman and then president of the Royal Aeronautical Society, he had a loyal and amused international following, which he was never to lose despite the perils to his reputation that pursued him.

The National Archives have still to release the full contents of the Sempill file from Official Secrets Act protection. Might he have been a 'double agent'? Who more likely than he to have prised forth, under the influence of pink gins at the Atheneum, tell-tale indiscretions as to what might be going on in Japanese shipyards and tempting forth smug boasts about the performance of new Japanese aircraft models in the China war?

Why was he such a protégé of Winston Churchill, and why such an embarrassment that he could not be prosecuted as a Japanese spy? The 'official' explanation is that to do so would have been to let on that Bletchley Park was reading the Japanese Embassy diplomatic code, including a cable from Tokyo to the London embassy approving the renewal of payments to Lord Sempill. On the other hand, the embassy was manned in 1941 by diplomats of an Anglophile cast who were doing an excellent job for Britain extolling to their superiors at home the way the nation was fighting back against Hitler, and how high was morale among the populace, at a time when the embassy in Berlin was doing little better than parrot Nazi propaganda. The London Naval Attaché, Captain Taiichiro Kondo, was a fluent speaker of English, described by all who knew him as a perfect gentleman and a really nice person. Only when Japan signed up to the Tripartite Pact did the Admiralty shy away from its friends at the embassy. Kondo and the others rued that day, and continued to send Tokyo upbeat reports on the British predicament.

It seems that one of these gave notice to Tokyo of the super-secret North Atlantic Conference of August 1941, when Churchill, his service chiefs and others sailed across the Atlantic in the battleship *Prince of Wales* – then proudly sporting the scars from its duel with the *Bismarck* – secretly to meet President Roosevelt on the heavy cruiser *Augusta* at an obscure cove on the Newfoundland coast. Another leak gave Tokyo a very fair summation of the outcome, the principal fruit of which was the North Atlantic Charter, the conceptual document that led to the NATO. All it had needed was for Tokyo to tip off Berlin that there was an Anglo-Saxon summit, and Admiral Doenitz could have positioned a wolf pack of U-Boats at their rendezvous point. However, there was no tip-off.

The 'unofficial' explanation of the 'Sempill Affair' became that here was an eccentric individual naively mixed up with the proverbial dirty armaments procurement and advisory business, who had somehow failed to acknowledge how the Anglo-Japanese Alliance, which had elevated him to celebrity status, was now as dead as his own mission – a mouse swallowed live passes out dead. On his return to the UK, there could have come the sense that he was the unfortunate dead mouse.

Back in Japan, they recalled Napoleon's slur on the British, 'perfidious Albion'. Sempill may have shared the anger and disappointment of his Japanese friends.

The Japanese Navy Grows its Wings

The story of how Japanese naval aviation shed its 1920s reliance on foreign advice and aircraft imports has three strands: a prophetic admiral; a very successful procurement system; and the China war as stimulus. This all came together in the 1930s largely unrecognized by the world.

The combination was to result in a war-winning collection of naval aircraft models, for which we will use their Allied names as usually encountered by the Pacific War reader, but on introduction at least including their official designations in parenthesis out of respect to the progenitors.

The most celebrated and successful were the three types the IJN supplied to their principal aircraft carriers before the outbreak of the Pacific War. They were in the specification, design, prototype or testing phase during the 1936/37 period when the debate between battleships and aircraft carriers could have been won. These were the Zero fighter, the Kate torpedo bomber and the Val dive bomber.

What was initially called the Zeke in American designation (to the IJN, the Mitsubishi A6M Type Zero carrier fighter) became familiar to the airmen of both sides as the Zero after its year of acceptance for production; in Japanese 2600, or 1940 in the Western usage. The Kate (Nakajima B5N Type 97 carrier attack aircraft) was accepted for production at the end of 1937 (or 2597 in Japanese chronology), while the Val (Aichi D3A Type 99 carrier bomber) was conceived not long after the Kate but was not accepted for production until 1939.

The Zero was at first unbeatable in aerial combat. Its range was three times greater than the German and British models of that time at just over 1,000 nautical miles, or 1,675 miles with the aid of a fuel drop-tank slung under its belly like a bomb. It could climb faster and more steeply than any rivals of that time, which made it the perfect defender of the carriers it protected. It was sleek, nimble and lightweight. It needed no catapult to launch, even from a third of a flight deck length. Its importance was as much strategic as tactical due to its range. Their unprecedented long range allowed Zeros to escort from Formosa across the South China Sea to the Philippines the bomber force that destroyed most of MacArthur's fleet of Flying Fortresses, thereby enabling Philippine operations to do without cover from the big carriers which could instead be used against Pearl Harbor.

The Kate was the world's most successful torpedo bomber, helped by its being armed with the world's best aerial torpedo, the Type 91. It could also act as a level bomber, performing in both roles at Pearl Harbor, where Kates sank the battleships *Arizona*, *Oklahoma*, *West Virginia*, *California* and *Nevada*. In their torpedo-bomber role, they also dealt the death blows to the carriers *Lexington*, *Yorktown* and *Hornet* in the great carrier battles of 1942, which together comprised half America's pre-war carrier fleet. Its range again was remarkable, even bearing the weight of a torpedo. On account of that burden, torpedo bombers were always the weak party when it came to operating range for combined strikes. Thanks to the Kate, the IJN could consistently out-range the American carriers with their combined strikes. By mid-1942, America began arming its carriers with a rival to the Kate called the Avenger, although American torpedoes were more or less useless until well into 1944.

The Val had the distinction of sinking more Allied warships than any other model of enemy aircraft. It was contemporary with the famous German Stuka dive bomber and the American Douglas Dauntless, which is usually reckoned to have had the edge over the Val for being able to bear 1,000lb bombs into battle. These were designed to wreck flight decks and hangars, as they did epically by torching the four Japanese carriers at Midway. In contrast, the Val carried a bomb not much more than half the weight, although most were designed to penetrate the hangar deck and explode in a carrier's vitals. In addition, lead planes often carried fragmentation bombs designed to explode on impact, decimating anti-aircraft batteries and wrecking plane handling gear. Following them into the attack, the aircraft loaded with armour-piercing bombs plunged down in their successive dives.

Meanwhile, the IJN had been leading the pace with other naval types such as land-based medium bombers, flying boats and float planes. Phenomenal range was again the key.

The Betty (Mitsubishi G4M Type 1 attack bomber) was a cigar-shaped, twin-engined, land-based bomber with a range that rivalled the four-engine American B 17, or Flying Fortress, and with a speed designed to outpace most fighters at the time. It came into production in 1941. It was torpedoes from the Kanoya Group of Bettys that finished off the *Prince of Wales* and the *Repulse*. But the Betty was no 'fortress' itself. The trade-off for a phenomenal range was a rash lack of armour protection. Its fearful crews called it the 'Flying Lighter'; the Americans 'The Zippo' after a popular cigarette lighter.

Often voted the best flying boat of the war was the four-engine Emily (Kawanishi H8K Type 2 flying boat), the first of which were distributed to naval reconnaissance outposts in early 1942. Its range well exceeded even that of the Betty at 3,888 nautical miles. It could carry a pair of torpedoes or two 1,746lb bombs. Unlike other Japanese models, it was of rugged construction and hard to shoot down. It and its predecessor, the Mavis, were the only four-engine aircraft to have been developed for production by the IJN.

Of a range of small seaplanes, the Jake (Aichi E13A Type 0 reconnaissance seaplane) was the most interesting. With a crew of three, the single-engined float plane had the phenomenal endurance for the time of fifteen hours and a range of well over 1,000 nautical miles. Designed for catapulting off cruisers, battleships and seaplane carriers, these float planes performed the fleet reconnaissance role in the Pacific for the *Kido Butai*, thereby saving from that role much diversion of strength from the air groups of the attack carriers. In contrast, the US carrier task forces committed a squadron of dive bombers to the scouting role. At the Battle of Santa Cruz in October 1942, that meant 25 per cent fewer dive bombers for attacking the Japanese carriers once the battle proper began. Thanks mainly to the Jake, the IJN retained a superiority of fleet-borne reconnaissance capability throughout the war.

Did these planes spring from the blue, like a Prometheus unbound, or was there a long, slow stewing in the engineering oven? How did a nation dependent upon importing or building aircraft under license in the 1920s suddenly, in a decade, become world class at aircraft design?

There were many reasons, but two stand out: the influence of Yamamoto as visionary and driver, and a brilliant procurement strategy.

If there was a Promethean moment, it came in 1932 with the establishment of a Naval Air Arsenal under the command of the Yokosuka Naval Base, which brought all testing, research and development under one big canopy. This happened during the couple of years Yamamoto headed the Technical Bureau of the Naval Aviation Department.

Top of the agenda was a new arrangement for managing competition for naval aircraft orders. Called the Prototype System, it invited two firms to compete by producing prototypes that would be expected to meet specifications demanded by the Navy. The IJN would then test the prototypes and award the contract to the most able. The big difference was that the loser could participate in production, for example in the supply of engines. The Japanese Army was even permitted to order from Nakajima modified versions of Mitsubishi fighters. It was a system ideal for nurturing an indigenous Japanese aircraft industry. While winners definitely won, losers still found roles. Firms learned to work together and to learn from one another; state and enterprise were locked together.

The first fruit of the Prototype System came with the highly successful predecessors to the Betty medium bomber and the Zero fighter – namely the Nell and the Claude. Both went into production in 1936.

The Claude (Mitsubishi A5M Type 96 carrier fighter) was 'in design, structure, and performance among the best fighters and certainly the best carrier fighter in the world at the time, and it gave Japanese aeronautical engineers the confidence that they could meet the highest standards', in the words of Mark Peattie, a leading authority on the development of Japanese naval aviation, to whose *Sunburst, the Rise of Japanese Naval Air Power, 1909–1941* we are much indebted here.

The Claude was such a success that even as it was first being issued to squadrons in 1936, the specifications were already being drawn up for the Zero. Promethean impulses were suffusing creative energies thanks to the inspiration of success.

The Nell (Mitsubishi G3M Type 96 medium attack bomber) had as its chief distinction a very long range at 2,365 nautical miles. To great enthusiasm, the plane entered service in the spring of 1937 just in time to participate in the early phases of the China war, wherein it shocked the aeronautical world with the distances of its transoceanic flights from Taiwan and Kyushu against targets in China. As the army began advancing up the Yangtze River after securing Shanghai, the Nells could be moved forward to mainland bases, from which they could penetrate to most key points in China, in particular the Chinese Nationalists' new capital of Chungking on the upper Yangtze.

Historically, the Nell was a very important aircraft for another reason. Around its performance peaked and then died the early 1930s myth avowed by a wide international following that bombers could outfly fighters. This received its 'bonfire of the vanities' in late 1937, when Chinese fighters began shooting down Nells in droves. In sacrificing everything to range over protection, the Japanese bombers caught fire almost from the first shot to the fuel tanks.

Fortunately for the future of long-range bombing, the Japanese Navy had almost concurrently been hard at work on a carrier fighter. From fighters being used primarily for shooting down scouting aircraft, foreseen now was a more ambitious capability, that of having the range to accompany carrier bombers to their objectives as escorts.

Mitsubishi was one of the two firms invited to meet the specifications laid down by the IJN with a prototype for it to test. This called for optimum speed, range and manoeuvrability. The design team was headed by Jiro Horikoshi (who went on to mastermind the new fighter's successor, the Zero) at the company's aeronautical works near Nagoya.

Horikoshi's single-engine all-metal monoplane made its debut as a prototype in January 1935. It won the competition, and after much testing and modification was adopted by the Navy in autumn 1936 to become known to the Allies as the Claude. It too entered the China war in late 1937, initially escorting carrier bombers, then accompanying Nells from advanced land bases gained by the advance up the Yangtze. After being withdrawn from the long-range role due to mounting losses, the Nells were now able to resume their missions. The Claude had put fighters back on the aeronautical map and saved the bombers.

No sooner was the revolutionary new fighter's success registering in the supreme test of combat than heads came together at Yokosuka with the aim of devising something far better still. The resulting 'specs' called for the range and endurance to cover Nells on their long-range missions, with consequently less reliance on advanced fighter bases, along with the speed and hitting power to knock down incoming bombers and the nippiness in dogfights to overcome enemy fighters. Features were called for that seemed to make the achievement of the 'specs' impossible. So thrown by the challenge was Nakajima that the manufacturer dropped out of the competition. Horikoshi's team at Mitsubishi refused to give up, seeing innovation as the key to success. A prototype was ready by March 1939, and even exceeded the standards of the specifications. By June 1940, the Zero began entering the China war. The fighters supplied to the Chinese Nationalists by the US and the Soviet Union were driven from the skies.

It had been the aim of Yamamoto in 1932 to make Japanese naval aviation independent of foreign help, able to stand on its own and even become supreme. He realized that for it to become the primary arm of the IJN, there first had to be the right aircraft for it to deserve that distinction, and indeed the right manpower to fly the beasts (which we will come to in due course). Hence the challenging specification standards set and the prototype system as a means of scientifically and expertly testing the prototypes.

While the debate raged between the 'gun lobby' and the aviation apostles, the latter already knew that thanks to the Nell and the Claude, the nation had become capable of competing with the best that rival powers could produce. Thanks to the specifications drawn up for the Kate, Val, Zero, Betty and Emily, similar achievements across the whole range of naval aircraft types was work already well in progress. Aeroplanes could now become ship-killers and outrange (*autoreenji* as rendered into Japanese spelling for foreign loan words) everybody else's.

A third dimension to the argument would cite the many who acknowledged that one day, even very soon, naval aviation would reign supreme. In that case, the aviationists argued, why not assume it and be prepared for it? After all, it took three to four years to produce an aircraft carrier. In that time, the IJN could expect to have all the improved aircraft models fully tested and in production, so why not order more flight decks ready for them?

Another strand of argument open to the aviationists was to say that the Navy could hardly become ready to go to war with America having just seen most of the fleet knocked about by a typhoon and currently being subjected to substantial modification as a result.

Indeed, in the mid to late 1930s, Japan chose to take much of its fleet out of operation in order to modernize key units, even to the extent of rebuilding its existing battleships. It also went about modifying those units that seemed at risk from typhoons due to top-heaviness.

There was also the most obvious argument of all: why persist obsessively with battleships when the IJN could not in all honesty expect to even attain parity in that department? Why not gain an edge in aircraft carriers instead?

The perspective from Yokosuka could see how America lagged about 35,000 tons short of its carrier quota in 1935. As we shall explore in Chapter 4 ('Phantom Fleet'), in 1935 there were only two facilities in Japan ready for building super-battleships, whereas there were at least ten slipways and construction docks suitable for churning out aircraft carriers.

Yamamoto as visionary

Yamamoto's aerial dreams seem to have sprung from the considerable time he spent in America. He had already made the rank of captain when, in 1923, he visited the US Naval War College. His experiences of America – first studying at Harvard from 1919–21, then touring America's industrial centres and oil fields, and his initial posting as an assistant naval attaché – may well have spurred a decision later in 1923 to change his specialty from gunnery to aviation.

In particular, the career prospects for a gunnery specialist might have seemed rather blighted now that Japan had been cut down to 60 per cent of the battleship strength of Britain or America. The possibility of aviation offering less-competitive career prospects could have been a consideration. He was also remembered for prophesizing the future importance of oil supplies and air power during lectures he gave to the IJN's Navy War College following his return from Harvard. As an attaché in Washington, he had been around at a time of enormous public interest in the future of aviation thanks to Lindbergh's epic flight across the Atlantic and the achievements of other aviators of the 1920s. Also worth considering was how at that time, General Billy Mitchell was trying to prove he could sink battleships with aircraft – to great controversy and with publicity to match.

Following his second visit to America, this time as a naval attaché in 1923, Yamamoto took up the post of vice-chief of the lakeside Kasumigaura ('Misty Lagoon') naval air station, which had recently been the location for the Sempill mission and could therefore be called the cradle of Japanese naval aviation.

There followed further diplomatic postings for Yamamoto, first again as Naval Attaché but now in the rank of captain at the Japanese Embassy in Washington from 1926–28, and then as a rear admiral participating in the London Naval Disarmament Conference of 1930. Between these appointments, he was posted to command the aircraft carrier *Akagi*, and after the London conference became head of the Technical Division of the Aeronautics Department at Yokosuka between 1930 and 1933, with the impact we have already noted. There followed another carrier command, that of 1st Carrier Division (which included the *Akagi*), before being sent abroad as naval advisor to the Japanese delegation at the preparatory talks for the 1935 London Naval Conference, after which he returned to the Aeronautics Department as its head.

Such an interwar summary of his career shows how he was almost exclusively used by the IJN in two roles: disarmament talks and naval aviation. His influence stemmed from these two specialties, such that he became Navy Vice-Minister in the government in 1936 and Commander-in-Chief of the Combined Fleet in 1939.

If a further dimension to the debate is needed, it would be that the apostle of naval aviation had risen in status by 1936 to a level that his voice could not be mocked.

For example, in the early 1930s, air power extremists set their hopes on long-range land-based naval air power. Yamamoto initially supported such aspirations. In aviation theory, it was then the day of the bomber supremacy school. There was a very orthodox streak to Yamamoto. He believed in the great sacred cow of the Japanese naval mindset, the 'decisive battle'. This is hardly surprising, for he fought as a young ensign at the Battle of Tsushima, where Admiral Togo met the Russian Baltic Fleet that had steamed halfway around the world to defeat Japan but was almost entirely lost under the guns of Togo's battle line.

The Americans were expected to combine their Atlantic and Pacific fleets to first cross the Pacific in defence of the Philippines and then to bombard Japanese cities. Mostly built of wood and paper, cities like Tokyo were not only the centres of population and industry, but notoriously vulnerable to firestorms of obliterating intensity. There was an in-built national cultural fear of foreign fleets taking advantage of Japan's exposure to intrusion or outright attack from the sea due to population centres clustering along the coastline, whereas the centres of the home islands are invariably mountainous and more thinly inhabited and resourced. This had propelled its will to join the modern world, if only to end unwelcome exposure to gunboat diplomacy.

The IJN strategy against any American surge in their direction across the Pacific was, as we have said, one of attrition. The American battle line would be whittled down by attacks of submarines, aircraft and light surface units before ever encountering the regrettably lesser force of Japanese battleships, whose quality would nevertheless be raised by virtually rebuilding them.

Yamamoto was fascinated with the chains of central Pacific islands that the IJN had won off Germany after the First World War. These 'unsinkable aircraft carriers' could become springboards for long-range air attacks on the advancing foe. It was this obsession that spurred him to demand a suitable bomber when he became head of the Technical Division in 1930. The result was the Nell and its successor, the Betty. The timing of the Nell coincided with the international debate about the future – or non-future – of fighter aircraft in the face of the widely fancied notion of the bomber becoming king of the skies. In such a climate, it was easy for the air power extremists to get carried away and argue shrilly for the scrapping of all big-gun ships, and even for that matter of aircraft carriers. None of this helped the naval aviation cause. If one wanted to win the argument, one had to believe in aircraft carriers.

Until the Claude and Zero came along, carriers could only serve up a thin soup. They needed fighters to protect themselves and those they were escorting. They also needed fighters with the range of their bombers so they could escort the bombers. Until that happened, the carrier was little more than the battle line's scouting force.

Here we come to one of the Pacific War's great ironies, one that is still not well understood and the real reason why aircraft carriers still command the sea today. The sinking three days after Pearl Harbor of the *Prince of Wales* and the *Repulse* off the coast of Malaya by flocks of Nells and Bettys, based at Saigon across the Gulf of Siam from Malaya, has been heralded then and ever since as the event that doomed the battleship. In actuality, it represented the sole occasion that a moving capital ship, namely a battleship or large carrier, was sunk by land-based aerial forces in the Pacific War. Level bombing from a great height of ships underway by large land-based bombers rarely ever scored a hit, while large land-based torpedo bombers proved easy targets for defending fighters and anti-aircraft fire.

The Malaya sinkings were therefore a one-off event. The protecting Australian Buffalo Brewster fighters failed to show up in time, while the Japanese airmen were an elite force with the training of the China war behind them. It was their state-of-the-art torpedoes that sank the ships. They were more easily able to close within decisive launching range because the *Repulse* was equipped with out-of-date AA defences, and the first hits on the *Prince of Wales* disabled power to some main AA turrets.

In subsequent attacks by Betty torpedo bombers against American warships under way, the bombers were mostly massacred by Wildcat fighters and AA fire.

The further irony of the episode is that the two British capital ships were all but doomed anyway, which has never been properly pointed out.

They sailed into the jaws of a well-prepared attrition trap. They first evaded a line of mines specially laid across their likely route, and next lines of scouting submarines, which nonetheless reported their course. As night fell, Jake cruiser float plane scouts shadowed the ships, guiding Admiral Ozawa's five heavy cruisers with their eighty deadly 'Long Lance' torpedoes – and escorting destroyers likewise armed – for a planned night attack, as was the IJN specialty. This was obverted when one of the searching navy bombers from Saigon illuminated Ozawa's flagship, thinking it had found the British force. The flare it dropped into the night was to guide in fellow fliers for a torpedo attack. Ozawa squawked out an alarm to Saigon, which called off the intended night air attack in favour of a daylight attempt next day. The British were a mere 15 miles away at the time, and an escorting destroyer was said to have reported seeing the flare. Assuming that any further attempt at concealment from the air was doomed, Admiral Tom Phillips had already given the order to set off home for Singapore, but only after first changing course further westward to give the spotter planes, while they were still in contact, the illusion that he was still sailing for the coast. It was while he was on this course that he so nearly ran into Ozawa before heading south for Singapore.

A night battle with Ozawa had been averted even as the Japanese force was coming into radar range of the British. This truth only emerged after the war. The aircraft that cheated Ozawa of his victory caught the *Prince of Wales* and *Repulse* the next day and sent them to the deep, along with Admiral Phillips.

Phillips was disparaging of the risks to battleships from aircraft. Naval intelligence had failed to brief him properly on Japanese proficiency in torpedo bombing, if indeed they knew anything of it in the first place. Posterity has tended to acquit him from blame, on the basis that risking all to sink the Japanese invasion fleet represented the only chance of obverting the disaster that followed: the fall of Singapore with its 100,000 defenders. He gambled wisely but he lost all. One of his greatest critics, Admiral Cunningham, who commanded the Royal Navy's defence of Crete in 1941 and the subsequent withdrawal from the island, averred that 'it takes three years to build a warship, but three hundred to rebuild a tradition'. In the halls of Etajima, these sentiments would have been well appreciated, as that is exactly what IJN graduates were taught to respect. Tom Phillips was indeed unlucky, because his fate at the hands of land-based air forces was not to be repeated.

It was naval aircraft flying off carriers that sank most of the Imperial Japanese Navy during the course of the Pacific War. The land-based US Army Air Force made continual and extravagant claims, but rarely was there any substance to them. The most notorious case was when they tried to claim responsibility for the victory at Midway, where their huge four-engined bombers splattered the ocean from far too great a height, only to miss with every one of their bombs. In no way did that inhibit much of the American press from being taken in by the USAAF's false claims. Even after the war, the myth died hard.

The best that Japanese land-based planes ever achieved against either carriers or battleships thereafter was sinking the light fleet carrier *Princeton* at Leyte Gulf and a few escort carriers in the final year of the war as victims of the kamikazes.

By the middle and late 1930s, both American and Japanese naval thinking was beginning to push aside notions of land-based air supremacy as any kind of easy sea power fix. They appreciated how a land base is vulnerable to surprise attack from seaborne aerial forces, as the Pearl Harbor raid so dramatically proved, and later that on Truk in the Caroline Islands. What was needed was a mobile platform. Range thus became less of a consideration. One could outrange an enemy carrier force by all means, but a carrier task force did not need to outrange land-based air resources when it could sneak up close under cover of darkness, as per Pearl Harbor, or exploit a weather front, as Admiral Sherman did in his bold raid on Rabaul in November 1943.

The proof of the pudding historically lay in the fact that not one of America's game-changing Essex-class carriers was sunk, despite the best efforts of the kamikazes in particular – mangled and part-incinerated as some of them were, notably the *Franklin* and *Bunker Hill*.

Critical Mass and the *'Aucun* Factor'

There comes a point in carrier warfare when critical mass takes over. The more flight decks on the water, the more state-of-the-art aircraft in the air, the more superbly trained and experienced air crews flying them and the more advanced the control, communications and detection systems, the less the risk of anything untoward happening to them. In every conflict between the Pacific War and the Second Iraq war, America put its carriers in the front line and never lost a flight deck. Nor has any other nation lost an aircraft carrier.

In this chapter, we have primarily dwelt on the rise of aircraft development and their seaborne platforms, the longbow and the arrows to use our earlier analogy. Now we must write of the archers themselves.

Aircrew training in Japan concentrated on creating an elite band of airmen but neglected the creation of a reserve to draw from in the event of extended conflict. The logic of this was fundamentally sound, in that underlying it was the awareness that Japan could only hope to triumph in a short war, thus applying superior skills from the outset. However many less skilled pilots the IJN trained, they could never be expected to suffice in a long war against America, let alone against America and Britain combined. Denied his 'decisive battle' victory in the Central Pacific at

Midway, Yamamoto found himself drawn into a war of attrition in the South Pacific, which sucked the IJN's prized naval aviation elite into almost total destruction.

By the time that Nimitz was ready to surge across the Central Pacific to Japan with his Essex-class and Independence-class carriers, the IJN found itself in the junkyard. From being the elite of the planet, Japanese airmen became cannon fodder, barely trained and now flying obsolescent models they were shot down in droves. There was no way the IJN could catch up. Everything conspired against them as they were run ragged as the relentless American advance surged onwards. Aviation fuel in desperately short supply forced limitations on pilot training. Materiel shortages held up production of the actually very competent new aircraft models being developed. By the end of 1943, the auxiliary aircraft carriers feeding fighter aircraft to far-flung island bases had to be switched to convoy escort in order to preserve the tankers that fuelled the war effort.

There were presentiments of what could unfold, not least among the carrier admirals themselves. Yamamoto has been criticized as igniting the American nation with his 'sneak attack' on Pearl Harbor, thereby – albeit unintentionally – exorcising it out of isolationism into a superpower almost overnight. However, as the *Kido Butai* sailed on its mission across the North Pacific, the pilots and their chiefs hoped above all to catch the US Pacific Fleet's three carriers at the Hawaiian base. They were cheated of this hope. Consequently, they were to be fed into the South Pacific meat grinder over the next two years, and most died.

The commander of the *Kido Butai*, Admiral Chuichi Nagumo, appears to have been pessimistically aware of the lack of properly trained aircrew reserves. After his victory in the Battle of Santa Cruz at the height of the Guadalcanal campaign in October 1942, he was in Truk lagoon when visited by a destroyer commander who had distinguished himself in night battles at Guadalcanal. Both were long-time destroyer and torpedo men. Commander (later Captain) Hara congratulated Nagumo on his victory. Nagumo confessed that it had not been decisive enough. As indeed it was not, for during the battle, most of the remaining elite fliers of the *Kido Butai*, including their leaders, were shot down in flames. It had been a Pyrrhic victory and boded ill for the conclusion of the war.

The Hara/Nagumo exchange at Truk after Santa Cruz is an insight into the mind of Nagumo when he faced impossible decisions during the Battle of Midway. He did not survive the war in order to explain his actions at Midway. The exchange indicates a possessive concern for his airmen, an awareness that after them lay little worth flying. Such may explain one of the great puzzles of the Midway battle – why he did not accede to the frantic signals of his 2nd Carrier Division commander, Rear Admiral Tamon Yamaguchi. After a scout plane that had been catapulted from the heavy cruiser *Tone* revealed at least one American carrier in ambush position, Yamaguchi wanted to dispatch immediately his near deck-ready squadrons of dive bombers against them from his pair of carriers, the *Hiryu* and *Soryu*.

Nagumo opted instead to accept the risk of an American strike, because the falsely reported position of the sighting had indicated the American force on the outside of its range. He thereby judged that he had time to ready full deck loads for a combined strike against the American task force from all four Japanese aircraft carriers, once the other two – the *Akagi* and *Kaga* – had completed rearming their Kate bombers with torpedoes. The dive bombers aboard the *Soryu* and *Hiryu* would be ready to strike much sooner.

Meanwhile, aircraft from the earlier strike against the American air base on Midway atoll could be landed and stowed below flight decks in the hangars for refuelling and rearming, so they could be hurled as a second strike against the American carriers. Waiting in order to dispatch a full co-ordinated first strike was a risk, but there seems to have been a presentiment at work – his fliers being an irreplaceable force, a once-only capability for securing total and decisive victory against America. That could only be achieved with an all-out co-ordinated attack. There was also the precedent of the Battle of the Coral Sea the previous month, when a co-ordinated attack was thought to have sunk both American carriers (in actuality only the *Lexington*, because the *Yorktown* survived to fight at Midway).

A commander, if he is any good, prides himself on his men. While a destroyer man himself and unexpectedly placed in charge of airmen – albeit well advised by the likes of his chief of staff Ryunosuke Kusaka, air commander Minoru Genda and leader of the Pearl Harbor raid, Commander Mitsuo Fuchida – Nagumo listened to his innermost fears. However reluctant he was to accept the new primacy of naval aviation, nonetheless he would have known how irreplaceable his aircrews were.

This and the record of his comments to Commander Hara in Truk lagoon may give insight into his much-criticized decision at Midway. One can assume that Nagumo was imbued with the IJN's 'decisive battle' fixation. One can also surmise that as commander of the elite First Air Fleet, he had uncomfortably realized that nothing much to compare with its air crews lay beyond it. Consequently, would not anyone have accepted the risk he took?

For here were American carriers in range. They had cheated him at Pearl Harbor by their absence, but now at least openly lay under his paw to crush. It had to be all or nothing. Anything less than a totally decisive result would fritter away the winning card in his hand and leave the American enemy with a carrier 'fleet in being', as tenuously became the case after Nagumo's hard-won victory at Santa Cruz. To give the man his due, he chose to take the risk he did because the sighting report received mistakenly placed the American fleet at or beyond the extremity of its air range. It seemed he still had time to act.

If asked, as Churchill did of General Weygand after the German panzer divisions broke through the French front in May 1940, 'Where are your reserves?', his reply would have been the same, 'There are none'. But it was not Nagumo's fault that Japan had failed to provide adequate reserves of aircrews.

For Japan to have developed critical mass (i.e. the Phantom Fleet, as proposed in Chapter 4) in aircraft carrier recruitment in the countdown to the Pacific War, it needed to address the question of building up reserves of trained aircrews, either by doubling or trebling the highly skilled front-line cadres that it entered the war with in late 1941, or at least finding an acceptable compromise strategy between recruitment of front-line elite and reserves.

If we peer at what historically was ordained, we can hypothesize Phantom Fleet prescription from that. For example, in August 1941, the IJN brought forth a plan for training 15,000 pilots a year, although that came far too late for it to have any hope of mustering an adequate war reserve. But what if it had started building up such reserves four or five years earlier?

In the 1930s, barely 100 pilots joined the fleet in any one year, such that, according to historian Arthur Marder, 'when war came, there were between 3,000 and 4,000 navy pilots, of whom 1,000–1,500 were trained for carriers. There were not enough pilots to man all available aircraft and maintain a comfortable reserve.' The reason for this lay in the extremely tough qualifications for flyers. According to fighter ace Sakai Saburo, he was one of only seventy accepted for flight training at Kasumigaura. There had been more than 1,500 applicants. The rigours of the training course weeded out more. The accident rate was also high in service due to the intensity of continued training in the most testing conditions. And then there was the China war, with its inevitable casualties.

The pre-war average number of flying hours in the IJN was two or three times that of Allied training. That was the measure of the human resource that flew in the open door at Pearl Harbor and raged all across the Pacific in 1942, the year that shook America and its allies to their core.

Given the prescience of the Japanese admirals as to their doubts about their chances in a war with America, what drove the decision to attack Pearl Harbor? The answer is Yamamoto – and such is universally accepted. So let us return to the admiral.

As we encountered in the first chapter, here was a man among the best brains in the IJN and the prophet of naval aviation, but imbued in the conservative IJN tradition, with the need to win a Pacific-wide war by annihilating the primary enemy fleet.

That fleet, on 7 December 1941, was anchored off Ford Island, Pearl Harbor. In order to succeed, the Japanese carriers would need to sink the US Pacific Fleet's three aircraft carriers and destroy the fleet's fuel reserves stored in tank farms. In the event, the US carriers were absent and the tank farms went unmolested. The raid thus failed. All Yamamoto succeeded in doing by eliminating the US battleship force as a factor in the early stages of the war was to unite Americans in a thirst for revenge. Isolationism died overnight in the mud and flames of Pearl Harbor. America did not miss its battleships once they had gone.

Chapter 3

Shadow Fleet

'The Japanese aircraft carriers Junyo and Hiyo illustrate the perennial obstacle to international attempts at effective arms limitation: cheating. Lord Chatfield had predicted this while attending the Washington Conference in 1921. The Japanese were to become the masters of the clandestine. Only they thought of building fleet aircraft carriers as merchant ships in order to increase the number shortly after the outbreak of war.'

(Andrew Lambert, ed., *Warship*, Volume IX)

On the French Riviera, hardly an hour goes by without a cruise liner edging across the horizon, suggesting that there may well be hundreds of them at large on the 'seven seas' of the world today. Imagine how if the Third World War broke out they would all be out of business, other than those requisitioned as troop ships or for conversion into auxiliary naval vessels, even into aircraft carriers. To the practised eye, they might as such seem to be lacking the carrying capacity for anything much more than helicopters or jump jets, given the demands of today's advanced naval jet aircraft for increased flight deck length. But remove the smoke stack and some superstructure, and the layman can imagine a nefarious quick fit of the sheep into wolf's clothing. Out then with the bingo halls, swimming pools, nightclubs and gyms, and in with the hangars, aircraft-size elevators and superimposed flight deck.

The Japanese did not invent the idea of converting vessels into aircraft carriers, as we have seen in the last chapter. Britain had been first to convert a liner, the *Argus*, before laying down the first actual purpose-built aircraft carrier, little *Hermes*. Japan's own claim to distinction was to have completed the first vessel in the world to be built from the outset as an aircraft carrier – the *Hosho*. There was no other purpose-built carrier completed by the time the Treaty came into effect. Everything else, apart from the much delayed *Hermes*, were conversions, including America's little *Langley*. That remained so until the appearance of the *Ranger* for the US, *Ryujo* for Japan in the early 1930s and – belatedly – HMS *Ark Royal* in 1939 for the Royal Navy.

There were to be no more conversions completed until 1941, when the European war was already two years into its course. In that year, Britain achieved great success protecting Gibraltar convoys with its first escort carrier, *Audacity*. During the same year, Japan completed the conversions of one fast naval auxiliary into the light fleet carrier *Zuiho* and liner *Kasuga Maru* into the auxiliary carrier *Taiyo*. America, in June 1941, commissioned its first conversion of a merchantman and named it the *Long Island*. The sole conversion to join the Pacific Fleet in 1942, it notably ferried the first thirty-one aircraft into Henderson Field on Guadalcanal following the airstrip's completion shortly after the landing of the 1st Marine Division there early that August.

What is it that so distinguishes Japan's record in this business of creating pearls out of sows' ears? It lies in the amazing fact that at the outbreak of the Pacific War, Japan had completed, or was completing, no less than seventeen hulls specially designed for speedy conversion at fitting-out docks and thereby leaving slipways and construction docks more or less free for keel-up new-builds. At 1942 values, the conversions could be expected to weigh into the balance of naval power a total capability of about 500 aircraft, or more than the fleet carriers of the Pearl Harbor striking force. That, of course, was provided that all seventeen were actually converted.

These clandestine 'hulls in the water' are known to historians of the Pacific War as the Shadow Fleet. It is a remarkable story never properly told. Rather, the Shadow Fleet is afforded brief or reluctant entries which to a greater or lesser extent disparage the admittedly modest attributes of the converted vessels. They universally fail to acknowledge their role in drawing out the Pacific War by providing the edge in keeping the US Navy busy in the South Pacific for well over a year, instead of surging across the Central Pacific on the direct route to Japan as they were to do in 1944.

All of the 'Shadow Seventeen' were conceived from the outset as vessels designed for conversion into front-line fleet carriers. That most of the conversions failed to meet that standard was due to them being two slow by Second World War fleet standards. They could keep up with the pre-war battleships, but not with modern battleships and carriers. Then, due to the very early start to the Shadow Fleet programme in the mid- to late 1920s, designers failed to allow for advances in aircraft design requiring of carriers greater speed in the water or catapults for launching the aircraft.

On the other hand, this disappointment was balanced by a positive realization – the need for auxiliary carriers to perform ancillary roles that would not divert fleet carriers and thereby dilute their overall attack strength.

In contrast, Allied mercantile conversions were much slower and smaller. They were intended for the anti-U-Boat role, as convoy escorts. Once they appeared in number, they turned the tide of the Battle of the Atlantic. They were also found to come in handy in many other roles, such as aircraft ferries, for training air groups, for joining the naval auxiliary groups that serviced the fast carrier task forces – their role being to replenish their air groups with new planes – and not least for providing close-in air cover and ground support for amphibious landing forces.

Their larger and faster Japanese peers were often similarly used, except that seven of the seventeen proved fast enough to attempt fleet carrier roles, as might two others if they had not been sunk before they could be converted. The Allied so-called escort carriers usually came with catapults, unlike the much larger and faster Japanese conversions.

The expression 'escort carrier' needs explanation. Any vessel specifically designed to escort convoys had the word 'escort' as designator. The Japanese conversions were never intended to work as such, albeit that late in the war they were committed to a convoy escort role. There was a world of difference between them, the Japanese conversions being the better part of two-and-a-half times the tonnage of those of the Allies, and near half again the speed. We will explore the Allied conversion concept in more detail at the end of the chapter.

The British were similarly challenged by the need for more fast fleet carriers, but they eschewed the temptation to convert the *Queen Elizabeth* and *Queen Mary* transatlantic super-liners, which were four or five times the size of the Japanese liners and unlike them, as fast as an average modern fleet carrier. It was a close call between conversion to carrier and adaptation to fast troop transport role. In the end, the latter won due to the necessity for safely transporting vast numbers of American GIs to Britain in the two-year build-up to the Normandy landings. The *Queens* were so fast they could outrun the U-Boats by sailing on their own rather than being tied to slow-moving convoys. Both survived the war undamaged, except for ramming and sinking the escorting light cruiser *Curacoa*.

We will now review Japan's 'Shadow Seventeen', finding therein two basic categories – naval auxiliary conversions and passenger liner conversions – as the Shadow Fleet table at the close of the chapter demonstrates.

The table shows what units had been planned for conversion and thereafter became 'hulls in the water' to be dressed up in whatever merchant or naval guise was adopted for them, namely as passenger liners or tenders for either submarines or seaplanes. Of the seventeen shown, we see that twelve actually became aircraft carriers. A further pair of seaplane carriers only missed conversion to light fleet carrier status when – still in service as seaplane carriers – they were sunk, as likewise were the first three ocean liners in their interim early wartime role as troop transports. That also was to be the fate of a later liner, *Brazil Maru*. Nonetheless, all seventeen were units clandestinely designed for rapid conversion to capital-ship status in the countdown phase before hostilities. Only shortage of fitting-out facilities in Japan allowed the fates of war to catch up on those in the rear of the conversion queue.

The table shows the Shadow Fleet in the order of vessels being laid down and where they were constructed under their 'shadow names': Shinto shrines in the case of the liners and historic place names in the case of the naval auxiliaries. To the left are shown construction times and locations. To the right are the same for the conversions, which in some cases proceeded while the vessels were still on the stocks. Their displacement tonnage is shown, and their speed as carriers, as well as their operative air strength – in the case of the seaplane carriers, first as seaplane strength and later as light fleet carriers. In the case of the two sunk while still acting as seaplane carriers, we show the number of seaplanes carried first when the vessels were operated solely as such and later when the lower deck became occupied by midget submarines.

Upon becoming carriers, the ex-liners were given 'hawk' names and the ex-submarine tenders 'phoenix' names. The seaplane carriers alone remained under their Shadow names. After all, had they not been carriers of a sort all along?

The Naval Auxiliaries

Obviously, were one to choose between a merchant vessel such as a liner for conversion or a fast naval auxiliary like a submarine tender or seaplane carrier, the better ship would emerge in the naval rather than the merchant guise. Too many compromises with the shipping line complicated the potential re-genesis of an ocean liner into an aircraft carrier. It also proved so in practice, although with a dramatic if controversial exception, as we shall come to with the *Junyo* and *Hiyo*.

Whereas three liners had been subsidised in the late 1920s in return for designs quickly convertible to carriers, the first actual conversion of a Shadow Fleet unit did not begin until January 1940. Not unnaturally, first choice was a naval auxiliary as that did not mean taking a liner off the lucrative trans-Pacific passenger route. Chosen after a long hiatus was the unfinished second ship of a two-ship class of submarine tenders, the *Takasaki*. It was re-named *Zuiho* ('Lucky Phoenix') upon the completion within a year of its fitting out as a light fleet carrier. It became the model for all subsequent conversions of fast naval auxiliaries to light fleet carrier, features of which included powering by a pair of destroyer steam turbines which on a heavy cruiser-size displacement gave a useful top speed of 29 knots, justifying deployment as a light fleet carrier. Other features were a single hangar, no island and two elevators, but minimal protection in order not to sacrifice a knot of speed, the carrier's speed and agility being considered its best defence against bombs and torpedoes.

Of similar displacement to the latest heavy cruisers *Tone* and *Chikuma*, its water-line length was much the same, even 2 metres longer. This gave it sleek and photogenic lines, unlike those of the stubbier-looking liner conversions.

The 'Lucky Phoenix' proved a successful unit, surviving the big carrier battles, first at Midway in a support role and next at Santa Cruz, this time more grandly alongside the mighty *Shokaku* and *Zuikaku*. There it performed the role of dedicated defence carrier, flying six Kates for reconnaissance and anti-submarine (A/S) patrol and twenty-one Zero fighters for strike force escort and combat air patrol. The Battle of Midway had taught the need for a flight deck cleared at all times for combat air patrol and A/S comings and goings.

There was, however, a not-inconsiderable speed differential, such that the Battle of the Philippine Sea found the *Zuiho* grouped with two other light fleet carrier conversions in the vanguard with Admiral Kurita's battleships and heavy cruisers. The lesser speed of the light fleets made them more compatible to being teamed with the faster battleships. *Zuiho* was finally sunk at the Battle of Leyte Gulf in October 1944, again this time in company with the *Zuikaku*.

In contrast, consider the quick fate of its sister *Shoho* ('Happy Phoenix'), sunk in its very first combat operation in a support role at the Battle of the Coral Sea in May 1942. It began life riding the waves as the submarine tender *Tsurugizaki* in the late 1930s, before following the *Zuiho* into conversion facilities at Yokosuka Navy Yard. The conversion lasted throughout 1941.

Next into the same Yokosuka facilities went an earlier submarine tender that had been ordered in 1931 – rather than in 1934 like the other two – this being the *Taigei* ('Great Whale'). It re-emerged towards the close of 1942 as the light fleet carrier *Ryuho* ('Dragon Phoenix'), despite receiving a bomb hit while in the shipyard during the famous Jimmy Doolittle Raid of April 1942. It survived the war afloat. The *Taigei* had the distinction of being the first naval auxiliary designed for rapid conversion, the order being placed in 1931. Photos taken of it as submarine tender show at first glance that it seemed to need nothing much more than a flight deck and repositioning of the funnel outboard to become a 'flat top'.

The air component of the initial duo, at 27 operational for each, was equivalent to the addition of a third carrier to the Soryu-class, the latter rated at fifty-four aircraft each operationally. As a trio, their combined operational air strength could exceed that of a seventy-two-plane Shokaku-class large fleet carrier. There lay the wisdom of the decision to convert these three naval auxiliaries. The 'Phoenixes' weighed into the Pacific arena when it counted for Japan the most.

Looked at from another perspective, compare the pre-war line-up of naval auxiliary hulls in the water suitable for light fleet carrier conversion – namely seven – with America's belated effort at front-line-worthy conversions, namely the nine-ship Independence-class. None of the latter became fully operational in the Pacific until the second half of 1943, their appearance coinciding with the first Essex-class large fleet carriers.

The Independence-class light fleets were conversions of unfinished cruiser hulls sitting on the stocks. The idea had been that of no less than President Roosevelt himself as an expedient for augmenting US strength in the Pacific in a hurry. By early 1944, the 'nifty nine' were able to plug a 300-plane suffusion into the fast carrier fleet's strike capability.

Also ordered as part of the same 1934 naval replenishment programme that eventually brought the *Soryu*, *Hiryu*, *Zuiho* and *Shoho* into the war were three other fast naval auxiliaries that were to begin life as seaplane tenders. These were the *Chitose*, *Chiyoda* and *Mizuho*.

The Seaplane Carriers

Here we come to the shadiest of the Japanese Shadow Fleet guises, that of the seaplane tender. In most navies, a seaplane tender was typically a vessel that *tended* float planes and flying boats floating on the water alongside, rather than *carrying* them on board. Unlike an airfield, the tender could move base by sailing to another port or anchorage, which conferred a great advantage in terms of extending the range of their scouting role. Popular candidates for tender were the old 'four-pipers' in US service. These were First World War-vintage four-stacked destroyers converted to a seaplane tendering role. As such, seaplane tenders were a category excluded from the respective aircraft carrier tonnages allocated each nation by the Washington Treaty. Yet someone forgot to attach a size limitation other than the blanket 10,000-ton limit on all warships except for the quota-limited battleships and aircraft carriers.

Hence the preposterous IJN response to what they saw as a window of opportunity. They built heavy cruiser-size ships able to carry from 22–24 seaplanes, while calling them tenders. When converted to the light fleet carriers *Chitose* and *Chiyoda*, they could operate thirty aircraft. These were in either incarnation aircraft carriers. Nevertheless, the world was content to class them as seaplane tenders, and it is under that designation they are listed in all the main references, including *Jane's Fighting Ships* and Watts & Gordon no less.

If float planes were close to useless in the striking role, they were nonetheless capable of long-range reconnaissance, anti-submarine patrol and as pickets warning of incoming air strikes. That saved diverting fleet carrier air resources to fleet support roles. The 'Chi Chis' became prized fleet units. Float planes in the IJN could be deployed as the eyes of the fleet in a longish-range reconnaissance role. The *Chitose* was part of the Vanguard Group at the Battle of Eastern Solomons, for instance. There, it was heavily damaged but escaped to Truk.

The 1934 Order included a third seaplane carrier, the *Mizuho*. The 1937 Order added a fourth, *Nisshin*. Each was designed to be rapidly convertible along the same lines as *Zuiho*. But that was never to be. The *Mizuho* was caught by a submarine early in the war and *Nisshin* succumbed to air attack while on a Solomons sortie, orders for which the codebreakers opened.

After the Midway disaster, conversion was begun at Yokosuka of the *Chitose*, following that of the *Ryuho* there. *Nisshin* was scheduled to have followed the *Chitose*'s conversion at these same fitting-out facilities at Yokosuka. *Chiyoda*, meantime, was converted at Sasebo. Useful as these fast warships were in the role of seaplane carriers to the fighting IJN, the desperate need to replace lost flight decks after Midway rode all before it.

In their first battle as light fleet carriers, they were teamed with the *Zuiho* as the 3rd Carrier Division, each hurling nine bombers, nine fighter bombers and twelve fighters into the Battle of the Philippine Sea in June 1944. All three survived the battle.

Their names were not changed after conversion due to the heroic reputation built up by the *Chitose* in the South Pacific earlier in the war. Its crew felt strongly on the issue. Chiyoda is the district of Tokyo that includes the Imperial Palace, the Diet and other glories of the capital city, so that was not a name to lose lightly either.

The 3rd Carrier Division reappeared at the Battle of Leyte Gulf as part of the carrier decoy force with which Admiral Ozawa lured Admiral 'Bull' Halsey's US Third Fleet away from the approaches to Leyte Gulf, so that the Japanese super-battleships and heavy cruisers could slip in through the San Bernardino Strait to slaughter the invasion shipping in the gulf. When Halsey's carriers caught up with the decoys, all three bit the bullet, as did that last of the Pearl Harbor veterans, the *Zuikaku*.

On the basis of the initial sighting report of the Japanese carriers being four in number, Halsey assumed from prior intelligence that one was indeed the *Zuikaku*, but the other three were brand-new Unryu-class fleet carriers, unknowing of the fact that not enough carrier plane crews were left to man the new boys. As this was a decoy force, the three Shadow light fleet carriers were sacrificed instead.

Thereby arose the Shadow Fleet's last great act of deception. It even came close to winning 'decisive victory' for Japan by opening the door to Leyte Gulf for the *Yamato* and its gang of battleships, heavy cruisers and destroyers. If Admiral Kurita had rode on into the Gulf, before that day's sun had set their guns and torpedoes could have massacred the greater part of shipping the Allies needed to transport troops and their supplies to future beachheads further up the sea road to Japan. The kamikazes could then have slowed up any recovery from what would have become a logistical nightmare. Why Kurita turned tail instead we shall come to in the next chapter.

Meanwhile, we will move on congenially to the topic of the liner conversions listed in the Shadow Fleet table.

The Liners

If the expedient of building fast naval auxiliaries as suitable 'hulls in the water' held most promise for quality conversions, the IJN's ocean liner scam proved the most ingenious. First, there were the exciting economics. One got a carrier-to-be more or less at half price. It would pay its way from passenger fares while still in the guise of liner. Secondly, there were three Mitsubishi slipways at Nagasaki suitable for sizeable liners. All one needed to do was make these liners fast enough and bludgeon the shipping line into design specifications more friendly to conversion needs – if less sympathetic towards passenger management. As we shall see in a couple of cases (the *Hiyo* and *Junyo*), they were to build up to *Shokaku* size.

The kind of international prestige that drove nations post-war to create their own national airlines attached itself in the interwar era to passenger liners. These were immensely expensive to build and equip, although taking a lot less time than a warship of equivalent size. In Japan's case, they were only affordable if generously subsidised by the government, just as many nations underwrote national airlines after the war.

The notion of converting liners was not entirely original. The Royal Navy's first full flight-decked aircraft carrier, HMS *Argus* – known to sailors as the 'Ditty Box' – had originally been laid down in a British yard in 1914 as a fast liner for an Italian shipping line. It was purchased by the Admiralty, and after the requisite design changes emerged as the first proper full-length flight-decked aircraft carrier in the world. The intention was that it serve as the 'eyes of the fleet' against the Imperial German Navy in the North Sea: it was aptly named after the 100-eyed watchman of Greek mythology.

This first of the world's conversions to aircraft carriers proved far too slow for fleet work, but played a heroic role in the Second World War as an aircraft ferry, notably on dangerous Malta convoys that fed fresh Spitfire squadrons to the beleaguered island base in the hours of its mortal peril.

Perhaps in Japan the liner 'penny' first dropped in the officers' mess at Kasumigaura air base up the coast from Tokyo, where the Sempill mission – see Chapter 2 – was ensconced shortly after the Great War.

Not long afterwards, the liner conversion recourse arose during discussions between the shipping line Nihon Yusen Kaisha (NYK) and Japan's Ministry of Transport. The result was that the ministry subsidised three 17,000-ton liners for use on NYK's trans-Pacific run to San Francisco, providing NYK co-operated with the IJN on a design capable of express-speed conversion into aircraft carriers in the event of war. In that contingency, passenger traffic would cease and the ships would have no other use than as fast troop transports.

The three liners were the *Asama Maru*, *Tatsuta Maru* and *Kamakura Maru*. They were all built by Mitsubishi at Nagasaki, and went into service each side of 1930. They were named after famous Shinto shrines.

While the Pacific run to America stayed open until Pearl Harbor in December 1941, the Atlantic run became dodgy for peacetime traffic with the outbreak of war in Europe in September 1939. The result was that the *Asama* trio went to the back of the conversion queue and a trio of liners intended for NYK's European service in effect jumped to the front. Only one had been launched by the time Hitler marched into Poland.

The European service liners were the *Nitta Maru*, *Yawata Maru* and *Kasuga Maru*, in that order of being laid down at Nagasaki on the two slipways that matched their keel length. This work proceeded between May 1938 and January 1940. The 1938 trio compared to the 1928 trio were very slightly larger, of the same speed but sporting a single funnel instead of the two on the earlier class. They too bore the names of Shinto shrines. Likewise, they were subsidised in return for designs capable of rapid conversion to carriers.

Kasuga Maru, being still on the stocks, proved the natural first choice. It was requisitioned before completion and converted between May and September 1941 into the auxiliary aircraft carrier *Taiyo* ('Goshawk', literally 'Great Hawk') at Sasebo. The other two followed on from its conversion, *Unyo* ('Cloud-borne Hawk') by April 1942 and *Chuyo* ('Heaven-bound Hawk') the following November. All were short order jobs, and as such deficient on quality grounds. Kure Navy Yard was given the conversion job, each following on successively from the other at Kure's fitting-out facilities.

The order for conversion was part of a panicky response to the 1938 Vinson Act's inclusion of new carriers for the US Fleet.

While their speed of 21 knots was very impressive by Allied escort carrier standards, it was not enough for their originally intended fleet carrier role. On the other hand, the burden and risk of aircraft ferry duty would not now need to be borne by the fleet carriers. Auxiliary carriers could also perform the role of training naval air crews.

Ferry duty was an honourable calling for a carrier, because delivering aircraft at great risk to distant island air bases helped beef up the defence line, behind which the Mobile Fleet lurked ready to pounce on any penetration of the island base chain. Without any conversions at the outset of the war, America was forced to use precious fleet carriers, thereby exposing them to air or submarine attack. The most celebrated case was when Churchill called for help in resupplying Malta with Spitfires.

Admiral King twice lent Churchill the fleet carrier *Wasp* for fast runs to flying distance from Malta, before transferring it to the Pacific theatre, where it was desperately needed. As an island fortress and air-sea naval base, Malta sat astride Rommel's line of supply between Italy and North Africa, but it could only be resupplied by the Royal Navy from either end of the Mediterranean – Gibraltar to the west and Alexandria to the east. The island's heroic defiance uniquely earned it the George Cross medal. It was said of its long defence against the worst that the air forces of Hitler and Mussolini could hurl at the island fortress that Malta had nine lives. The *Wasp* saved two of them. That the Royal Navy lost the fleet carriers *Eagle* and *Ark Royal* to U-Boats in the Mediterranean, and had HMS *Illustrious* and *Indomitable* very badly beaten up by air attack, demonstrates the level of risk to the *Wasp*. Within a year or so, there were escort carriers that could take on such risks.

Interesting in the case of Japan's liner conversions was how both the 1928 and the 1938 trio were all built in Mitsubishi yards at Nagasaki, as we shall see so importantly in our next chapter. So also were the next two when shortly after the start on the Taiyo-class came a green light for subsidy of two smaller liners of 13,600 tons for the Osaka Shosen Kaisha's (OSK) South American service. The *Argentina Maru* became the *Kaiyo* ('Sea Hawk'), while the *Brazil Maru* was sunk early in the war before it could be taken in hand for conversion. Instead, the Japanese purchased the German liner *Scharnhorst*, which was sheltering from the Allies in Kobe. It was transformed into the *Shinyo* ('Godly Hawk').

The liner conversions typically ferried land-based naval aircraft, and on occasion army aircraft, to far-flung island air bases, most importantly to Truk. While not leading charmed lives in this role, their fast speed relative to that of US submarines kept them mostly out of harm's way. They were not tied to slow convoys, sailing independently or in groups with their own kind. The results were most impressive, judged by the number of planes delivered to the major outlying bases in the Central Pacific and at Rabaul. Here were three carriers, later five, plying back and forth between Yokosuka and Truk on a monthly basis, bar the odd interruption to the routine. The strategic importance of their work has been missed in most accounts of the Pacific War.

Indeed, the liner conversions were the means by which in 1943/44 the IJN built up the deployment of the First Air Fleet. This was a land-based naval air force set up under Admiral Kakuji Kakuta to defend the Philippines and the Central Pacific bases as fears grew that the augmentation of American fleet carrier strength might see the focus shift from the South West Pacific (then at the stage of the aerial siege of Rabaul) to the Central Pacific. Leading talents of IJN naval aviation, such as Minoru Genda, were recruited to mastermind the new air fleet.

We have shown in Chapter 2 how two persuasions had flourished in naval air circles. The earlier one envisaged long-range bombers using island air bases to savage the advancing US Pacific Fleet in its sweep through the Central Pacific. The later persuasion came to see carrier-based air power as paramount. In practice, both would obviously be exercised, even in co-ordination. The loss of four fleet carriers at Midway inevitably heralded a greater reliance on land-based air power. Suddenly, the value of the liner conversions leapt as a result.

Their success in feeding the land-based build-up was matched by their survival through 1943 when engaged in the ferrying role, despite them being hunted ceaselessly by submarines tipped off by the codebreakers as to their routes and destinations. It was a combination of their speed and defective American torpedoes that led them to lead relatively charmed lives for so long, to the great frustration of the submariners and the codebreakers. In December 1943, however, all five auxiliary carriers were shifted to First Escort Command following the decision to adopt convoying in protection against American submarines – losses to them having become insupportable after the Americans finally fixed their torpedoes and multiplied the number of their marauders. Particularly crippling to the war effort had been the loss of tankers.

Of the five auxiliary carriers, the *Chuyo* did not make it into First Escort Command. It was sunk by the submarine *Sailfish* at the end of the year. The other two Taiyo-class carriers were sunk while protecting their convoys, as also was the later conversion *Shinyo*. They were now so much more vulnerable tied to slower vessels, added to which US submarine headquarters at Midway – having broken the merchant vessel code – now knew even better where they were headed. Despite this, there were relatively few losses among those convoys they shepherded. This has been revealed recently when the tabular record of movements (TROMs) for the auxiliary carriers appeared on the internet, courtesy of CombinedFleet.com.

Judging at least from *Kaiyo*'s record of movement, it performed great service in covering important convoys with its planes and preserving itself from damage into the bargain. That latterly it was switched to training air crews in home waters explains its survival, albeit being finally sunk in shallow water.

Thanks to its lesser displacement tonnage and two destroyer turbine engines, the *Kaiyo* was graced with better speed at 23 knots. This might well have qualified it for a front-line fleet role and for a more noble end. It might well also have achieved much if equipped with catapults.

Time now to turn to a dramatic pair we shall call 'The Olympians' – liner conversions that did fight as full-blown attack carriers alongside the fast fleet carriers and light fleet conversions. Only with the *Junyo* and *Hiyo* can we best satisfy our self-appointed mission of defending the Shadow Fleet in refutation of its many disparagers. For this we need to return again to the germinal period of late-1930s decision-making on Shadow Fleet matters.

'The Olympians'

Quietly in the background, a dialogue had been ongoing between the NYK line and the Ministry of Transport, and in due course with the Navy Ministry. It involved NYK's passionate determination to match or exceed competitor passenger lines in America, Canada and indeed Germany (vide the foresaid *Scharnhorst* liner). Liners like the *President Coolidge*, the *President Hoover* and Canada's cheekily named *Empress of Japan* had been adroitly robbing the *Asama* trio of much good business.

An ample state of high excitement was further raised when Japan found itself awarded the holding of the 1940 Olympics. For this great national challenge, Japan surely deserved a pair of super-liners in time to compete and for the nation to 'show the flag'?

The Ministry of Transport saluted this politically charged vision. When negotiations faltered over the level of subsidy, the Navy Department stepped in and the deal was signed. The government would pay 60 per cent in return for a design capable of speedy conversion to carrier. The *Kashiwara Maru* was laid down accordingly on the No. 3 Mitsubishi slipway at Nagasaki on 20 March 1939. Nearby, carefully shrouded in the secrecy of sisal wraps, lay the growing super-battleship *Musashi* on the company's No. 2 slipway.

The consortium behind NYK opted for Kawasaki Shipbuilding Ltd at Kobe for the other clandestine vessel, the *Izumo Maru*. This was laid down eight months later, the delay having been caused by the need to free the slipway by launching the large fleet carrier *Zuikaku*. At Kobe, there was just one large slipway available, a factor we return to in the next chapter.

The IJN had many requirements in return for government subsidy: double hulls; provision for ease of additions to compartmentalization; extra fuel capacity; space arrangements encouraging rapid installation of aircraft hangers and elevators; extra conduit diameters for housing the greater number of electric cables necessary for a carrier; tanks fore and aft for eventual storage of airplane fuel; and a bulbous bow such as was introduced in the plans for the super-battleships and the Shokaku-class fleet carriers, so they could manoeuvre more quickly when under attack.

The engine arrangements were complicated, and for that reason disappointed the IJN in practice.

Alas, passengers were never to wonder at certain oddities of the liners' internal structure, such as super-giant head room (above what became the hangar decks) and the way passenger accommodation was all crammed into the centre in order to ease future installation of aircraft elevators bow and stern.

The reason why they were never to nibble at *sushi* and sip their *sake* in the luxuriously appointed state rooms was that Japan's Olympian liners were not yet launched when news came of the fall of France to Hitler in June 1940. In reaction to that, there followed Washington's Two-Ocean Navy Act of June 1940. As we have seen in the last chapter, that act promised eventual US naval supremacy in both the Atlantic and Pacific. The IJN duly requisitioned both ships from NYK and conversion was ordered that October. They were launched within three days of each other in June 1941, and completed in mid-1942. In contrast, the carriers ordered by the Vinson 1940 Act could not reach the Pacific War at peacetime rates of construction until 1945/46.

Secrecy ruled. The Diet passed the project in 1938 as the 'Large Size Superior Ships Construction Programme'. The Mitsubishi order was for 'No 1001 Ship' and the Kawasaki order for 'No 1002'. What sort of ships was a question evaded. There was much shipbuilding going on then, and much of it was about equipping Japan with 'superior ships'. Foreign naval attachés in the Tokyo embassies might well have just yawned, even more so if told these were to be special liners for the Olympics ('Well dear boy, at least they have tied up two of their few long slipways such as they can't slide forth more of those vicious looking heavy cruisers!')

Like the other liners, the pair were to receive 'Hawk' names as aircraft carriers. *Kashiwara Maru* became *Junyo* ('Peregrine Falcon') and *Izumo Maru* was renamed *Hiyo* ('Flying Falcon'). The hawk names could be wrongly transliterated *Hayataka* and *Hitaka*, as the Allies knew them for much of the war. Also, like the other liner conversions, they were designated 'auxiliary aircraft carrier', or at least the *Junyo* was until redesignated a fleet carrier after Midway. The *Hiyo* emerged three months later than its sister and received the fleet carrier designation from the outset.

Some comparisons seem in order here. The standard displacement of the two whoppers was 24,150 tons, against 26,675 tons for Shokaku-class large fleet carriers, or not very far off at all, and a lot larger than Soryu-class medium carriers at around 16,000 tons. On the other hand, the air strength was an operational forty-eight, compared to seventy-two and fifty-four. Therein lay the penalty for not building a carrier as a carrier from keel up.

The other half of the price was that even with the top speed attained on its trials of 25.63 knots, the *Hiyo* could not expect to keep up with Shokaku and Soryu-class carriers. In contrast, the two classes of fast fleet carrier enjoyed a design speed of 34 knots and could show it, powered as they were by the marine equivalent of race car engines and sporting the sleek profiles of cruisers rather than the stubby hulls born of liners.

However, not all of Japan's fleet carriers could race around at the speed of destroyers. Rated below 30 knots were *Kaga*, *Ryujo* and the light fleet conversions. After Midway, the loss of its two carriers there caused the 2nd Carrier Division to be reformed; initially that was with the *Junyo*, *Hiyo* and *Ryujo*. The latter was lost in the Battle of the Eastern Solomons in August 1942, and in replacement the slightly sluggish *Ryuho* did not emerge from its Yokosuka conversion yard until near the end of the year.

In now presenting their battle history, we explore the merits and demerits of a carrier 'slow division'.

When in October 1942, Admiral Kondo led the Mobile Fleet from Truk lagoon, not to be denied, 2nd Carrier Division brought ninety-six additional aircraft to add to the 171 of the 1st Carrier Division (*Shokaku*, *Zuikaku* and little *Zuiho*). Admittedly, their contribution fell to forty-eight when the *Hiyo* developed engine trouble and retired to Truk after having topped up *Junyo*'s complement of aircraft to the maximum before departing. What planes could not be transferred were diverted to nearby land bases.

In the subsequent Battle of Santa Cruz, the remaining four met the *Enterprise* and *Hornet* in battle. The American combined capacity of 150–160 aircraft had been somewhat reduced by losses in the lead-up to battle. In the event, the aircrews of the 1st Carrier Division crippled *Hornet* and damaged the *Enterprise*. Chugging along in the rear of 1st Carrier Division came the *Junyo* group. Its attacks further damaged *Enterprise* and forced the abandonment of the *Hornet*, which was finished off by pursuing Japanese destroyers. Clearly, if the other half of the slow division had not called off sick, the odds were on *Enterprise* being taken off the chess board too. Santa Cruz was a Japanese victory, if dearly bought in savagely heavy losses of irreplaceable veteran airmen, but was rued as not having been decisive. Such a victory would have left the US with no carriers and having to abandon Guadalcanal, much as the Royal Navy would have had to extract the Marines and Paras from the Falklands in 1982 if they had lost the carriers HMS *Invincible* and *Hermes*, these precariously providing the only air cover in defence against Argentinian land-based air attack from the Patagonian mainland opposite the Falklands. (There was much in the Falklands campaign that was analogous to the six-month Guadalcanal fracas.)

As a further example, at the Battle of the Philippine Sea, the 2nd Carrier Division included the slow coaches *Hiyo*, *Junyo* and *Ryuho*. There, Admiral Ozawa enjoyed his advantage of a superior striking range for his aircraft, and from having better scouting resources to search for and stalk from afar Admiral Spruance's vast carrier fleet off the Mariana Islands. There, the US Fifth Fleet was guarding an invasion armada and therefore tied to its apron strings. Spruance had first to defend himself and hopefully shred Japanese air striking power in the course of that process before risking pursuit into the wastes of the Philippine Sea, lest the Japanese outflank him and imperil the invasion shipping.

In the next day's battle Spruance did spring forward to the attack as the Japanese fleet retreated, but not in such desperation as to leave behind the slow 2nd Carrier Division as babes to the wolves. All three Japanese carrier divisions together met the aerial onslaught. The always unlucky *Hiyo* collected a single torpedo hit, fires from which ruptured a gasoline tank. It went under after a massive explosion, the third carrier loss in a battle that truly doomed Japan, *Taiho* and *Shokaku* having succumbed the previous day to submarine attack. The *Junyo* escaped with its distinguishing lopsided funnel disfigured by a bomb hit. The *Ryuho* also was damaged.

Fighting slow divisions in contiguity with fast divisions was a common occurrence in naval warfare. The British may have done without their pre-Dreadnoughts at Jutland, but the Germans included them in the rear of their line. All but one reached home safely. A more modern example was Admiral Somerville's response to the prospect of Japanese carrier raids on Ceylon in April 1942. His R-class battleships were too slow to keep up with his two fast carriers and one fast battleship, so he teamed 'the old tarts' – as he called the 'R's – with the equally slow light carrier *Hermes*.

When not with the Mobile Fleet, both *Junyo* and *Hiyo* were very active like the other liner conversions on aircraft-ferrying missions, again sparing precious fleet carriers the risk of loss to American submarines, which ruthlessly hunted the liner conversions aided by the codebreaking successes of US Intelligence. The *Hiyo* was caught this way outside Tokyo Bay by the submarine *Trigger* in May 1943, but survived, while *Junyo* was twice torpedoed and survived.

An additional point in favour of the *Junyo* is that a forty-eight-aircraft group was much more useful than the paltry twenty-seven to thirty carried by the light fleet conversions, whatever their superior speed.

Preceding its great hour of glory at Santa Cruz, the *Junyo* exited Truk lagoon in October 1942 with eighteen Val dive bombers as its main strike component, twenty-one Zero fighters for escort and defence, plus nine Kate attack planes capable of taking off armed with torpedoes if the wind was brisk enough, otherwise with bombs, or as reconnaissance. The limitation on the death-dealing Kates was the only concession made for the *Junyo*'s inferior fleet speed. That squad's leader, Lieutenant Yoshiaki Irikiin, however, has been credited as finishing off the *Hornet* with a devastating torpedo hit. He left no record as he perished in the assault.

This limitation on the number of Kates was compensated somewhat by the 'slow division' adopting a different mode of attack to that of the 1st Carrier Division, whose practice it was to fly off two balanced deck-loads in successive attacks with co-ordinated strikes of Vals, Kates and protective Zero fighters, the better to divide and confuse the defence. These highly skilled multi-carrier co-ordinated strikes were what the Japanese were best at and the Americans were unable to emulate during the great 1942 carrier-to-carrier battles.

In the case of the 2nd Carrier Division (our 'slow division'), the dive bombers were to deliver a massive first strike in the hope of immobilizing flight decks and slowing the enemy carriers for a successive weaker strike of torpedo planes to skim in just above the waves and deliver the death blow.

When the next great battle for Guadalcanal came in mid-November, the 'slow division' was all that Yamamoto had left at Truk to provide seaborne air cover, and that from afar and therefore ineffectively. Attacking the convoy the Japanese pilots were defending was the damaged USS

Enterprise, still unable to use the forward elevator that had been knocked out by the jar of a *Junyo* bird's near miss in October.

The *Junyo*, in company with *Zuikaku*, also covered the evacuation of Guadalcanal in January.

How important the 'slow division' was to the balance of power in the Pacific in the six months following can be instanced by the following line-up of flight decks. On the IJN side, the big fleet carriers were *Zuikaku* and later the *Shokaku* (following repairs to it from four bomb hits at Santa Cruz), on the US side the *Saratoga* (by year's end returned from the submarine damage inflicted the previous August) and *Enterprise*, which lingered in its damaged state in the South Pacific until relieved by British carrier HMS *Victorious*.

The balance overall, however, was in favour of Japan, thanks to the pre-war decision to nurture a Shadow Fleet. The *Junyo* and *Hiyo* were reinforced with the light fleet carrier *Ryuho*, initially in a dedicated scout and defence role like *Zuiho* had provided for the fast division at Santa Cruz, where it fielded eighteen Zero fighters and a flock of nine Kates in the scouting role. This was a homogeneous and powerful force, and by April their air crews had been replenished, albeit with crews of far less ability than those shot down in droves at Santa Cruz.

So, why was there no carrier fight in 1943? None were more disappointed than the crew of the *Victorious*, no doubt little aware of their good fortune given the heavy odds against them. The usual reason given is that the US had lost four of its Pacific Fleet aircraft carriers in 1942, and the remaining two were insufficient in strength to risk them against Japanese land-based air power. The Japanese also found their air crews burnt out in the furnace that was 1942, and their training programmes proved inadequate at furnishing properly qualified replacements. They were reluctant to risk their remaining flight decks. Twice they yielded to the temptation of diverting carrier squadrons to land bases in the South Pacific rather than risk those precious flight decks.

They worried, ironically, that America also had a Shadow Fleet. This question had first arisen during the Battle of Midway, when there seemed more US carriers than there should be opposing them. Some substance to the notion could later have arisen when the first escort carriers appeared in the South Pacific. America's first such carriers had ferried in the initial Marine aircraft squadron to the Henderson Field air base on

Guadalcanal after its capture in early August. Then in early 1943 came the converted oilers *Sangamon*, *Suwannee* and *Chenango*. They and their sister *Santee* had helped the fleet carrier *Ranger* deliver air support to the North African landings along Morocco's Atlantic coast. Once that Allied first priority was over, the *Santee* was diverted to hunting German raiders in the wastes of the South Atlantic. The other three hot-footed it to the South Pacific.

Too slow for fleet work, they could at least take the dangerous ferrying chore away from the fleet carriers, provide close-in support for invasions and carry out a host of other chores. Yet adding their aircraft to the line-up still did not balance the books in terms of the respective orders of battle.

Ironically, it was the remains of the IJN's 'slow division' which survived the war. The *Junyo* was the sole survivor of the Japanese carriers that fought at Santa Cruz. Only it and the *Ryuho* of Admiral Ozawa's Mobile Fleet at Philippine Sea remained afloat, albeit both heavily damaged. In the closing weeks of the war, Admiral Halsey's carrier armada ranged up and down the eastern seaboard of Japan seeking insatiable revenge for what the IJN had so treacherously wrought at Pearl Harbor.

For the *Junyo*, the atom bombs came just in time. Now at peace, the ship lay at anchor off Sasebo. There, 'the big crappy Jap carrier' was much photographed by the conquerors before being scrapped in 1946. Stripped from *Junyo* was its bell, which now adorns an atrium of Fordham University in New York.

As for the 1940 Tokyo Olympic Games for which the *Junyo* was conceived to serve, they never happened due to the war in Europe. Indeed, there were no Olympic Games until 1948, in London, where a Japanese athlete won gold in the prestigious final event – the marathon. Tokyo was finally awarded the 1964 Olympics.

Meanwhile, post-war Japan ironically became the leading shipbuilding nation in the world, a living example of phoenixes rising from their ashes.

Allied Conversions – Better Late Than Never!

We have already touched on Allied efforts in the conversion field and noted their belatedness, their different objectives and the smallness and slowness of the vessels themselves, but of their eventual vast numbers we have written little.

The sudden impetus for producing conversions of merchant hulls arose from a phenomenon known as the 'Atlantic Gap', a mid-ocean band about 500 miles wide that could not be given air cover from land, where Admiral Doenitz directed his U-Boats to form packs operating at night on the surface. Like a pack of wolves, they would tear into a fifty-ship convoy and torpedo ship after ship. The limited escort vessels would be run off their feet, unable to persist in any serious hunt after contact.

The closing of the Atlantic Gap with air cover became the decisive event that won for the Allies the near six-year-long Battle of the Atlantic. It was the little escort carriers that made the big difference in the gap's closure. Sailing with the convoys, or in hunter-killer groups contiguously, their planes forced the U-Boats to submerge rather than be sunk by bombs and rockets, thereby losing for the submarines the advantage of a higher surface speed than the convoy. Doenitz had to call off his mid-ocean wolf packs from the vital North Atlantic, rescheduling them to hunt on less-protected but less-frequented trade routes. From August 1943, sinkings fell off to a trickle of what they had been, particularly as long-range shore-based air cover was also extended. The hunter-killer groups nosed into any remaining gaps. From the carriers attached to the convoys took off and landed a steady stream of Avenger bombers and Wildcat fighters. These were the guardian angels of the merchant marine. By 1944, the North Atlantic was so safe that children evacuated from Britain in 1940 to the US and Canada were able to return – on the escort aircraft carriers.

The standard reference (Wragg) catalogues 132 escort carriers built by the US, of which forty-five were for the Royal Navy and eighty-seven for the US Navy. Additionally, the British converted some ships on their own. What staggers the imagination is how they could have manned them all. Was this a case of massive overkill? In a way, perhaps that was so, but it has to be remembered that losing the Battle of the Atlantic was the only way the Allies could lose the war.

For the Allies, losing the Battle of the Atlantic became a glaring prospect following the fateful first quarter of 1943, when convoy losses escalated alarmingly and the U-Boats were proliferating faster than ever. The escort carriers almost arrived too late, while those few that were early birds got diverted to other priorities such as the North African landings rather than being vectored to the rescue of North Atlantic convoys entering the Atlantic Gap.

While the need of convoy protection was the most urgent reason for American yards churning out so many of these escort carriers, there were other considerations, such as how to transport vast numbers of planes to Europe or to Pacific bases. They also provided flight decks for training carrier pilots and gave close support to amphibious invasion forces until air bases could be captured and land-based aircraft flown in as cover. Every one of the escort carriers was put to good and urgent use.

The US Navy called these carriers by a number of names. Formally, they were designated CVEs, or escort carriers, in honour of their primary role. For those who sailed in them, the initials ruefully stood for 'Combustible, Vulnerable, Expendable' due to their reputation in the early days for blowing up when hit. More fondly, they were known as 'jeep carriers' for their small size, or 'Woolworth carriers' for their downmarket provenance.

There were two main classes of escort carrier that did most of the work in the war: the Bogue-class and the Casablanca-class. The former were conversions of standard Maritime Commission C3 hulls at 8,390 tons, with a top speed of 18 knots and capable of operating twenty-eight aircraft, or alternatively transporting over sixty, according to type. The latter were all built by the Kaiser Ship Yard in Washington State and bore much the same attributes as the Bogue-class carriers.

The forty-four Bogue conversions were originally intended for the Royal Navy under the Lend-Lease Act, and indeed thirty-four fought for the British Empire as the Attacker and Ruler classes. Ten of those closer to being ready were held back after Pearl Harbor for American use, and the same number ordered for the Royal Navy. The American escorts won quick fame in the Atlantic, first the *Bogue* itself with the North Atlantic convoys, then the *Core*, *Card* and *Croatan*, who under able commanders led mid-Atlantic hunter-killer groups, mostly around the Azores, killing off several of the large 'milk cow' U-Boats which acted as tankers extending the range and patrol time of the attack boats. At this time, the North Atlantic route became the responsibility of Britain and the Mid-Atlantic that of America, having suddenly become both important and sensitive following the North African landings of Operation Torch and the need to move American troops and supplies into the Mediterranean.

The fifty-odd Casablanca-class carriers were less conversions than keel-up projects, albeit using a merchant ship profile. The name ship of the class was aptly baptized. That all-time movie classic *Casablanca* had just been rushed into release in November 1942 to take advantage of the publicity about the Allied landings in North Africa, those around Casablanca on the Moroccan coast having been the responsibility of the US Navy under Admiral Henry Kent Hewitt. The class came to be named after Second World War victories.

Visionaries of the escort carrier were Admiral William 'Bull' Halsey and President Roosevelt himself. Halsey was famous for being the archetypal 'flying admiral'. In 1940, he recommended the need for converting merchant or tanker hulls to aircraft-carrier status as he felt the fleet carriers would find themselves run off their propellers with all the manifold tasks that would be so urgently found for them. But it was the president who drove Halsey's notion into action and sustained it. As an example, when the West Coast shipbuilder Henry J. Kaiser proposed to the Bureau of Ships that they commission from him thirty vessels that he could guarantee completed in six months, he was rebuffed. He took the matter to the president, this time offering fifty to fifty-five. They were all produced and fought in the war. These were the escort carriers of the foresaid Casablanca-class. Almost every one of them was retained by the US Navy and reserved for the Pacific War.

There were two other classes. The earliest was the four-ship Sangamon-class. These were larger vessels converted on the slips from the US Navy's Type 3 oilers, such as sustained the Pacific Fleet's fast carrier task forces in action. Only four were reluctantly selected for this due to the U-Boat emergency temporarily overriding fleet oil replenishment needs. Being designed as oilers, the class was still able to stow considerable volumes of oil from which they could refuel their thirsty escort of destroyers. They were also larger. As mentioned, they contributed to the carrier-borne air cover off Casablanca, with three of them then being bustled off to the South-West Pacific to help Halsey.

They gave stalwart service as a single-class escort carrier division in the front lines of the Pacific War from the late stages of the Guadalcanal campaign to the very end, latterly suffering terribly from kamikaze raids. Being rather classier than the other 'jeep carriers', and from having experience of events at Guadalcanal, they tended to be favoured as command cores, particularly as the constant worry for any task force commander was his destroyers running low on fuel, and here with the Sangamon-class he had the oil for them.

In the Leyte campaign, the close-in air support for the landings was delivered by sixteen escort carriers in three groups. Their leader, Rear Admiral Thomas L. Sprague, sailed with the first group, which included the four Sangamon-class. In the next chapter, we reveal what happened to the third group under his namesake and Naval Academy classmate, Rear Admiral Clifton A.F. Sprague, and how the other two groups rushed to its rescue.

In the closing phases of the war, twenty Commencement Bay-class escort carriers began joining the fleet. At last, here was an escort carrier of a size to match the Japanese auxiliary carriers, although still of lesser speed. But again, as with the Sangamons, an oiler type of hull had been specified. And again, spare fuel oil could be carried.

Due to their slowness, the Allied escort carriers could not work with the fleet's fast carriers, but they could do a lot of often very dangerous work in support of operations, thereby freeing the fast carrier forces for a safer, more-distant role and for wide-ranging raids on Japanese bases.

In the final chapter, we explore how this factor came into increasing play as the numbers of escort carriers built up in the Pacific. The CVEs could have played a role in the final decisive battle between the IJN and the US Navy, as we propose in the final chapter, 'Mother of all Carrier Battles'.

*   *   *

But before we can project alternative history, we have much ground to cover. So onward to two chapters; and two big questions. Firstly, what if Japan had dedicated all its longest slipways and construction docks to the production of fast fleet carriers, forgetting about everything else that was big, including super-battleships, heavy cruisers and particularly liners and fancy fast auxiliaries? Secondly, how might they have possibly 'gotten away with it' by avoiding the kind of situation that would invite an arms race in aircraft carriers with America and Britain?

SHADOW FLEET, 1927–44 – Vessels designed for quick conversion to aircraft carriers

Early Liners (NYK)	Laid to launched	Converted to carrier	Tons	Speed (knots)	Aircraft
Asama Maru	Nagasaki, Sept–Oct 1928	sunk, no conversion	16,950	21	(27)
Tatsuta Maru	Nagasaki, Dec 1927 – Apr 1929	sunk, no conversion	16,950	21	(27)
Kamakura Maru	Nagasaki, Feb 1928– May 1929	sunk, no conversion	16,950	21	(27)
Naval auxiliaries (submarine tenders)					
Taigei	Yokosuka, Apr–Nov 1933	Dec 1941–Nov 1942, there	13,360	26.5	27
Takasaki	Yokosuka, 1935–June 1936	Jan–Dec 1940, there	11,262	28	27
Tsurugizaki	Yokosuka, 1934–June 1935	Jan 1941–Jan 1942, there	11,262	28	27
Naval auxiliaries (seaplane 'tenders')					
Chitose	Kure, Nov 1934–Nov '1936	1943–1944 at Sasebo	11,190	29	30
Chiyoda	Kure, Nov 1936–Nov 1937	1942 –1943 at Yokosuka	11,190	29	30
Mizuho	Kobe, May 1937–May 1938	sunk, no conversion	10,929	22	12/24
Nisshin	Kure, Nov 1938–Nov 1939	sunk, no conversion	11,317	28	12/24
Later NYK Liners					
Nitta Maru	Nagasaki, May 1938– May 1939	June–Nov 1942 at Kure	17,830	21	23/27
Yawata Maru	Nagasaki, Dec 1938– Oct 1939	Nov 1941–May 1942 at Kure	17,830	21	27/30
Kasuga Maru	Nagasaki, June–Sep 1940	May–Aug 1940 at Sasebo	17,830	21	27/30
NYK Liners for the 1940 Olympics					
Kashiwara Maru	Nagasaki, Mar 1939– Nov 1941	Oct 1940–May 1942, there	24,140	25	48
Izumo Maru	Kobe, Nov 1939–June 1941	Oct 1940–July 1942, there	24,140	25	48
OSK Liners for South American trade					
Argentina Maru	Nagasaki, 1938	Dec 1942–Nov 1943, there	13,600	23	24
Brazil Maru	sunk, German liner substituted	Sep 1942–Dec 1943 at Kure	17,500	22	33

<u>Notes</u>: On conversion to carrier, most shadow unit names changed. These can be found in the text of the chapter. We assigned names given to Shadow Fleet conversions to the keel-up light fleet carriers proposed in the Phantom tables (see next chapter).

Chapter 4

Phantom Fleet

'November 1st, 1940, Nagasaki. The tide was slowly rising, and the water beneath the ship's bow began to reflect the red of the rising sun ... Serikawa struck the launching bell ... Two groups of workers rushed to either side of the keel to remove the last remaining blocks. Watanabe held his breath. As the curtains began to part, the hills on the far shore of the harbour appeared in the mist. His heart was beating frantically. Once the curtains were fully opened, the harbour came into view – the first time the sea had been seen from the slipway in over two and a half years.'

'October 24th, 1944, Battle of Leyte Gulf. A long line formed along the edges of the deck of people waiting their turn to jump. The ship tilted suddenly, stirring up a large wave as the vast hull swung to port. The bow pointed down into the water, with the stern towering prominently above the rest of the ship. The crewmen still clinging to the wreck under the darkening skies of sunset were gradually moving further toward the stern as the bow plunged into the sea.'

(Excerpts from *Battleship Musashi* by Akira Yoshimura)

At dawn, Japan's ultra-secret second super-battleship proudly splashed into the rising sun, but four years later slid ignominiously beneath the waves in the last of the light, a victim of torpedo bombers in the greatest ever naval battle in history.

The *Musashi*, as it was to be named, was laid down in March 1938 on Mitsubishi's No. 2 slipway at Nagasaki, which had been hugely strengthened and extended back into the mountain side in response to ultra-secret briefings from IJN naval construction bigwigs. Manager for Mitsubishi on the project was Kensuke Watanabe, a shipbuilding engineer blessed not only with the intense professionalism of his trade, but also with superb security and public relations skills. He was a committed company man and meticulous problem solver.

Watanabe would become the perfect manager for the genesis of a Japanese super-battleship, but only if his pride could rule and nerves could survive the ordeal of this massive responsibility and brainstorm all the problems that arose. He recounts how he would awake screaming in the night after undergoing recurrent nightmares. These were of an appallingly realistic nature. One night he dreamt of the launch going catastrophically wrong:

> *The launch platform collapses. The concrete foundation below erupts as the weight of the hull bears down on it at 19.3 tons per square metre – and then the 862-foot long battleship capsizes through its concealing hemp curtains in turn toppling the gantry cranes onto the slipway alongside, thereby also destroying the future carrier Junyo. The air is rent with the clamour of doom as hundreds of workmen are crushed in a great wine press of blood gorging into the harbour.*

Watanabe would wake up and try to carry on.

At the actual event, the concrete under the launching platform did start fissuring as the supporting blocks were removed during a long dark night of launch preparation. The gold braid and royalty among the morning's visiting celebrities dreamed otherwise in outlying luxury inns, where they had been discreetly located as part of the security plan.

All went swimmingly well, except maybe for the mini-tsunami caused by the leviathan's impact wave when it entered the water. Across the narrow channel, a large surge washed water up under the foundations of low-lying wooden houses, surprising residents as it spurted up between their tatami mats. They tried to evacuate their homes, only to be shoved back inside by some of the hard-case 1,800 marines shipped in from nearby Sasebo Naval Base to make sure nobody in camera range on that fortuitously misty autumn day's dawning caught a peak of Battleship No. 2, or at least not until its purpose-built tug manoeuvred it to the outfitting dock and other tugs brought the *Kasuga Maru*, a Shadow Fleet liner (the future carrier *Taiyo*) as recently launched by Mitsubishi, into a position screening it from that part of town. On the other side, a special warehouse had been built to mask the fitting-out phase from the American and British consulates only about 700 yards away.

For Watanabe and those of the militaristic bureaucratic state he had to satisfy, there was a security nightmare: how to hide a super-battleship that was half as much again the size of Germany's *Bismarck* and *Tirpitz*, and almost twice the size of the new American and British battleships.

All this while it was being constructed inside a large city and busy international port. From a spy's single snap-shot showing the length of the ship, its basic specifications could be extrapolated.

Unknown to the Allies until the end of the war, the 18.1-inch guns of the *Yamato* and *Musashi* had a range of very nearly 26 miles, or over the horizon from sea level. To allow gunnery officers to peer into the beyond, the rangefinder was perched atop the bridge tower fifteen decks above water level. The helmet of Star Wars villain Darth Vader was partly inspired by a Yamato-class battleship's fighting top, as was the film's theme of a Death Star at large.

The battleship's extraordinary 128ft width was dictated by the needs of its guns, not least their tremendous kick upon being fired. That width was too wide for the Panama Canal; should America seek to match it, the only other route to the Pacific was around South America by way of Cape Horn.

The displacement of 68,200 tons (we use Yoshimura's figure, as his is from the specifications sent to Mitsubishi on 1 July 1937 by the Bureau of Naval Construction) was very close to twice the Washington Treaty's 35,000 ton limitation on battleships. For their part, America and Britain went on wedded to the Treaty after Japan's withdrawal. Their new battleships attempted to adhere to this limitation, the White House not being aware how the *Musashi* and its fearsome sister *Yamato* could hover just outside the American 16-inch gun range. From there, they could pick off their antagonists one by one as their massive projectiles tore into machinery and munitions spaces and ripped open the underside of the hulls with the 'underwater shots' for which the IJN specially designed their naval shells. The optical gear was way in advance of anything the Allies had (or at least until they installed range-finding radar), and the three big gun turrets could be co-ordinated for engaging three separate targets.

Mercifully, such an encounter was never to happen, even at the Battle for Leyte Gulf from 24–26 October 1944, when the pair underwent their true baptism of fire. The *Musashi* never made it to the Gulf, succumbing to massed carrier plane attack. The best it achieved was attracting the attention of the American pilots as a lame duck lagging behind the speeding fleet. *Yamato* was thus spared any crippling damage and so made it through the San Bernardino Strait into the approaches to Leyte Gulf, off the coast of the neighbouring island of Samar.

After dawn, the *Yamato* and its retinue surprised groups of flimsy American escort carriers alongside Samar. In consternation, those with a view from battle stations made out the ominous tower of the *Yamato* and the pagoda masts of its consorts looming over the horizon. The only advance warning had been a pre-dawn jabbering of nearby Japanese voices on the radio. The first big shells splashed around them soon after.

Where were the big fast fleet carriers and the great escorting battleships of Admiral William ('Bull') Halsey's US Third Fleet that was supposed to be blocking access, Rear Admiral Clifton Sprague frantically radioed to the Seventh Fleet? His boss, Admiral Thomas Kinkaid, with the rest of Seventh Fleet, was mostly on the other side of Leyte Gulf and its battleships were low on ammunition after a night-time fight with the southern Japanese pincer force. Kinkaid radioed Halsey the same desperate enquiry.

The truth was that Halsey had blithely raced off with everything into the Philippine Sea in overnight pursuit of the Japanese aircraft carriers that had been deployed as decoys for that very purpose. Consequently, he presented the IJN's super-battleships and heavy cruisers with an open door to the hundreds of transports and other ships that comprised the Allied invasion fleet crowded into Leyte Gulf. All that stood in the way were these 'jeep carriers' – the very lowliest and slowest of all the various species of aircraft carrier – and their gallant retinue of destroyers.

Yamato's guns thundered away at the escort carriers until three American destroyers valiantly charged the Japanese columns in a suicidal torpedo attack, USS *Johnston* in the lead, followed by the *Heerman* and *Hoel*. The *Johnston* torpedoed lead heavy cruiser *Kumano*, forcing its retirement from the pursuit, its sister *Suzuya* in attendance. Finding the *Hoel*'s torpedoes closing in, the mighty battlewagon *Yamato* turned tail, using its top speed to outrun them. This steered it out of the fray, or more importantly out of sight of it. As a result, Admiral Kurita was no longer in control of the battle. With the American carriers mistakenly identified as fast fleet carriers from this distance, rather than slow escort carriers, Kurita called off the chase and ordered his fleet to regroup around the *Yamato* before heading on towards the Gulf. Subsequently, in a decision unaccountable to this day, he changed his mind and headed for home.

The *Johnston* sank with heavy loss of life, including that of its captain, who was a member of the Cherokee nation. His heroic charge had seen off the mighty *Yamato* in its one and only meeting with American warships (other than the submarine that nicked it a year or so before). Meanwhile, the escort carrier aircrews had stopped three more heavy cruisers, which were scuttled in the withdrawal. In a last heroic action, Commander Evans on *Johnston* spoiled a destroyer squadron's torpedo attack on the force. As his destroyer went down, it and the remnants of its crew were saluted from the bridge of a circling Japanese destroyer.

Before this, the two super-battleships spent most of the war in Japan's Central Pacific naval base in Truk lagoon, where Admiral Yamamoto's flagship became known to sailors as the 'Yamato Hotel' due to its air conditioning and commodious appointments. When the *Musashi* belatedly joined it there in early 1943, the admiral checked out of one hotel and into the other.

Part of the reason for the *Musashi*'s late arrival had been last-minute design arrangements to make it a better command vehicle. Rumour suggested these included improvements to the air conditioning and to the kitchens.

There were two rationales for their inactivity. The first was to preserve both for the 'final decisive battle'. The second was the fuel they consumed. For as soon as the arrival of the large Essex-class carriers – the 'Essex Surge' – occurred, and for want of having broken American naval codes, there was no way other than by hunch or brilliant deduction to know where the US might strike next. To 'roar about' speculatively in search of the 'decisive battle' would deplete increasingly scarce fuel supplies.

The first hint of the size of the monsters occurred when a long-range spy flight overflew Truk in preparation for the planned February 1944 raid by Admiral Spruance's fast carrier forces. Between clouds, the photographs revealed one of the beasts: the *Musashi*. The *Yamato* was then undergoing submarine damage repair in Japan. From the prints, a length estimate could be calculated. This indicated that the guns designed to exploit such dimensions could be of a calibre alarmingly larger than the 16-inch guns of the modern American battleships, although such an estimate was unconfirmed. Revelation would only come when the war was over.

Nonetheless, there was no panic, only an immediate dedicated urge to hit it from the air as soon as possible.

Yamamoto was dead by this time. His successor was Admiral Koga, a pre-war supporter of the super-battleship project. Alarmed by the spy flight, Koga took off with his precious baby and the rest of the fighting fleet for a more distant and safer lagoon, such that only the fleet's 'servants' – the train of auxiliaries – found themselves left to suffer the fury of Spruance's raid on Truk.

The 'Death Star' that had become a luxury hotel moved first to Palau, thence ever further westwards until the hour of sacrifice drew nigh. This caution betokened how the advantage of the initiative lay now with the Americans. The IJN could only react or it could run.

Carriers as Stars of the Show

Compared to the spates of print lavished over the decades on Japan's two super-battleships, only a trickle by comparison has honoured the two large fleet carriers that the 1937 Order also conceived into being. These were to be the *Shokaku* at Yokosuka Navy Yard and *Zuikaku* at Kawasaki's Kobe yards.

Their war record in comparison was heroic and strategic, no Pacific War authority denying it. Their air groups contributed 37 per cent of the assailants at Pearl Harbor. Next, their air groups sank the carrier *Lexington* in the Battle of the Coral Sea and damaged the *Yorktown*. Damage they suffered there removed them from the order of battle at Midway.

After that setback, the IJN reassigned the surviving air crews of the lost carriers to reinforce the formidable pair and to man the newly arriving flight decks of the Shadow Fleet. As such they fought the six-month Guadalcanal campaign.

The awe of their brooding presence in Truk lagoon to the north constantly obliged Admiral Ghormley to position the US carrier force south of Guadalcanal in order to give air support to incoming convoys reinforcing and supplying the hard-pressed US Marine garrison on that island, otherwise only defended by its stationery airstrip, Henderson Field. This exposed America's last remaining fleet carriers to the perils of 'Torpedo Junction'. Here large I-15-class Japanese submarines lurked, some equipped with scouts in the form of mini-float planes. Submarine torpedoes first sent the carrier *Saratoga* out of the war for four decisive months, then sank the carrier *Wasp* and put the battleship *North Carolina* out of the six-month campaign. There were also many near squeaks.

When the Guadalcanal campaign peaked in October 1942 at the Battle of Santa Cruz, the *Shokaku* and *Zuikaku* engaged the last two American carriers in the Pacific. The *Hornet* died as a result and the *Enterprise* was damaged. The first attack wave co-ordinated all of *Shokaku's* torpedo planes with all of *Zuikaku's* dive bombers against the *Hornet*. It has been acclaimed as the best-co-ordinated naval air strike of the war. It was led by the leader of the torpedo bombers at Pearl Harbor, Lieutenant Commander Shigehara Murata. He did not survive the closely contested assault.

The US Navy was by comparison slow to master such co-ordinated strikes by two or more carriers. Murata's strike was a masterpiece.

In contrast, the second Japanese strike was not well co-ordinated. Between the first deck-load being dispatched and the second, a pair of American scouting dive bombers had landed a bomb on the little *Zuiho's* rear, rendering it incapable of receiving landing aircraft.

What has never been properly acknowledged is not that a carrier was thereby put out of operative action, but how the success was doubly crowned by probably saving the *Enterprise*. That valiant American scout planes' attack had unnerved Admiral Nagumo into believing a big raid could be on its way towards him (causing nightmares of another Midway). Therefore, he brooked no delay in impelling the second strike. The *Shokaku's* contribution of dive bombers was ready to go: so away they went. The *Zuikaku's* complement of torpedo bombers not yet being ready to roll, they followed a little later. Its torpedo-bearing Kates, by attacking alone, consequently failed in their purpose. It did not amount to a co-ordinated strike.

On that circumstance hinged the whole six-month Guadalcanal naval campaign. Lieutenant Birney Strong, the American scout bomber pilot whose bombing of *Zuiho* indirectly saved the *Enterprise*, was recommended for the Congressional Medal of Honor, but was fobbed off with the lesser Navy Cross. Yet here was an individual's act that was decisive to the outcome of the whole war, if but the action of a mere human pawn on the chessboard. Yet this pawn's act led indirectly to the rebuff of the opposing queen.

The *Shokaku* was heavily damaged at both Coral Sea and Santa Cruz, but the *Zuikaku* on both occasions escaped untouched by dodging into concealing rain squalls. There were over-optimistic battle reports from

American pilots. Yet back at Pearl Harbor, the codebreakers frustratingly recorded the *Shokaku*'s retreat to home waters for repair after taking three bomb hits at Coral Sea. Frantically, submarine ambushes were set en route. Its return to the fray after repairs was likewise despondently revealed by the codebreakers.

Admiral Nimitz, in his Pacific Fleet headquarters at Pearl Harbor, was free in proclaiming that the happiest day of his life would be when he heard that 'those two ships' could be scratched from the Pacific order of battle. He meant the hard-fighting 'Shockers', not the super-battleships his forces for so long never met.

The survival of the 'Shockers' from the carrier battles of 1942 as carriers-in-being crowned them as queens of the chessboard until the completed Essex-class carriers arrived fully worked up with aircrews trained. This began from early autumn 1943.

The achievement of the *Shokaku* and *Zuikaku* was that they were the major factor – albeit with the support of Shadow Fleet units – in partly freezing the Pacific War for most of 1943. A recap will be helpful here.

After Midway, the US went on the offensive by seizing Guadalcanal at the lower end of the Solomon chain of volcanic islands, which were acting as a springboard for Japanese efforts at cutting off Australia. The somewhat optimistic US intention had been to move on to Rabaul at the top end of the chain. It took another eighteen months before 'Fortress Rabaul', Japan's base in the South-West Pacific, could be written off, during which the American public endured snail-like progress of their forces up the Solomon ladder because there was not yet an ample force of carriers available to project advances beyond the range of supporting land-based aircraft. There could be no jumping off into the wide blue yonder until most of the initial batch of eight big Essex-class flight decks under construction on the eastern seaboard were completed and fully worked up for action in the Pacific.

Imagine what eight of the 'Shockers' could have wrought in terms of extending the conflict, if all eight amply preceded in time the nemesis-to-be of the Essex Surge – that forthcoming instrument of America's revenge for Pearl Harbor. How that could have succeeded we examine next.

By the logic of slipway and construction dock availability, eight 'Shockers' were indeed the number achievable in that timeframe. But how could that be done? First, the 1937 Fleet Replenishment Order called for a pair of super-battleships and a pair of large fleet carriers. Secondly, the successive 1939 Order specified a further pair of super-battleships and a third carrier.

In 'Phantom Scenario', the traditional 'Big Four' shipyards (more anon on those) could build instead eight large fleet carriers and no battleships. It could have been more dramatic than that, because the aggregate of all launch facilities available could have contributed a large number of medium fleet carriers, and in particular two shipyards that in reality were tied up building a heavy cruiser and a seaplane carrier. In addition, there were four lesser slipways available for up to a dozen light fleet carriers if two of these at Nagasaki were not assigned to producing the liners introduced in the last chapter.

One can imagine some of the key points Yamamoto could stress during the debate between big guns and carrier aircraft. One was the wastefulness in tying up Japan's few large slipways or construction docks with super-battleships: the *Yamato* and *Musashi* averaged thirty-two months on their launch pads, as against eighteen months for the carriers *Shokaku* and *Zuikaku*. Latterly, a mere nine months was achieved for the medium-size Unryu-class carriers.

The other problem was that at only two out of the traditional Big Four yards was it possible to produce a super-battleship at all. For Japan to lay down more than a single pair of them at a time, special docks needed to be constructed, entailing a delay of two years or more.

The table demonstrates the alternative capabilities of a 300-metre slipway or construction dry-dock in Japan for the period 1938–45 in terms of 'going super-battleship' or instead proceeding all out building carriers. Note particularly how a medium carrier laid down following the launch of a repeat Shokaku-class large carrier is shown completed simultaneously due to much shorter launch and fitting-out periods. Therein can be seen the efficiency in switching to medium fleet production once war seemed certain.

We can now proceed to build the Phantom Fleet, the aim being to complete enough aircraft carriers to realize the '1,000-plane air-sea armada' that we have imagined Admiral Yamamoto promising the Naval General Staff he could deliver before the close of 1941 as a way of persuading them to go all-out constructing carriers and to forget about battleships and other big gun ships in entirety.

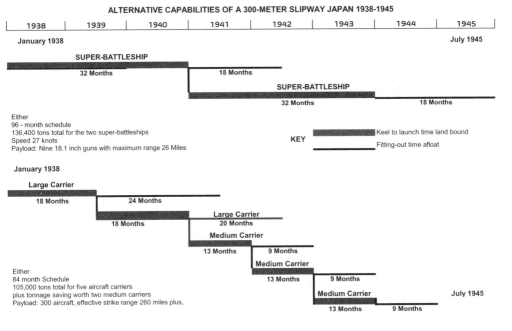

ALTERNATIVE CAPABILITIES OF A 300-METER SLIPWAY JAPAN 1938-1945

We do so by adhering to the following self-imposed set of rules in building our Phantom Fleet:

Slipway Rule: there would have had to be a slipway (or construction dry-dock) of the requisite length available and unoccupied at that time, long enough for carriers (albeit any vessel planned or just begun to be cancelled or pushed aside).

Diet Rule: we will not exceed the overall displacement tonnage (as proxy for both cost and supplies, steel being in even shorter supply than Yen) in fulfilment of the 1937 and 1939 Fleet Replenishment Orders that were agreed by the elected legislature of the Japanese Empire, the Diet.

Fitting-out Rule: whereas fitting-out docks and other facilities that work on ships launched and in the water are easier to adapt and replicate than slipways and construction dry-docks, the total months these were engaged in fitting out large warships in the 1939–45 frame is an expression of skilled human resources and available engineering plant.

Japan's slender shipyard capacity could compete with America's vastly greater resources provided the moral of Aesop's fable about the race between the hare and the tortoise is the analogy. In their race, Mr Tortoise crawls along while Mr Hare enjoys a long lunch and a siesta, only to wake up to find Mr Tortoise a few inches from the finish line, and he, Mr Hare, not even started yet.

In other words, if Japan could use the six years between the 1937 Fleet Replenishment Order and the accelerated fruition of the Essex Surge in the second half of 1943 to exploit its very limited shipbuilding resources in order to churn out aircraft carriers, and waste none of those resources on battleships, heavy cruisers and liners, then flight decks could be amassed to match or exceed the 1,000-plane strong air-sea armada that got hurled at the Japanese homeland three-and-a-half years later. In the interim, the IJN could be its own unstoppable air-sea armada, staking out positions in the Pacific and Indian oceans that would daunt any Allied comeback.

How this scenario could have unfolded – call it 'Phantom Scenario' – requires first a look at the product itself – what sizes of carrier – and next a close look at the shipyards to assess the availability of slipways and construction docks for producing those sizes of vessel. Thereby we reckon the *potential* according to the Slipway Rule. When we are done with that, we can apply the Diet Rule to reckon how much of that production would have been politically and economically *possible*. Finally, we check that within the parameters of the Diet Rule we satisfy the Fitting-out Rule by making it *accomplishable*.

We have already seen how there were three general types of Japanese fast fleet carrier. Our three models and where they would be spawned would have been as follows:

1. The large Shokaku-class of 25,675 tons that we have been describing. They were named after cranes (the '-*kaku*' word endings), the bird being a metaphor of the emperor cult. Their speed was 34 knots. In 1942, they each operated seventy-two aircraft with nine spares. They were also the best-protected of the Japanese carriers produced up to that point.

Their keel length was 236 metres (all length measures are taken from the 'perpendiculars', or length of keel resting on the slipway rather than overall length). Suitable for that were launch facilities at the Big

Four, namely the Navy Yards at Yokosuka and Kure at 300 metres each, Mitsubishi at Nagasaki (275 metres) and Kawasaki at Kobe (250 metres). While these figures are found in sources, all we know for certain is the keel lengths of warships historically laid down and launched from them, which is all that is important. For simplicity of expression, we continue to quote slipway lengths with confidence, that caution having been stated.

The *Shokaku* and *Zuikaku* averaged eighteen months on the slipways and two years fitting out. The latter could have reasonably been reduced in the case of repeats, if as proposed the first four big carriers were immediately followed on with another four laid down as soon as the first batch were launched and tugged off to the fitting-out docks.

In contrast, the *Yamato* and *Musashi* hogged two of those construction facilities, from laid-down to launch times, for an average of thirty months and were over four years in the works overall. The reason is that more goes into a battleship hull than a carrier hull. However, fitting-out time for a battleship in comparison to hull-work is considerably less, whereas superimposing hangars, flight deck and complicated systems on carriers can comprise more work than simply building and launching a hull. In a throwback to the last chapter, we find that one of the attractions of the Shadow Fleet had been that by putting hulls in the water, nine to eighteen months' production time was thereby saved. All they had was the conversion time.

2. The medium-size type that began with the *Soryu* and improved with the 17,300-ton *Hiryu* in turn inspired the model for the Unryu-class. Called after dragons (the '-*ryu*' word endings), they could zip along at the same speed as the *Shokaku*. *Hiryu* in 1942 operated an air group of fifty-four aircraft with nine spares.

Lengths for both were 206.5 metres. There were 225-metre slipways at Kure and Nagasaki available pre-war, and from May 1942 a dry-dock at Yokosuka capable of building a pair at a time. As a means of accelerating wartime production, we show the Big Four yards turning out Unryu vessels latterly (as the comparisons table dramatizes to impressive advantage).

We estimate turnover time for the first Unryu pair ordered in 1937 at less than for the *Hiryu* and less still for their repeats, because historically such was achieved with the Unryu-class, thanks to standardizing and simplifying the design, as well as these carriers being given the topmost priority as wartime production.

We envisage the first four following the configuration of the *Hiryu* and receiving dragon names. Experience of the *Hiryu* in practice would next prompt an evolution of the design reflecting that of the historical Unryu-class but receiving mountain and volcano names, as happened with them after the Unryus had been launched and named. In the modified guise, the island would be fitted starboard and forwards, and the carriers given just two elevators rather than three.

Production would accelerate as the Big Four yards became available. The later units, it is proposed, would become the sustainability factor; the ongoing way of replacing war losses.

3. Light carriers like the *Zuiho* were 11,000 tons or more. It is proposed that any yards suitable for the length were employed from 1938 onwards launching full-speed light fleet carriers from keel up, with no messing about with Shadow Fleet conversions of fast naval auxiliaries, but we do steal the names of the Shadow units for the proposed keel-up new-builds at Nagasaki and Sasebo.

The historical *Zuiho*'s air group in 1942 was twenty-seven with three spares. For keel-up equivalents reckon more, or conservatively thirty plus spares (not much more because of the single hangar-level limitation on such a light tonnage). Speed would be ideally close to the *Shokaku* and *Hiryu*.

Zuiho's length was 185 metres. A 200-metre slip was available at Yokosuka, and one in excess of 162 metres at Sasebo. In addition, Mitsubishi at Nagasaki launched three Shadow Fleet liners using at least two slipways of 170/180 metres or more, or close enough to be easily extendable. Given an immediate dedication to simple standard designs, we estimate a turnover time of eighteen months keel-to-completion for light fleet carriers from 1939 onwards.

With a dozen of them logically available by the close of 1941, here was a great way of maximizing the capabilities of four lesser slipways. But once the medium fleet carriers began appearing in larger number, these lesser slips could be turned to other priorities, such as fast fleet oilers, for which one interesting design in the case of the Tamano-class provided for the oilers additionally carrying fourteen replenishment aircraft for the carriers.

There is the reasonable criticism that proposing a dozen light fleets mimics in hindsight an American recourse, the Independence-class of light fleet carriers. Belying that is slipway logic; there was no other way to go if the foresaid four lesser slipways were to be engaged in all-out carrier production.

Having set out the specifications for our three classes, or sizes, of aircraft carrier, some background notes may be helpful at this stage.

The limitation on Shokaku-class production was that initially at least there were only the four large facilities, and two of these had been allocated to super-battleships. The other limitation was that it took a long time to build such a large and complex vessel. A Shokaku was a quality peace-time build. In contrast, the Unryu-class were quantity wartime-builds. They could be churned out faster. And on an aircraft-per-ton basis, they perhaps surprisingly had the edge over their larger mates, although that was at the expense of inferior protection.

The peacetime IJN believed passionately in superior quality as a means towards compensating for inferior quantity. But even then, there had been a tendency towards making an exception in the case of carriers. This was considered from two points of view: first, safety in numbers for a highly vulnerable type of warship; and secondly, the determination to retain parity with the US in fleet carriers.

It thus seems logical in the circumstance of the super-battleship strategy being discarded, that the IJN would have adopted standardized, simpler designs much earlier on, and especially so in the long countdown to war with America.

Ideally, a carrier fleet would include no light fleets at all, as their air groups were insufficient at twenty-seven to thirty planes in the case of the Japanese conversions, and at up to thirty-three in the case of the American Independence-class carriers.

* * *

In all, nine of the Independence-class carriers were built, and that astonishingly over the course of only a year and every one by New York Shipbuilding Company. They contributed a punch of 300 planes to the

Pacific War. They were the fries to the hamburger of the Essex Surge, but only as a desperate stop-gap measure. Who placed them on the table was no less a figure than President Roosevelt himself. After his Pacific Fleet battleship force had been sunk or smashed by the air groups of six Japanese carriers at Pearl Harbor, he was shocked to learn that only one new American fleet carrier was scheduled for completion until 1944, which was at least two years away. He proposed, and then forced into being against intense professional Navy opposition, the Independence-class as a means of plugging the gap while the shipyards worked night and day on hurrying forward their Essex-class big brothers. Mr Hare had finally woken up to Mr Tortoise's progress.

The hare in this predicament called forth the age of Rosie the Riveter, a somewhat mythical folk heroine made famous by a popular song, a *Saturday Evening Post* cover by America's favourite artist, Norman Rockwell, and the poster of Rosie flexing a bicep as used in War Bond drives. She became in due course the symbol of American womanhood entering equality, as the 'gals' swarmed into war production to replace men drafted off to war. Rosie personified 'America – Arsenal of Democracy', a slogan of the era.

* * *

Japan had no choice but to consider light fleet carriers from the earliest times. This was due to the dearth of long slipways; Mr Tortoise had short feet.

Light fleets represented a splendid opportunity for the IJN in the short term. They might take longer to build than Independence-class carriers, but the four slipways available (as aforesaid, two at Nagasaki and one each at Yokosuka and at Sasebo) could turn out a dozen light fleet ships between 1938 and the close of 1941, with air groups collectively worth 360 aircraft. In other words, they could kick off with light fleet carriers on the basis of going for flight decks anyway you can and as fast as you can; but only if you can, which is the factor we later consider when applying our Diet and Fitting-out game rules.

American light fleet carrier production slowed down after 1943, once the Essex-class began appearing in the Pacific. Likewise, Japan could have turned over these shorter slips to other needs once Unryu-class medium carrier fleets and the second generation Shokaku-class began joining the air-sea armada at the rate of almost one per month.

We now proceed to the promised overview of the shipyard launch potential in Japan, the arbiter of our first limitation factor on the size of the Phantom Fleet.

The Shipyards

From the earliest times of the modern era, Japan concentrated on building a strong navy and large mercantile fleet. The progress of the private sector was stimulated with subsidies and naval orders. As an early example, laid down just before the First World War were the battleships *Fuso* at Kure and *Yamashiro* at Yokosuka, the *Fuso* briefly becoming the most powerful battleship in the world. To make sure all went right for the important duo, navy yards were used. Japan fielded a total of five navy yards: Kure on the Inland Sea, Yokosuka in Tokyo Bay, Sasebo on the southern island of Kyushu and Maizuru on the Japan Sea, while Ominato in the north only handled repairs. The only navy yards producing capital ships were Kure and Yokosuka. Sasebo built mostly light cruisers, and Maizuru destroyers.

In order for the next pair of battleships to help influence the outcome of Great War hostilities, the contracts were awarded to commercial yards – Mitsubishi in Nagasaki for the *Hyuga* and Kawasaki in Kobe for the *Ise*. From that time, we can talk of the Big Four shipyards. The famous 8-8 Project called for class quartets. These were to be laid down in successive pairs, the first pair at Kure and Yokosuka, the second pair at Nagasaki and Kobe. The successive quartet was to follow that sequence.

In the interwar period, the same pattern adhered to the four-ship heavy cruiser classes (Takao, Myoko and Mogami-classes), as that was all anyone was building in 'big ship' size because of the Treaties. Only with the next pair came any break. The *Tone* and *Chikuma* were both awarded to Nagasaki, where Mitsubishi had been quick to scent the changing political and military climate, eagerly seeking to make itself ready for rearmament. As the major liner producer, it was sensitive to how the Japanese Navy subsidized the mercantile shipping lines, most particularly if an aircraft carrier could be conjured forth from a liner hull. It was wise therefore to invest in long slipways. In contrast, Kawasaki was sensitive to how after the First World War, a great surfeit of shipping lay unused and orders were hard to come by.

Often overlooked is how heavy cruiser production ceased at the Big Four yards in the post-Treaty phase. The reason is that it had to do so once battleships could be built again. As the model-maker well knows, a battleship might be three times the tonnage of a heavy cruiser but their lengths are much the same. Nonetheless, such was the influence of the gun lobby that the immediately pre-war 1941 Fleet Replenishment Order included a pair of Ibuki-class heavy cruisers in preference to medium fleet carriers. They were allocated to secondary yards at Kure and Nagasaki.

As for aircraft carriers, a more complicated situation arises which we can best address on a shipyard by shipyard basis (starting where we just left off with the most interesting example, Mitsubishi at Nagasaki). We rate each centre's contribution by the number of carrier-borne aircraft the flight decks produced by these yards could operate in 1942, historically the year of the four great carrier battles.

Nagasaki

Mitsubishi had on offer at Nagasaki at least four slipways suitable for aircraft carriers.

Instead of the super-battleship *Musashi* on the 275-metre Slipway No. 2, we have Mitsubishi contracted to build two Shokaku-class large fleet carriers in succession, just eighteen months on the slipway for each (compared to thirty-one months for the *Musashi*). We follow with two quicker-to-build Unryu medium fleet carriers. Slipway No. 2 thus provided 252 planes to the air-sea armada.

On the 225-metre Slipway No. 3, the liner *Kashiwara Maru* had been laid down in March 1939. This was converted while still on the stocks to the shadow fleet carrier *Junyo* by early 1942, rated as worth forty-eight aircraft operationally but in the slow lane speed-wise. With Japan out of the Washington Treaty, there was no point in wasting slipway space with slow Shadow Fleet units (Japan was at war, even if only in China at that stage).

Instead, Mitsubishi is contracted with a two-carrier succession of medium fleet ships on Slipway No. 3. Given the earliest possible start – March 1938 – the first might make Pearl Harbor in time and the second

Midway. That would entail fourteen months on the slip for the first and twelve for the repeat. Fitting-out time is reckoned at sixteen months for the first, but down to twelve for the repeat. Four Unryus would thus be available in time to meet the Essex Surge, and two more before the close of play. The total wartime value was 324 planes.

Likewise, nothing should ever have come of the liner deal with the NYK line for the *Nitta Maru* (future auxiliary carrier *Unyo*), *Yawata Maru* (*Chuyo*) and *Kasuga Maru* (*Taiyo*), the latter seemingly to have followed *Nitta Maru* on its slip; nor for the OSK line's *Argentina Maru* (*Kaiyo*) and *Brazil Maru* (sunk before conversion).

Instead, we propose that the two slips are commandeered for keel-up light fleet carrier production and given an even faster turnaround by Mitsubishi. It seems that two slips at or in excess of 175 metres are inferable from the keel length of the liners, and which we will call No. 4 and No. 5 (for want of a source on actual length and identity).

Consider a production of six light fleet carriers at large before Pearl Harbor, but after March 1941 carrier production ceasing, being thenceforward switched to fast fleet oilers more aptly perhaps to perceived operational priorities.

We can use the aircraft carrier conversion names given to Shadow Fleet liners, namely the *Taiyo*, *Chuyo*, *Unyo* and *Kaiyo*, for these six keel-up light fleet carriers with a plane value of 180.

To summarize, Mitsubishi's contribution to the Phantom Fleet for the duration of the Pacific War could have been two Shokakus, eight Unryus and six Zuihos – 16 fleet carriers with air groups totalling 756 aircraft.

Yokosuka

Yokosuka Navy Yard in Tokyo Bay lay at the heart and head of Japanese naval aviation. Major naval air bases were clustered nearby. To Yokosuka was awarded the lead ship of any new carrier class, and also the first light fleet carrier conversions. It was generously equipped with a jumbo 300-metre facility big enough for the largest carriers, plus one of 200 metres suitable for light fleet carriers and two of 150 metres, one of which was extended to 270 metres and on which the *Unryu* had been laid down on 1 August 1942 (but with no time to complete a follow-on before mid-1945).

Planned to be ready by 1940 was a monster dry-dock for building super-battleship No. 3. The *Shinano*, as it became, was cancelled after Pearl Harbor and the sinking of HMS *Prince of Wales* and *Repulse* – for Yamamoto, the great acknowledgement that all along he had been right.

Initially, it was planned instead to build pairs of Unryus two at a time inside the dock. The loss of flight decks to dive bombers at Midway then occurred. Work was resumed on the super-battleship *Shinano* but as an armoured flight deck super-carrier. The first Unryu pair so allocated were cancelled. In Phantom Scenario, however, there are no super-battleships, therefore we can *theoretically* proceed with Unryu-class pairs inside the dock following its completion. We know when it opened for business from the lay-down date for the *Shinano*, 4 May 1940. That would make it worth four medium fleet carriers between launch of the first pair in June 1941 and completion of the second pair, a great way of sustaining the armada after it began to undergo battle losses (how this might run aground on Diet and Outfitting Rules we shall in due course be unwelcomely apprised).

A late start on Unryu production could also become the case at the 300-metre facility, which would first be preoccupied with turning out in succession a pair of Shokaku-class large fleet carriers, the launch date of December 1940 for the second one being the lay-down time for the first Unryu, with two follow-on successors possible before the end of the war in 1945.

The 200-metre slip could churn out fast naval oilers to keep the armada on the go and above all succour its fuel-starved escorting destroyers. Repeatedly through the Pacific War, destroyers running low on fuel became cause for carrier task forces breaking off battle, or withdrawing before joining battle. Aptly fitting out facilities could have converted the submarine tenders *Tsurugizaki*, *Takasaki* and *Taigei* into fast fleet oilers. These were already either complete or in advanced state in 1937, and therefore not cancellable unlike the *Nitta*-class Nagasaki liners which were only to be ordered the following year.

Thus, Yokosuka Navy Yard's logically possible wartime contribution to the Phantom Fleet could have been two Shokakus, seven Unryus and three fast fleet oilers, with air groups collectively of over 600 aircraft.

Kure

Kure was the second of five Naval Districts set up in 1889, having been chosen thanks to its position in the secluded Inland Sea. It became the naval base and naval shipbuilding centre specializing in developing new classes of battleship and heavy cruiser, as well as all aspects of submarine warfare. Sometimes called the Japanese Pearl Harbor, like the US Hawaiian base it enjoyed the proximity of a large city, in its case Hiroshima.

Naturally, it was awarded the job of building super-battleship No. 1, or *Yamato*, as it was called after its launch. But first, its 300-metre construction dock had to be adapted. Our Phantom Scenario requires a Shokaku-class carrier laid down instead, the earliest date for that probably being November 1937, with a second such following on from its launch in August 1940, with completion by March 1942. In succession to that, like the other Big Four yards, it could be expected to turn out fast-build Unryu-class carriers, of which two would be the contribution of the dock that built the *Yamato* before August 1945. Their combined contribution could be 252 planes.

Kure could contribute a 225-metre slipway for Unryu-class production from early on, providing the seaplane carrier *Nisshin* was cancelled before it was laid down in November 1938, having figured in the 1937 Order. Likewise, the 1939 Order would have to forget the light cruiser *Oyodo* and the 1941 Order's the heavy cruiser *Ibuki*. Following the latter on the slip would come an Unryu-class called *Aso*, thereby confirming an alternate capability for the production of medium fleet carriers and indeed the opportunity of an early start on such. That early start permits five medium-size fleet carriers before mid-1945 carrying some 250 planes.

Kure's contribution to the Phantom Fleet could therefore have been two large and seven medium carriers, their air groups contributing 522 aircraft. That compares to a poor actual contribution to naval aviation.

Kobe

Kobe's actual record in turning out aircraft carriers for the IJN is an example of what could be achieved when carrier followed carrier on the slipway. Shipbuilders Kawasaki could only offer a single slipway long enough for any carriers. At 250 metres, the No. 4 slipway was not considered adaptable for a super-battleship, such that the Navy Ministry looked toward Sasebo instead. A problem at Kobe is how it half-rings a bay, with high ground rising behind and valuable realty, some of it involved in crucial war production.

On the other hand, 250 metres was big enough for large carriers, with Kawasaki actually churning out the seaplane carrier *Mizuho* and large carriers *Zuikaku*, *Hiyo* and *Taiho*, followed by the Unryu-sized *Ikoma*. The huge *Taiho* makes an interesting case: 238 metres of its keel would have been resting on the slipway, with 22 metres of pre-launch deck length in over-hang.

Instead, we award Kobe a Shokaku as was laid down in late May 1938, and a follow-on successor of the same ilk. That leaves time for two more Unryu-class, and in turn the axing of the *Hiyo* and *Taiho* – no Shadow Fleet units nor armoured flight decks were needed for the Phantom Fleet, as its best defence would be high speed and manoeuvrability, combined with supremacy in the air.

A tribute to Kawasaki Shipbuilding at Kobe is that its actual contribution in aircraft carrier hitting power compares very closely to the needs of our Phantom Fleet scenario potential. Consider if the other three out of the Big Four had been so carrier productive. The Kobe contribution to the Phantom Fleet could have been two Shokaku and two Unryu carriers, with a total of 252 planes.

Sasebo

Sasebo had been Admiral Togo's base for the Combined Fleet, commanding as it did the approaches to the southern home island of Kyushu and to Korea. Between Sasebo and Korea, the Russian Baltic Fleet had passed through the Straits of Tsushima bound for Vladivostok.

The Navy Yard was not Big Four, but it had experience and know-how undertaking pre-war carrier rebuilds in the case of the *Kaga* and *Akagi*, and later also with conversions. It also featured a slipway reputedly of 200 metres, which was tied up producing a new class of light cruiser. In Phantom Scenario context, the Agano-class carriers were irrelevant. The story was that the IJN had wanted to replace the elderly light cruisers which served as flagships for destroyer squadrons. Instead, the IJN could have done better by building more of the Akitsuki (more familiarly

Terutsuki) destroyer-class, which were designed as anti-aircraft escorts for carrier forces. These could have been additionally used as destroyer squadron flagships, as indeed had Admiral Tanaka in his *Terutsuki* during the evacuation of Guadalcanal and Admiral Akiyama in *Niitsuki* at the Battle of Kula Gulf. The need for the 'moon class' (moon in Japanese is *tsuki*) had been foreseen before 1938.

The 200-metre slip at Sasebo would have been available before 1939, when the *Agano* was ordered. That would have permitted the facility to turn out two or three light fleet carriers of Zuiho length before 1942, and a further five before the end of the war.

Sasebo's contribution would thus amount to six light fleet carriers with a total of 180 aircraft.

Keeping count, the five centres had the *potential* over seven years of laying down and launching eight large Shokaku-class aircraft carriers, twenty-five medium Unryu-class and up to twelve of the light Zuiho type, every one of them with a speed qualifying them for fleet status. The total count for their air groups would amount to 2,380 aircraft, or more carrier aircraft than Admiral Halsey's fleet carriers deployed in the final months of the Pacific War off the coasts of Japan.

That much is permitted as *potential* under the Slipway Rule, but was it *possible* on the basis of the Diet Rule? Here we encounter the grand entrance of the Treasury Chief. In the case of arms procurement proposals, treasuries throughout history have been ruthless trimmers, the axe-men of lore.

Before we present tables showing all these aircraft carriers, we need to identify what units on the historical order of battle we can axe in order to make way for the alternative construction we have set our minds on. Let us take each of the pre-war historical Fleet Replenishment Orders in turn, and see what tonnages we can save in order to earn more flight decks.

1937 FLEET REPLENISHMENT ORDER

What is proposed is to axe the super-battleships, from which we gain colossal savings – 136,400 tons for the two, plus an additional 10,784 tons for a special transport for toting their guns about and a special tug. Next, we winkle out a seaplane carrier usurping a slip needed for medium-carrier production at Kure. Cancel that for another 11,100-ton saving. Totting all that up, we can pencil in 158,284 tons worth for extra new aircraft carriers from the 1937 Order.

The first pair of Shokaku-class carriers already appear on the 1937 Order. They are slated for Yokosuka and Kobe. So, we hold onto them. We need a further pair instead of the two super-battleships; one can be for the Kure Navy Yard and one for Mitsubishi at Nagasaki. Deduct from the above savings 51,350 tons. Next, we need a pair of medium fleet carriers off those secondary yards at Nagasaki and Kure that are long enough for them, and then a pair to follow them – all four being achievable from the balance.

So far, so good; the foresaid potential for large and medium carriers passes the Diet Rule test.

Regrettably, the balance left over will not stretch to the dozen light fleet carriers that the slips can in theory deliver. For the four permitted keel-up light fleets, we must restrict the Order to just two Zuiho-class carriers from Sasebo and two from Nagasaki, and hope a successive year's budget can realize funds for more.

Admittedly, we have strayed 4 per cent over the 158,284-ton savings made above (a mere nothing by the yardstick of conventional naval procurement). Should, however, the Treasury Chief get pernickety, it could be asked if it isn't better to end up with an extra light carrier than a surplus doing nothing? One can imagine the rubbing of hands, mannered way with words and nuancing of threats:

'Might not His Excellency, the honourable Minister, consider that maybe he risks an affront to Admiral Yamamoto who has promised us his prophetic vision of a thousand-plane air-sea armada for the emperor's shield in protection of our nation's peace and thereby its divine mission in achieving the projected Greater East Asia Co-Prosperity Sphere: we beg you not let bean-counters quibble, Your Excellency, surely not over a handful or two of the humble peasant's rice.'

Cancelling the entire battleship programme would also include plans for two super dry-docks for building them; one at Yokosuka and the other at Sasebo. We cannot put a tonnage figure on these dry-docks, but suffice to say that it is proposed the budget for each be spent instead on expanding fitting-out facilities to be better able to meet fitting-out needs of both

Good Guys

dmiral Tomisaburo Kato

Admirals Yonai and Yamamato

dmiral Tomisaburo Kato was a Navy minister from 1915, then leader of Japan's elegation to the Washington Naval Conference in 1922; he returned to become rime Minister, but died within a year.

He debuted the so-called 'treaty-faction' in the Navy, those in favour of the Vashington Treaty terms. In the 1930s it was led by Admiral Mitsumasa Yonai s Navy minister and Admiral Isoroku Yamamoto his vice minister.

Such was the fury of the opposing 'fleet faction' that Yonai appointed Yamamoto ommander of the Combined Fleet to reduce his exposure to assassination. There e could hole up in the 'iron tower' of flagship *Nagato*.

Almost to a man, their 'treaty faction' deplored any war with the US as nwinnable.

Admiral Kanji Kato

Admiral Nobumasa Suetsugu

First leader of the 'fleet faction' was Admiral Kanji Kato, who served on th
Japanese delegation to the Washington Naval Conference alongside his namesak
Tomisaburo Kato. He was particularly antagonistic towards Yamamoto, who use
his influence to hobble Kato's career.

Much nastier among the 'fleet faction' was Admiral Nobumasa Suetsugu
an intriguer and a thorough fascist. Adherents of the faction tended also to b
battleship men and Tripartite Alliance supporters. Suetsugu engineered a purg
of liberal-minded senior naval men, including Yamamoto's best friend, and egge
on the police to arrest left-wing intellectuals.

Prince Konoye, in traditional dress at his Tekigaiso villa, confers with Foreign Minister Matsuoka (centre), Army Minister Hideki Tojo (right) and Navy Minister Zengo Yoshida (centre right). The main topic was probably whether Japan should join the pact with Germany, which Yoshida bitterly opposed and resigned upon incurring a nervous breakdown.

Prince Konoye in 1937 was photographed dressed up as Hitler at a fancy dress party prior to his daughter's wedding. Shock reverberated around the world.

Japan's Emphasis on Long-Range Planes

Early naval aviation effort, as spurred on by Yamamoto, began a dedicated focu on long-range models for both land-based bombing and for scouting. Experienc of the China War later saw need for long-range fighters both to protect thes bombers and to arm a growing carrier fleet.

The twin-engined Mitsubishi 'Nell' (above left) had a range of 2,356 nautical miles, soon exceeded Mitsubishi's 'Betty' (above right) at 3,256nm. Between them their torpedoes sank *Prince of Wales* and *Repulse* off the Malay coast, flying a huge distance from Saigon airfields.

The four-engine Kawanishi flying boat coded 'Mavis' (above) sported a range of 2,590 nm. Th improved on that a few years later with the 'Emily' (below right), range 3,888 nm, widely regarded the best flying boat of the Second World War.

The most successful reconnaissance float plane was the Aichi 'Jake', typically flying off heavy cruisers, two of which could carry five float planes. Crew of three, endurance in air 15 hours, range 1,128 nm.

Japan's Carrier Planes

'Zero' fighters were Mitsubishi's contribution towards winning the Pacific War. For range and agility in combat, the Zero outclassed all.

ikewise for the range, the 'ate' torpedo bomber won urels as the nemesis of five US ttleships and three US carriers it of six available in 1942

The 'Val' dive bomber (left) was almost as good. In contrast to the US 'Dauntless' (below), it lacked retractable landing gear and the capacity to carry a 1,000 lb bomb.

Fast Fleet Carrier Option

Taigei as submarine depot ship (above). As converted to *Ryuho* carrier (below).

Seaplane carrier *Chitose* (left) fought in this aspect in 1942, before conversion to light fleet carrier much like *Ryuho* (above).

Junyo as photographed by the Allies after the war at Sasebo, the last surviving IJN carrier from 19 battles. It was a shadow fleet addition to the Kido Butai.

Fast liner *Nitta Maru* (above) was one of three ordered just pre-war for Japan-to-Europe passenger trade, but designed for quick conversion to auxiliary aircraft carrier.

The three conversions, such as the *Taiyo* below, emerged in the flight-decked configuration as below. In ferrying fighters to overseas bases they saved the faster fleet carriers the risk while themselves surviving for a long time.

Super-Battleship Option

Yamato on trials, November 1941.

Admiral Yamamoto plotting the fall of shot.

Musashi's tower with range finder on top.

Yamato and *Musashi* at anchor in Truk lagoon, 1943.

Fast Carrier Option

Shokaku

Zuikaku

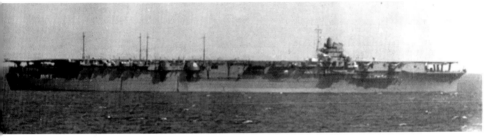

The sisters are usually described as nearly identical, although *Zuikaku* wore its island further forward and appears the better model for the six 'phantom' additional units proposed.

Katsuragi

Real time *Katsuragi* was the third vessel of Unryu class; the hull was much the same as *Hiryu* but the island was worn as for *Soryu*.

The light carriers had no islands.

Zuiho

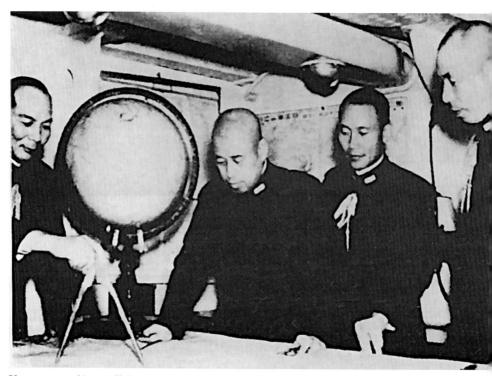

Yamamoto and his staff plot operations aboard *Nagato*, with Chief of staff Ugaki (left) and Yamamoto chess partner Yasuji Watanabe (right).

Admiral Jisaburo Ozawa pressed Yamamoto to combine Japan's carriers into a single 'shock and awe' carrier fleet. He succeeded Nagumo in command of it, impressing Americans as the most capable Japanese fleet commander.

Five Kido Butai carriers depart Staring Bay, Celebes, with their four battlecruiser escorts to raid the Indian Ocean, led by *Akagi*, astern *Soryu* then *Hiryu*.

At some point in the raid the *Akagi* photographer pointed his camera astern to *Soryu* (see below) to catch this rare iconic shot, which usually is published as its mirror image claiming that it is *Hiryu* astern, but it wore its island superstructure to port amidships whereas Soryu wore its starboard forward.

Battle of Midway Saga

Dive bombers from *Enterprise* smashed *Kaga* and *Akagi*, and *Yorktown* sank *Soryu* leaving *Hiryu* to fight back. *Hiryu's* eighteen dive bombers struck back at the *Yorktown*, followed by a strike of ten 'Kate' torpedo bombers which also found *Yorktown*.

Joichi Tomonaga led the attack. It scored twice but he was shot down by fighter ace John S. Thach

Dick Best. This dive bomb ace led the attack on *Akagi* and later in the day also hit *Hiryu*. He survived.

Yorktown hit and sinking; its dive bombers found shelter on the *Enterprise* and later that day shared in the torching of *Hiryu* (below).

Battle of Santa Cruz

Despite his defeat at Midway, **Admiral Chuichi Nagumo** continued to command the carriers at Santa Cruz, on 26 October 1942, for him a tactical victory in comparison, but a strategic defeat due to the loss in the battle of Murata and other leaders.

Shigeharu Murata, the IJN's aerial torpedo expert. His 'Kate' torpedo bombers sank five American battleships at Pearl Harbor. At Santa Cruz he led the co-ordinated strike that sank the *Hornet*.

A deck-load of fighters and dive bombers are seen here on the *Shokaku* ready to take off on the morning of the battle.

Battle of Santa Cruz

Zuiho conducting flight operations.

At Santa Cruz, light carrier *Zuiho*, used for scouting and fighter defence, had already launched most of its aircraft when Lieutenant Birney Strong's two-plane patrol hit the little carrier on the fantail. It was now out of the battle but afloat and mobile.

The attack panicked Admiral Nagumo. Whereas his first deck load had flown and then put paid to the *Hornet*, the second deck load was only ready to launch off one attack carrier. The torpedo bombers on the other were delayed. Result: no co-ordinated attack on *Enterprise*, which survived. Victory in the Pacific hinged on at least one US carrier surviving through 1942.

Hornet under attack by dive bombers and torpedo planes

Enterprise shown under attack, with a near miss by a Junyo dive bomber

Essex Surge

The famous shot of five *Essex*-class carriers lined up in Ulithi lagoon epitomised the 'Essex Surge' and the image became known as 'Murderers Row'. In real time they brought Japan to defeat. Two Independence-class light fleet carriers are visible.

Gambier Bay was the 19th jeep carrier completed by the Kaiser Yard and became the sole scalp of *Yamato* and its consorts at the Battle of Leyte Gulf

Admiral William Halsey.   Admiral Raymond Spruance.

nown as 'Bull' Halsey, the admiral won the pivotal Guadalcanal campaign, but his impetuosity ter in the war gave concern. Alternating in command of the Essex surge was the cautious Raymond pruance, the victor of the battles of Midway and Philippine Sea.

Essex Surge

USS *Neosho.*

The US Navy had nine of the thirty-one Cimarron-class 18-knot fleet oilers ready to fuel the flee before Pearl Harbor. Four on the stocks were converted to escort aircraft carriers, among the firs to serve in the war. The oiler *Neosho* is shown above, and below at Pearl Harbor next to flagshi *California*. It succumbed to the Japanese five months later at the Battle of the Coral Sea.

Oilers were the potential Achilles heels of the carrier fleets. Knock them out and the carriers had t go home, that is if they could. At Coral Sea, an older oiler, *Tippecanoe*, was also in support, so Admir Fletcher got home to Pearl Harbor.

the 1937 and 1939 programmes. In criticism of that, why forego being able to build two medium-size carriers at once in such docks as had at one point been planned? But the Diet Rule would make that impossible. Available largesses do not permit these dry-docks, as thereby we would be exceeding the 1937 and 1939 Diet allocations.

Some may find fault with the way 'sacred largesses' have been expressed by proxy in displacement tonnages. But displacement tonnage makes a good proxy. While it is only an expression of the tonnage of water displaced by the floating steel bodies of these ships, steel is money – big money. And steel does not grow on trees. Japan, in particular, was not resource-rich in steel. It relied on imports. The embargoes reduced these, particularly by ending imports from America. The country was left dependent upon a slender output from the pre-war territories of the Japanese Empire. One can only project wartime carrier production reliably by reference to what tonnage was historically expended in total naval construction.

The 1939 Fleet Replenishment Order, all of which was achieved (as was also indeed the case with the 1937 Order), benefited from two-and-a-half years of comparative peace and from steel stockpiling.

1938 SUPPLEMENTARY ORDER
Before we can proceed to the 1939 Fleet Replenishment Order, there is some in-between business to transact, namely what usefully to substitute for the seven liners.

These became ongoing around 1937–39, and did not appear on any orders sanctioned by the Diet for actual warships because they were not warships at that stage under their liner guises.

The only warship order for 1938 was a Supplementary Programme resulting in calls for two Katori-class training cruisers and a food supply ship (a third Katori was ordered under the 1939 Fleet Replenishment Order. The three training cruisers are fair game at 17,000 tons in total, as we shall see).

Meantime, let us see what fleet carriers we can gain from not subsidizing the seven liners.

The seven liners were ordered in three tranches. In 1937 for the NYK line came the Nitta Maru-class of three. In 1938 for the OSK line came the *Argentina Maru* and *Brazil Maru*, and for the NYK line the *Kashiwara*

Maru and *Izumo Maru*. The government subsidized the latter pair by 60 per cent. When expressed as a proportion of tonnage, that antes up 28,680 tons. We find no record of the subsidy level for the other five, so assume 50 per cent which puts another 42,280 tons into the game for a total liner subsidy saving of around 70,000 tons.

We choose to expend this on two Unryu-class, one from Kure and one from Nagasaki (the third such vessels from each) – reckoning on their appearance on the Pacific War scene by mid-1942 – and on three more light fleet carriers, one from Nagasaki and two from Sasebo's slip, these likewise available by mid-1942.

1939 FLEET REPLENISHMENT ORDER

With the programme for super-battleships not yet dead, we nonetheless find two of these listed again for the 1939 Order; one to follow on from the *Yamato* in its dry-dock at Kure, and the other slated for the new dry-dock at Yokosuka which became ready by May 1940. Therein lies a whopping saving of 136,400 tons.

Next, we find the armoured deck carrier that became the Kobe-built *Taiho*, which was 29,300 tons when completed. We cannot see any need for armoured flight decks in the Phantom Fleet. A carrier's best defence was its aircraft, followed by its speed and agility under attack. It was far less bombs bursting through flight decks that sank carriers, and far more aerial or submarine-borne torpedoes.

In discussing above the role of Sasebo as a Navy Yard, we questioned the need for new light cruisers being built. The 1939 Order was notable in ordering no less than six new light cruisers, of which the four-ship Agano-class could have contributed an aggregate of 26,608 tons towards new aircraft carriers and the two-ship Oyodo-class a further 16,328 tons.

Next, we find unworthy of largesse three Katori-class training cruisers, two being from the 1938 Supplementary Programme and one on the 1939 Order – 17,670 tons handily there.

The total savings of 226,306 tons will first have deducted from it 102,700 tons for four Shokaku-class repeats from the Big Four shipyards, but now at a faster rate of production. That leaves a balance of 123,606 tons for either seven medium-size fleet carriers of the Unryu-class, at 17,150 tons each, or six Unryus and two Zuihos. We propose adopting the second option, because in 1942/early 1943 there would be six slipways producing Unryu medium-size fleet carriers – the original secondary slips at Kure and Nagasaki, added to the Big Four slips at Kure, Nagasaki, Kobe and Yokosuka. That has all six on the scene well before June 1944. By continuing to patronize the Zuiho-producing factory on Sasebo's 200-metre slip, we can ensure another pair of them before the close of 1943 without running into the Diet Rule.

And how fare we this time in confrontation with the frosty stare of the Treasury Chief? We own up to being about 2,000 tons overdrawn, which at a tad less than 1 per cent is ant dung in the arms procurement business, where any such figure is amateur pickpocket stuff in a world where larceny is calculated in the volumes of super-bank scams.

1941 ARMAMENTS PROGRAMME

On the eve of war, in September 1941, Japan dreamt up another heavy Order, again persisting with super-battleships, such was the dedicated stubbornness of the big-gun lobby, and this time pathetically but a single carrier, the historical *Unryu*. There was no way it could all be realized, given that yards were crowded with work under the 1939 Order, such that under the influence of the defeat at Midway a year later, the whole programme was scrapped and substituted with another which called for sixteen Unryu-class carriers (finally no battleships!). Of these, three were fully completed in 1944 and a further three 80 per cent complete by early 1945 when work on them was discontinued.

Given that the Phantom Fleet would extend the Pacific War by a year or two, the crippling shortages of strategic materials would not have kicked in so early, such that we allow six more Unryus by the first half of 1945. There are no more because the plan for sixteen very much relied on being able to construct two Unryus at a time in the new Yokosuka super dry-dock, which we earlier anticipated the IJN cancelling in order to develop extra fitting-out facilities instead. Also, many of the sixteen were not slated for completion until 1946.

We have not extended our overview beyond early 1945 because after that date, as in 1944, actual events would have started to become tight. Therefore, it would be speculative to predict anything as being realizable after early 1945.

On now to the Fitting-out Rule. The umpire for this rule was a graphite pencil with lots of clean eraser on the end, two sheets of graph paper and a ruler for drawing in outfitting times chronologically. We first practised this methodology as a means of measuring outfitting capability on the historical record from 1939–45. Next, we projected an alternative capability, or 'Phantom Scenario'. Ending the frame in early 1945 seemed as far as one could take such a table, given that by then, war damage repairs would begin kicking in, thereby reducing dock time for fitting out new-builds, as it did severely in 1944.

REAL TIME IJN OUTFITTING PERIODS; REFITS AND CONVERSIONS INCLUDED

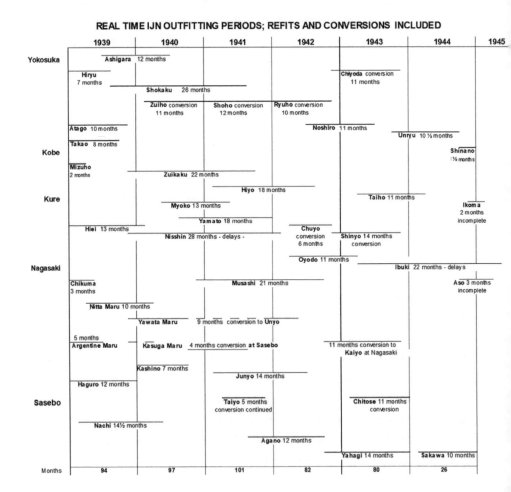

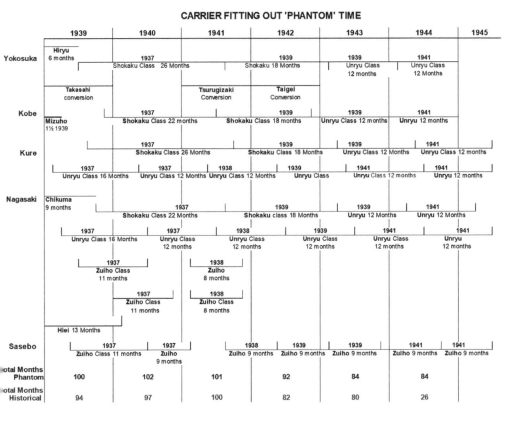

CARRIER FITTING OUT 'PHANTOM' TIME

These fitting-out studies are presented in the pair of diagrams shown in the tables. We comment below.

We omitted 1938 because all 1937 authorized construction would still have been on the stocks then and not outfitting.

On a 'months in the works' basis, the historical table demonstrates large warship fitting-out capacity in excess of 100 months a year. In Phantom Scenario, we have also opted for advanced expenditure on extra fitting-out facilities instead of on the two super-battleship dry-docks. Therefore, in any one year, total fitting-out time permitted in Phantom Scenario needs to keep within 100–120 months expended.

We included on the historical table any remaining carrier work covered by the 1934 Order, plus all the 1937 and 1939 Order outfitting work on battleships and carriers. We also included time on the seven Shadow Fleet liners' conversion times, and the extensive refit times from January 1939 on the battleship *Hiei* and six heavy cruisers. Astonishingly, the four Myoko-class cruisers had lavished on them close to a year's work in the dockyards. In Phantom Fleet scenario, priority would go to aircraft carriers, and anything needing modernization would need to wait until there was room at the bar. We were delighted to welcome *Hiei* back to the bar, as it and its three sister fast battleships were to serve the carrier fleet as escorts during the Pacific War. Its sisters had already been modernized. The *Hiei* reappears on the companion table showing Phantom Fleet outfitting. It is said to have been the emperor's favourite warship and was named after Mount Hiei, just to the north of Kyoto, in medieval Japan the stronghold of warrior monks.

Using another page of graph paper and the same ruler, but another graphite revolving pencil with a fresh rubber on the end of it, we lined up the Phantom Fleet outfitting times.

Although there was no possible way of predicting the outcome without risking brain haemorrhage, in the event the two tables fortuitously showed a neat match once they were complete. If we had anticipated a problem at all, it would have been with 1941. Surprisingly, the mismatch occurred in 1940. This we 'smoothed out' by removing 1940 light fleet carrier production at Yokosuka from the Phantom table and having the heavy cruiser *Myoko* make do with what it had. It was actually the last of the heavy cruiser modernizations. The *Chokai* was to have received one, but that was cancelled when war began. The lack of such work did not prevent it being the flagship that led the IJN to its great naval victory at Savo Island, the opening round to the Guadalcanal campaign.

There is the understandable objection that bottlenecks should surely be seen as less a national phenomenon, more a local one. Here must be taken into account that outfitting does not need to be confined to the location of launch. Frequently, launched vessels from Nagasaki and Yokosuka were towed to Sasebo, Kure or even Kobe for outfitting or for conversion. Nagasaki was a great launching location, but nearby Sasebo had good fitting-out facilities, having notable experience with aircraft carrier conversions or rebuilds.

Mission Accomplished

Our proposition that Admiral Yamamoto could have fulfilled his naval aviation ambitions by arguing successfully that Japan's naval shipbuilding capacity – limited though it was – could deliver our postulated 1,000-plane air-sea armada by close of 1941 has been met, at least to our satisfaction.

We have now launched and fitted out our Phantom Fleet, and commend the reader to the series of tables that take it stage by stage, first counting in the actual (historical) production of the Treaty years which had a collective striking value of 530–540 planes inclusive of three seaplane carriers. Next, our revisions to the 1937 Order are worth another 480 aircraft.

We next see the 1938 Order adding another five flight decks worth 198 aircraft, followed by the 1939 Order kicking in with a hefty 672 planes, and mostly all good by mid-1943, the eve of the Essex Surge. With the 1941 Order, we see the prospect of another 400 or so planes by the end of hostilities, or a nice way of replacing carrier battle losses.

*   *   *

Finally, a rogue factor to consider is whether Japan could have got away with the Phantom Fleet? Surely, the American hare would have woken up earlier to the Japanese tortoise's relentless progress; Washington rushing Rosie the Riveter forward to work hammer and tongs on an Essex Surge.

We answer that question in Chapter 5: 'Smoke and Mirrors'. Therein, the depressing answer is that yes, Japan could very well have got away with it.

While the Essex Surge was already in full spate thanks to the succession of Vinson Acts in Congress and the post-Pearl Harbor panic, in the circumstances of the Phantom Scenario it might have come far too late.

Furthermore, the Allied powers had little clue as to what eggs Tokyo was hatching in its nests. Were the shipyards producing super-battleships, regular battleships, battle cruisers, pocket battleships or the odd aircraft carrier, and in what proportions? The answer was a couple of the first and a couple of the last, but clever folk in their offices also persuaded themselves to believe in a Phantom clutch in the categories in-between.

Meanwhile, nobody measured slipways, which you did not need to gate-crash with tape measure in hand. All you needed was to check *Jane's Fighting Ships*, in particular the 1940 edition, to note the lengths of large warships the Japanese had been producing and where in Japan they were built. Therein lay the limitation factor in a nutshell. An irony is that the compilers and researchers at *Jane's* don't appear to have carried out that mundane chore themselves, for example by reading closely their own annual. But don't let us spoil a good story here – our next chapter reveals all.

First three tables for which art work is separate, namely aircraft carrier versus battleship production capability off a 200-metre slipway. The next two tables show first real-time fitting-out times and secondly 'Phantom' time fitting-out projections.

PHANTOM FLEET PHASE 1: Real time pre–war carrier strength from the Treaty era and pre–Pacific War, including two Shokaku-class large fleet carriers and three seaplane carriers.

NAME (translation)	CONSTRUCTION HISTORY	TONS	SPEED (knots)	AIR GROUP (1942)
Hosho ('Soaring Phoenix')	1919–22, Yokohama	7,470	25	14
KAGA (ancient province)	1920–28 (remake Sasebo, 1934–35)	38,200	28.5	72
AKAGI (mountain name)	1920–27 (remake Sasebo, 1935–38)	36,500	31	63/72*
Ryujo ('Prancing Dragon')	1929–31 (remake Yokosuka, 1934–36)	10,600	29	36
SORYU ('Sea-Green Dragon')	1934–37, Kure (300 metres)	15,900	34.5	54
HIRYU ('Flying Dragon')	1936–39, Yokosuka (300)	17,300	34.33	54
SHOKAKU ('Soaring Crane')	Dec 1937–Aug 1941, Yokosuka (300)	25,675	34.25	72
ZUIKAKU ('Fortunate Crane')	May 1938–Sep 1941, Kobe (250)	25,675	34.25	72

From the Shadow Fleet we preserve for the Phantom Fleet the *Chitose*, *Chiyoda* and *Mizuho* seaplane carriers (for details, see Shadow Fleet chapter), with a speed of almost 29 knots (but for the *Mizuho* 22 knots) and carrying twenty or so ship-borne float planes, each useful for carrier fleet reconnaissance and picketing; and the submarine depot ships *Tsurugizaki* and *Takasaki*, these completed at Yokosuka as 29-knot fleet oilers instead of light aircraft carriers, but to include accommodation and catapulting of fourteen reinforcement aircraft each for attack carrier replenishment, as in the Tamano-class design. As the text (see Chapter 3) makes clear, all five were begun preceding the 1937 Fleet Replenishment Order, and so would not take up slipways needed for 1937 carrier orders (unlike the *Nisshin* at Kure, which we axe). They belonged to the 1934 Order and were well advanced by 1937.

* Whereas both *Akagi* and *Kaga* had operational capability for seventy-two planes, the *Akagi* sacrificed nine in order to create stowage space for drummed fuel due to a lesser endurance compared to teammate *Kaga*.

Air groups for the thirteen units comprise 530–540 aircraft at 1942 loads.

PHANTOM FLEET PHASE 2: Extra carriers proposed in substitution for the super-battleships etc authorized by the 1937 Fleet Replenishment Order and to become operational by late 1941 (i.e. by the time of Pearl Harbor). Top speed for all carriers from now on is 34 knots.

NAME (translation)	YARD (length)	FOR COMPLETION	AIR GROUP (1942)
Zuiho ('Lucky Phoenix')	Sasebo (200)	June 1940	30
Shoho ('Soaring Phoenix')	Sasebo (200)	February 1941	30
Taiyo ('GreatHawk')	Nagasaki (175)	November 1940	30
Chuyo ('Heavenly Hawk')	Nagasaki (175)	November 1940	30
KORYU ('Shining Dragon')	Kure (225)	May 1940	54
UNRYU ('Cloud-borne Dragon')	Nagasaki (225)	May 1940	54
SHINRYU ('Godly Dragon')	Kure (225)	May 1941	54
KAIRYU ('Sea Dragon')	Nagasaki (225)	May 1941	54
RYUKAKU ('Whooping Crane')	Kure (300)	August 1941	72
CHUKAKU ('Heavenward Crane')	Nagasaki (275)	September 1941	72

Air groups for the two large, four medium and four light fleet carriers contribute a total of 480 aircraft, to which can be added the 530–540 (see previous table) from the historical carriers of the Treaty and pre-war era, thereby exceeding the Phantom Fleet strategic aim of a fully worked up '1,000-plane air-sea armada' by close of 1941. Successive phases will seek to double that.

NOTE. Air group figures to the right indicate units as large, medium or light carriers (as also in successive tables). For the keel-up light fleet carriers, we have poached Shadow Fleet names.

PHANTOM FLEET PHASE 3: Extra carriers proposed in substitution for the subsidies on seven Shadow Fleet liners (as had been planned in 1938) and to be added to the 1938 Supplementary Order. These were operational by mid-1942 (i.e. by the time of the Battle of Midway).

NAME (translation)	YARD (length)	FOR COMPLETION	AIR GROUP (1942)
AMAGI (see note below)	Kure (225)	April 1942	54
KATSURAGI (see note below)	Nagasaki (225)	April 1942	54
Ryuho ('Dragon Phoenix')	Sasebo (200)	May 1942	30
Unyo ('Cloud-borne Hawk')	Nagasaki (175)	September 1941	30
Kaiyo ('Sea Hawk')	Nagasaki (175)	September 1941	30

Air groups for the two medium carriers and three light carriers contribute a further 198 aircraft. As in Phase 1, all light carriers are keel-up new-builds.

We 'fast forward' the nomenclature change that historically took place in early 1943. Medium carriers now bear the names of volcanos and other mountains, as heavy cruisers and battlecruisers had previously. Amagi is a volcano range in the Izu peninsula. Katsuragi is a scenic mountain near Nara in western Japan. Historically, the second and successive Unryu-class units (*Unryu* itself was launched before the nomenclature policy changed) were named as such.

In the next table we see light fleet carriers receiving river names, as had traditionally light cruisers. As we anticipate having some of them cruising the trade routes causing a lot of trouble, anointing them with cruiser names seemed apt.

Some may quibble that, in usurping the actual place of the first seven Shadow Fleet liners that were all converted to carriers, we only show an overall bonus of about thirty aircraft, or an extra light carrier's worth, and show no timing advantage. We agree there is a choice. But add to the extra air strength the fact that these will be keel-up fast carriers of equal speed to their larger brethren. And it is better surely to go all the way with Phantom rather than Phantom and Shadow mixed.

PHANTOM PHASE 4: Twelve carriers proposed to substitute for the super-battleships and light cruisers authorized by the 1939 Fleet Replenishment Order, and all these operational by early 1943 (i.e. ahead of the Essex Surge). If not such, we mark them with a *.

NAME	YARD (length)	FOR COMPLETION	AIR GROUP
TOSA	Yokosuka (300)	January 1943	72
KII	Kure (300)	March 1943	72
OWARI	Nagasaki (275)	February 1943	72
HIZEN	Kobe (250)	December 1942	72
KASAGI	Kure (225)	April 1943	54
ASO	Nagasaki (225)	May 1943	54
IKOMA	Yokosuka (300)	January 1944	54*
KURAMA	Kure (300)	April 1944	54*
UNZEN	Nagasaki (275)	February 1944	54*
TOKASHI	Kobe (250)	December 1943	54*
Hirado	Sasebo (200)	February 1943	30
Chikugo	Sasebo (200)	October 1943	30*

Air groups for the four large fleet carriers, six medium and two light aggregate a strength of 672 aircraft, of which 438 could have been achievable operationally before the onset of the Essex Surge in late 1943, and a further 270 before June 1944, by when all eight of the original Essex batch and the nine US light fleet carriers had become engaged in the Pacific. Thus, by doing without super-battleships and some lesser irrelevances, Japan could have accumulated by the time of the June 1944 Battle of the Philippine Sea a carrier fleet of over 2,000 aircraft (provided no losses in the interim), compared to the US having accreted less than 1,500 (in the case of its fleet carriers at least).

The official 1944 change in IJN nomenclature has been brought forward here in the case of the large carriers, which are now called after ancient provinces. River names are now sported for light carriers; Hirado is the main river in Shikoku and Chikugo a river in Kyushu. At Big Four yards hereafter, production is to switch from large carriers to medium for greater efficiency and speed.

PHANTOM PHASE 5: Conservative estimate of further carriers theoretically conceivable in the 1941/1942 Orders (the latter year's order substitutive of the former) that in less stressed circumstances of Phantom Scenario could have been capable of completion by early 1945 (i.e. by the arrival of the British Pacific Fleet).

CLASS	YARD (length)	FOR COMPLETION	AIR GROUP (1942 STANDARD)
UNRYU-class**	Kure (225)	April 1944	54
UNRYU-class	Nagasaki (225)	March 1944	54
UNRYU-class	Yokosuka (300)	December 1944	54
UNRYU-class	Kure (300)	March 1945	54
UNRYU-class	Nagasaki (275)	January 1945	54
UNRYU-class	Kobe (250)	December 1944	54

Air groups for the six medium carriers could aggregate an additional 324 aircraft, or considerably more than what the British Pacific Fleet contributed to the campaign in the first half 1945. Alternatively, the late-war infusion can be seen as the ongoing capability for sustaining war losses.

A note here is not amiss on the Unryu-class. Sixteen of these medium fleet carriers were authorized after the Battle of Midway in 1942, inclusive of *Unryu* itself (the sole carrier authorized in 1941, but as of 1942 not yet laid down). Of the sixteen, all but six were cancelled, of which three became operational in the second half of 1944 and the others would have been in early 1945 but for the march of war. For the Phantom Fleet we envisage production of medium-size fleet carriers latterly spreading to the Big Four yards as a more efficient way of using slipway space than with Shokaku-class carriers. In this way, Japan could have fought the war with twenty medium carriers instead of a mere seven, of which two were Shadow units.

Suggested volcano and mountain names for the six are Iwaki, Kita, Hotaka, Daisen, Ishizuki and Kaimon, which presents a fair geographic spread over the Japanese home islands.

Chapter 5

Smoke and Mirrors

'The United States Navy knew far less about its principal maritime enemy than any reader today [1986] can learn about the supposedly secretive Soviet Navy in the pages of one of the open-source naval references ... Post-war investigation of Japanese ships and equipment revealed details undreamed of during the conflict.'

(A.D. Baker III ed., *US Naval Institute Guide to the Combat Fleets of the World*)

The irony in the above observation was how US Pacific Fleet intelligence knew a lot of the time where the Imperial Navy was headed, and even which divisions – even individual ships – thanks to breaking Japanese naval codes, but knew so little about the ships, their weapons and their sensors.

There were many reasons for US Navy scientific and technical intelligence lagging behind operational intelligence capabilities during the years counting down to war. For a start, tight security had been very effectively imposed in Japan from 1937 onwards, especially with the country being at war with China and with America bitterly opposed to Japan's adventure there. Spy fever was rife.

We saw one over-the-top example of that in the last chapter of how the *Musashi* was built and launched. That was not too far off being the general rule. Even within the IJN, the implicit order of the day amounted to 'Chinese rules' – no see, no hear, no talk. Specifications were downplayed. For example, the 18.1-inch super-guns were called 'special-type 16-inch guns'; torpedoes were represented as having ranges far short of actuality, and likewise with aircraft nothing was ever claimed that might 'scare the horses' at the embassies.

It was an offence to photograph one of His Imperial Majesty's warships, such that only one photograph of the short-lived super-carrier *Shinano* has ever been found. No clear image of *Musashi* has survived, only of *Yamato*.

The diplomatic convention of exchange visits to construction facilities and bases by naval attachés was observed, except that in the event much fancy footwork conspired to avoid showing the Tokyo attachés anything they would most want to see.

Scratching around the hen yard, foreign naval attachés had found themselves having to form an attachés' club in order to share and compare the few pickings any of them could glean individually. Periodically, rather convivial luncheons were the venue.

There was also a basic institutional ignorance on the part of Allied navies about naval shipbuilding in Japan. This extended to an apparent failure to take in data available in open-reference works. A yawning ennui over 'what the Japs were up to' might seem to have characterized intelligence bureaucracies in home capitals – the exception being the naval attachés and language officers attached to Tokyo embassies, who pried well despite all the handicaps facing them. Things fell apart when their reports and occasional key revelations reached their distant ministries. These commonly were ignored, disparaged or merely not circulated properly. Some examples follow.

The immediate pre-war US air attaché, Stephen Jurika, remembered how he found himself seated in the cockpit of a Zero fighter, an exhibit at an Army/Navy air show open to the public, probably that of January 1941 at Haneda airport. He took down all the data he could for transmission to Washington. Despite it being obtained from a metal plate giving the plane's vital statistics, this intelligence coup earned from Washington a stern reproof in reply. Jurika was told not to exaggerate because the specifications he had sent were deemed unachievable, even bordering on pure fantasy. The grounds stated were that the US had no aircraft to match (so, presumably what many Americans at the time saw as 'slit-eyed folk' could have produced nothing better was implied). Posthumously in his case, this tale has been doubted, although such air shows were staged by the armed services, and specifically that cited above.

Doubted or not, sources on the scene of the China war reported back about the mystery new super-fighter driving all else from the skies. Analysis of these reports should have prompted alarm about the phenomenal range and agility of the Zero. But there was probably only casual and sceptical analysis. The Chinese even passed on a competent report by their aviation experts who inspected a fairly intact Zero that crash landed.

Another espionage success by Tokyo-based US Embassy naval intelligence officer and ex-language officer Henri Smith-Hutton came as a result of a chance encounter at a tennis club. He recruited a Chinese student resident in Japan and of adopted Japanese name, who was treated as a native Japanese and included as a guest on student visits to warships. Japan was at war with his native China. The clandestine patriot was guided on how to undertake discreet eye-guess measures of the width of a torpedo tube on a destroyer his group had been invited to visit. A sailor had even bragged to the youth that the torpedoes did without air, using oxygen alone. Passed on to the Office of Naval Intelligence (ONI), this vital intelligence stirred no attention. It was not until after mid-war that the secrets behind the uniquely oxygen-fuelled 24-inch 'Long Lance' torpedo, with its incredible range, speed and accuracy, became revealed to the Allies, thanks to the salvage of an unexploded torpedo off a Guadalcanal beach and to prisoner-of-war interrogations. Yet here again, information about a closely guarded secret weapon had been delivered on a plate before the war had even begun. We will return shortly for more on this secret weapon.

The Chinese student agent also revealed how on a visit to one of Japan's four Mogami-class so-called large light cruisers, its five turrets mounted pairs of 8-inch guns when the current annual edition of *Jane's Fighting Ships* illustrated 6-inch guns in turrets of three guns apiece. This was not even particularly secret, there having been public admissions, also reported back by the naval attaché. Washington, however, dismissed the report.

When the *Mikuma* was sunk at Midway, it and accompanying sister *Mogami* were repeatedly reported by their assailants as being a couple of battleships, these mounting pairs of guns in their turrets. Only close examination of pictures taken by attacking planes showed clearly the configuration of Mogami-class cruisers. The IJN had re-gunned the four heavy cruisers after the Treaties elapsed, as also they did with the successive two-ship Tone-class. Thereby, the IJN had managed to achieve equality with the USN on heavy cruisers despite the 1930 London Treaty provisions. As a bonus, the IJN heavies carried 18 per cent more 8-inch main armament in aggregate. Their heavy-cruiser status was only to be officially recognised by the ONI after Midway.

An incoming British naval diplomat was able to sneak the first pictures of the brand-new seaplane carrier *Chiyoda*, having aimed his

Leica through the porthole of a liner while entering the port of Kobe. Another hired a small boat one night in Nagasaki. He reckoned, from the flash of welding torches visible through the screening curtains, that the vessel under construction was at least 720ft long, or a very definite battleship, with no maybes about it. He even figured accurately that the slipway length had been increased. Similar intelligence incoming to US sleuths did not inhibit a long and comprehensive report being worked up by Washington that trashed rumours of any battleship in the works at Nagasaki. The hapless report merited going all the way to President Roosevelt.

In practice, spying was discouraged by the US Embassy when Eddie Layton was posted to Tokyo before the war as assistant naval attaché, and particularly not using cameras. Admiral Nimitz's wartime intelligence chief was encouraged rather to become a social star with top Japanese naval brass. He recounts his friendship with Admiral Yamamoto and being invited to a 'duck fishing' party in a park dedicated to duck hunting, where admirals and their guests cast with nets at sitting ducks, cooked and ate them *sushi yaki*-style to copious drafts of Begg's Scotch whisky, with much good camaraderie. The admiral then proceeded to win a number of rubbers of bridge, helped no doubt by the whisky he seemed to be drinking along with everyone else, except that in Yamamoto's case, the brown liquid was in fact only tea.

An affable rapport between Layton and Yamamoto stemmed from the older man having likewise served as a language student and embassy naval attaché, and as such having been as smitten with American culture as Layton had been with Japanese.

On another occasion, Layton dropped by the Navy Vice-Minister's office and casually enquired of him why two fast naval oilers were taking such a long time in building. Yamamoto delicately changed the subject – perhaps the promising young American officer would care to be his guest at a Noh drama? He would not reveal that one oiler had been completed as a submarine tender and the other had been set aside until it could be converted to the light fleet carrier *Zuiho*. One Yankee hound dog at least was sniffing at the traces of the Shadow Fleet.

There was in Washington and Whitehall a seeming reluctance to engage with the niceties of the IJN's emperor-approved nomenclature policy, which usefully furnished its own giveaway as to ship types merely from reading the name and checking its derivation. Until June 1943, the official nomenclature policy for the IJN was to name battleships after the ancient provinces of Japan, or old names for Japan itself, such as Fuso. Battlecruisers and heavy cruisers were named after mountains and volcanoes, light cruisers after rivers and destroyers after atmospheric and other natural phenomena. Aircraft carriers were named after legendary flying beasts, such as phoenixes and dragons, or after birds with mythic attributes associated with the Imperial cult, such as cranes. The liner conversions were named after hawks. Exceptions were the conversions to aircraft carrier from capital ships, the *Akagi* and *Kaga*. These retained the battlecruiser and battleship name each had been launched under.

The IJN was very cagey about releasing names from 1938 onwards. If they had been more prescient of the future character of war at sea, and taken the Phantom Fleet route in 1937 instead of proceeding with the Yamato-class, a good ploy would have been to bring forward (as we have in the preceding chapter's Phantom Fleet tables) the June 1943 change in nomenclature so that large carriers received ancient province names, as had battleships before, and medium carriers mountain names, as had heavy cruisers, in order to foster the illusion they were building battleships and pocket battleships or battlecruisers of one kind or another – and fewer carriers.

With the light carriers continuing to bear flying beast names, the Allies might thus find comfort that Japan was still seemingly interested only in building carriers 'to pet shop sizes', as we shall shortly dramatize.

Last but not least, there entered a gratuitous disposition towards self-deception. In Allied recognisance, Shadow carriers stubbornly remained in their original guises as submarine tenders and seaplane carriers, and there was only the dimmest awareness until late in the war that the Japanese had been converting big passenger liners.

On the other hand, the Allies were quick to see Phantom carriers where there were none; it was a case of Shadows real and Phantoms false!

The Great Pocket Battleship Illusion

Should the Phantom Fleet have proven real, as we have outlined in the previous chapter it could have been, a necessary grand deception would be needed in order to bamboozle everyone. As important to hiding the switch of emphasis from great guns to mobile massed aircraft platforms would be to nourish the illusion that Japan was still committed like everyone else to the big gun. The sensitive time would have been 1938–41 for the Phantom Fleet to mask its purpose, or otherwise run the risk of setting off an international armaments race centred on carriers. If there was to be a secret fleet of new aircraft carriers, then there needed to be the illusion of Phantom battleships instead occupying Japan's limited slipways. In this the Allies needed no special assistance from Nipponese spin doctors and dissimulators.

The most astonishing example of the Allies 'seeing things' was a long-held conviction on the part of both Allied navies that Japan was engaged in building a class of pocket battleships similar to the Germans' *Deutschland*, *Graf Spee* and *Scheer*.

As a naval power, the Germans had a dreaded reputation as raiders of commerce on the high seas. Nations such as Britain and France with colonial possessions extending around the world needed very large numbers of cruisers to hunt down these raiders. The word 'cruiser' derives from that aspect of naval duties; the need to cruise the shipping lanes in protection of trade.

In contrast to the Germans, the pre-war planning of the Japanese never contemplated the diversion of key units to commerce raiding. Rather, the IJN was wholly dedicated to a decisive fleet action strategy. Its carriers, cruisers, destroyers, submarines and aircraft were designed for one purpose only – to whittle down the strength of the US battleship force in the course of its progress across the Pacific so that Japan's smaller force of battleships would stand a chance in a final duel between battle lines; a Tsushima defeat for the Yankees.

One set of weapons specifically designed for the 'decisive battle' scenario were the 8-inch gun Japanese heavy cruisers produced during the interwar era. Photogenic to a fault, they are still one of the most popular subjects for warship model-makers thanks to their undulating deck lines, raked back smokestacks, massive castle-like bridges, multiple gun turrets and enviable record in the war. Aptly called 'ferocious beasts' by Pacific War strategist H.P. Willmott, the IJN's heavies mounted ten 8-inch guns and sixteen torpedo tubes on a fairly well-armoured and compartmented frame which nonetheless could be driven to 34 knots by powerful engines, or as fast as many classes of destroyer. The ships could also survive much punishment in battle (unless perchance a bomb touched off their torpedoes). The torpedoes used were a secret weapon if ever there was one.

Alone of the navies of the world, the Japanese succeeded in developing an oxygen-fuelled torpedo. Designed to a 24-inch width (compared to the Allied 21-inch), it came to be called the 'Long Lance' (this appellation was coined by Samuel Eliot Morison and has stuck) because it vastly outranged and outshone anything the Allies could deploy thanks to the revolutionary way it was fuelled. In the ideal final battle, the eighteen heavies were to have fought under cover of night – executing a much practised technique against the American battleships that the IJN called 'long range concealed firing'. Once their torpedoes had been expended, they were to have turned their heavy guns to busting open American screening forces. Through the gap would pour massed squadrons of destroyers, each armed with sixteen deadly 'Long Lance' torpedoes, eight in the 24-inch tubes and eight reloads housed on deck rails ready to reload the firing tubes within twenty minutes. In practice, things seldom occurred in such an ideal way during the Pacific War. The closest it ever happened against battleships was off the coast of Malaya in December 1941, as we recounted in Chapter 2, once off Guadalcanal in November 1942 and when the *Mogami* burst through the screen and was able to launch at the American battle-line but missed during the October 1944 action in the Surigao Strait, often called the 'death march of the pagodas'.

Nonetheless, the super-torpedo so depleted Allied heavy cruiser task forces that by 1943 they were relying almost alone on light cruisers to fight the IJN in the later stages of the Solomons campaign. A participant of the night action off Tassafaronga, when four out of five of a squadron of large cruisers were torpedoed, went so far as to conjecture when writing a book about it in later life that as a secret weapon, the 'Long Lance' was of a shock value comparable to the Germans' V2 rocket.

The US was indeed lucky not to have lost the new battleships *Washington* and *South Dakota* in a night engagement off Guadalcanal. So great a wake did the two make at high speed, that 'Long Lance' torpedoes fired at them by the heavy cruisers *Atago* and *Takao* exploded astern when they hit the roil of the *South Dakota*'s wake. Its speed had been underestimated. As for the *Washington*, it wisely fled the scene.

Much as the heavies would have made great commerce raiders, they were battleship killers and nothing else. They were designed to be the Velociraptor that would tear the Tyrannosaurus Rex apart. In the decisive battle scenarios, all eighteen were expected to deploy and to fire around 300 torpedoes thanks to their unique reload capacity.

When the Japanese heavy cruiser *Ashigara* represented the emperor's navy at King George VI's Coronation Naval Review at Spithead in 1937, it was allotted anchorage next to the German pocket battleship representing Hitler. As a result, the *Ashigara* was immediately typecast in the media as a raider and its true purpose ignored.

There reigned only the perception that the *Ashigara* and its ominous ilk might act as a threat to an 'empire on which the sun never sets'; they might interfere with the passage of tea from China and India, with depressing consequences for the sacred 'cuppa' imbibed in British parlours.

But it was not just the British who deceived themselves. The Americans were seeing the same phantoms – pocket battleships or armoured super-cruisers. To document one example, a Government Printing Office publication of 1941 called *Military Intelligence Identification of Japanese Naval Vessels* listed pocket battleships building or completing as being of 12,000–15,000 tons, with a 30-knot top speed and armed with six 12-inch guns, or much the same specifications being dished up by *Jane's*.

So convinced became Washington that the Roosevelt administration persuaded Congress to enact the building of five Alaska-class battlecruisers, on the same basis as the French had in the late 1930s introduced the *Dunkerque* and *Strasbourg* as German pocket battleship hunters. The Japanese pricked up their ears. Why these American battlecruisers, they asked? Could that be to prevent the IJN's *Ashigara* and its sisters from closing on the American battle fleet, they wondered?

Delusion swung full circle. In September 1941, the Japanese Diet ordered a pair of battlecruisers in answer to America's Alaska-class order. The Japanese Naval General Staff shortly afterwards gave pause and asked itself exactly what role these ships were to play that could be so important as to clutter up slipways desperately needed for more carriers? The order was soon cancelled. Two of the Alaska-class, however, made the war in time; white elephants for the US taxpayer to wonder at.

Thereat we conclude one of the great farces in the history of naval arms procurement.

The progress of a well-armoured self-deception can be followed in the successive annual editions of that British bible of naval reference, *Jane's Fighting Ships*. Originally edited by Fred T. Jane, the annual grew to an internationally iconic status as *Jane's*. Its loyal browsers confidently assumed that the data, when it was not official, at the very least had been whispered by bona-fide spooks seated in scuffed leather armchairs at exclusive gentlemen's clubs in London's West End, discreetly whispering their revelations over well-shaken dry Martinis. A movie scenario could find no less than the Master of Sempill, he of the unofficial British naval aviation mission to Japan whom we met in the second chapter, dropping the first dread news of Tokyo having pocket battleships in the works.

Given the importance of the totally false pocket battleship deception to the book, it is worth tracing its progress through successive *Jane's* annual editions.

The *Jane's* 1940 edition reports four armoured pocket battleships being built at Yokosuka, Nagasaki, Sasebo and Maizuru, with dates for them being laid down given as between 1937 and 1938, despite no provision having been made by Japan for such a class of ship in either the 1937 or 1939 Fleet Replenishment Orders. The editor even adds weight to the annual's confidence in its data by repeating this news in his foreword to the edition.

The 1941 edition finds '*Chichibu* and two or three other ships building'. It does, however, accurately report a new class of light cruiser (as ordered in the 1939 Programme), but goes on to caution that 'evidence of the existence [of the light cruisers] is so slender that it is quite possible that these reports actually refer to the "pocket battleships" described on an earlier page'.

The 1942 edition repeats four 'Titibu-class' pocket battleships, confidently listed as *Takamatsu* laid down at Yokosuka in March 1937, *Titibu* at Nagasaki in March 1938, *Niitaka* at Sasebo in June 1938 and an unnamed ship in 1938 at Maizuru. It guesses that the four may become operational in a 1941–42 time frame.

Come the 1943/1944 edition, we find no change and again a confusion with Agano-class light cruisers, although the entry this time concludes that 'exactitude cannot be guaranteed. Design may be based on German pocket battleships.' It adds that the *Niitaka* had been reported as an aircraft carrier, all four possibly having been completed as carriers.

The 1944/1945 edition published at the close of the war hazards the opinion that the Unryu-class aircraft carriers might be conversions of the pocket battleships, if not of Yamato-class battleships. The IJN may have deliberately or accidentally aided in the deception by giving *Unryu's* five sisters province names rather than dragon names, the province names then cropping up in decrypted radio traffic that could have prevented the pocket battleship illusion from vanishing without trace.

Where there was a will, there was a way; those pocket battleships just never quite went away.

Fancy Tales of Chinese Merchants

As a proxy for the state of Allied intelligence-gathering, *Jane's Fighting Ships* proved almost as much in the fog over new battleships. The compounding factor was less a failure to pick up reliable news of new construction. That was quite difficult enough in the circumstances of over-the-top security on the part of the Japanese authorities. Rather, it had more to do with a puzzling ignorance of the Japanese shipbuilding record, its launching facility limitations and its nomenclature policy.

Again, a review edition by annual edition of *Jane's* will document a tale touched upon but never unfolded whole and in the raw.

The *Yamato* starts out in the 1940 and 1941 editions as laid down in March 1937 at Kure with the name *Nisshin*, although the latter edition notes '*Nisshin* also reported as an aircraft tender'. *Nisshin* was never a battleship name. The seaplane carrier of that name was actually laid down at Kure in November 1938, as was the *Yamato* a full year before.

The *Musashi* was laid down in Nagasaki at the end of March 1938 as Battleship No. 2 and not named until a very late stage. *Jane's* confidently awarded it the ancient province name *Kii* in 1941, and again in 1942. To Yokosuka Navy Yard *Jane's* was to award a battleship they called *Takamatsu*, laid down in September 1937, when in reality the aircraft carrier *Shokaku* was awarded Yokosuka's longest slipway that December, partly because of it not being suitable for a super-battleship. At Yokosuka, once a dry-dock had been built that was big enough for a super-battleship, the *Shinano* was laid down in it in early May 1940. But that was two-and-a-half years later. In the case of *Takamatsu*, that is not a name featuring in any list of ancient Japanese provinces and so should have been recognized as a phoney. Takamatsu is the principal city of Shikoku, the lesser of Japan's four home islands, and faces the Inland Sea.

Both editions warn of possible confusion on the part of sources 'between these 40,000 tonners and smaller armoured ships', for example pocket battleships. Possibly this was because they were reminded of having in the previous edition shown *Takamatsu* as one of the pocket battleships. Indeed, by 1942 the names and the yards are dropped.

Sasebo Navy Yard on the southern island of Kyushu is credited in 1941 with one of the battleships; they have the *Tosa* laid down there in 1939. The 1942 edition prefers to find *Tosa* at the Maizuru Navy Yard on the Sea of Japan. Yet at no time in their history did either navy yard produce a capital ship. The best that Sasebo could sport was a 200-metre or so slipway, just long enough for a light cruiser, whereas all that Maizuru ever produced was destroyers and such like. Admittedly, a super-dry-dock was slated for Sasebo as a cradle for a super-battleship, but it never seems to have had such a keel laid on it. This may have been because it was preferred to keep it ready for servicing or repairing super-battleships. On the other hand, Sasebo enjoyed fitting-out facilities sufficiently commodious to sustain the virtual rebuilds of the upper works of the carriers *Kaga* and *Akagi* in the late 1930s. Sasebo lies close to Nagasaki, such that sources citing Sasebo should have in fact instanced Nagasaki.

The 1942 edition of *Jane's* is fairly secure in the knowledge of Kure and Nagasaki being involved in the construction of four new battleships, given that Hull 111 (never named) followed on from the launch of the *Yamato* at Kure (as most sources aver rather than at Sasebo). That had not been the case at Mitsubishi in Nagasaki. The *Musashi* was not followed on after its launch in November 1940, much as it could have been. The launching scares blemishing the birth of the *Musashi* (that we described in Chapter 4) may well have argued against slipways in favour of dry-docks, such as were used at Kure for *Yamato* and at Yokosuka for *Shinano*.

Jane's, having finally begun to get it right by 1942, errs by persisting again in its belief of a battleship in the works at Maizuru.

The edition goes on to warn that the names *Kii* and *Satsuma* at Nagasaki, *Owari* and *Aki* at Kure and *Tosa* at Maizuru must be regarded as more or less speculative, coming as they did from Chinese sources. Those names would have smacked of good provenance at least, as all five were ancient provinces and had been used for prior battleships or those cancelled after the Washington Treaty. For his supper, the Chinaman in question had sung in tune at least. As confided to historian Arthur Marder by the head of British Naval Intelligence from 1940–42, Rear Admiral John Godfrey, 'It was simply very difficult to infiltrate agents, and the few we did have were usually Chinese merchants.'

Most remarkable is the omission of Kobe throughout the editions, given the foresaid inclusion of Sasebo and Maizuru. Unlike the last two, Kobe and Nagasaki had since the First World War been the other two Big Four producers of capital ships, starting with the *Ise* then *Kaga* in Kobe's case. Three others from the 8-8 Programme cancelled by the Washington Treaty were also awarded to Kawasaki Shipbuilding there. Kawasaki next produced the heavy cruisers *Ashigara*, *Maya* and *Kumano*, and later the carriers *Zuikaku*, *Hiyo*, *Taiho* and *Ikoma* at Kobe. These were all launched from the same slipway, often successor ships being laid down within days of the launch of the predecessor.

Astonishingly, anyone leafing through capital ship entries in earlier editions of *Jane's* would have found the importance of Kawasaki Shipbuilding at Kobe lit up as one of the Big Four capital ship yards, and how Japan divided its naval construction between its IJN yards and private enterprise yards for lack of facilities at the one and as a stimulus to the shipbuilding industry at the other. For Japan, it was important not just to challenge the world with a navy but also to sustain the nation with a first-class merchant marine. Giving the civilian yards good business helped keep their noses above water in bad times, and thereby still around in better times busily turning out merchant ships.

Jane's may have omitted Kobe and Yokosuka because it knew aircraft carriers were being produced at each. But to have awarded the navy yards at Sasebo and Maizuru battleship-status demonstrated a failure at consulting the recent historical record.

The 1943/1944 *Jane's* retains the five names and the three yards, and claims at least two vessels delivered. In the Foreword, the editor reports that two 45,000-ton battleships are believed to have been completed. He finds reason to suppose *Musashi* and *Yamato* for names, noting these to have been ancient provinces. By 1944/1945, there is still no inkling of the 68,200-ton displacements and the 18.1-inch super-guns. They advise that the names previously given as derived from Chinese sources 'can no longer be considered authentic and may be disregarded'.

No-one had yet cottoned on to what aircraft carrier the third ship of Yamato-class had been converted into. This was in fact the aircraft carrier *Shinano* that was torpedoed by the submarine *Archerfish* (it had been on its way from Yokosuka Navy Yard to be completed at Kure). *Jane's* speculates variously that the carriers *Taiho* or *Unryu* may have started out in life as Yamato-class. It then cites *Unryu*'s sisters, the *Amagi* and *Katsuragi*, as other carrier conversion possibilities.

Could Allied intelligence have been any better informed than the world's best-known authoritative open-source naval reference work? We can go all the way to the top on that question, because Winston Churchill left us his memoirs of the Second World War.

Not One of Winston's Finest Hours?

Few world leaders could have been better informed on naval matters than Churchill, twice First Lord of the Admiralty, both at the outset of the First World War and again at the start of the Second. A shared sense of fellowship underlay Churchill's relationship with President Roosevelt: FDR had served in the 1920s as Assistant Secretary of the Navy. In his confidential correspondence with Roosevelt, Churchill signed off anonymously as 'Former Naval Person' out of respect for their common experience.

Few more than Churchill enjoyed better awareness of what super-battleships could achieve in catching rival navies off-balance. He had been the driving force behind the five Queen Elizabeth-class dreadnoughts just prior to 1914. Four of them saved the Battle of Jutland two years later, where they hosted the largest guns, bore formidable armour and came close to the speed of the battlecruisers they were partly teamed with in the van of the fleet.

That was thanks to Winston's sagacity and nerve insisting on oil-fired engines and untested big guns. In the battle, HMS *Warspite* was hit harder than any of Admiral Beatty's nearby squadron of battlecruisers but staggered free of the battle without blowing up, as had disastrously three of the thinly decked battlecruisers, occasioning Beatty's laconic remark to his fellows on the bridge of the squadron's flagship, HMS *Lion*, 'There's something wrong with our ships today.'

In the great Winston's case, his famous grasp for detail tended to dim out anywhere east of British-governed India, as witness the post-war story that found him and President Eisenhower discussing the agenda in flight for the Bermuda Conference in 1953. Through the smog from his cigar smoke, Churchill's curious but Champagne-fired eyes lit upon the unfamiliar topic of Cambodia as a final item. He asked Ike, 'Who Is Dr Cambodia, and what does the devil want?'

Worried about Japanese naval power, we find Churchill querying Admiralty estimates of ongoing Japanese capital ship production on 10 March 1942. He expostulates to the Admiralty, 'Has Japan really the capacity to be working on up to eleven capital ships at once?' Well, if one was including as capital ships the non-existent shorter hull-length pocket battleships, the answer actually was 'yes'.

So, had British Intelligence been at work after all? In a way, it had. There were after all ten slipways or construction docks capable of turning out battleships from pocket-size to super-size, including carriers. That at least was something to go by if one knew the information in the first place. That could well have been so, for the British were very well represented in major Japanese ports as shipping line executives and marine insurers. Japan also imported cranes and other heavy engineering products from British industrial sources (these indeed annually among the leading full-page advertisers in editions of *Jane's*), which imparted a certain access and the ability to extrapolate capability. It was the view at the US Embassy in pre-war Tokyo that if the Russians had the best spy network thanks to communists embedded in industry, the British had the second-best.

Of course, by March 1942 the time for wishful thinking and racial putdown was over. The Japanese had surprised everybody, so what exactly was their capability? To answer that, fingers were licked and the pages turned on the *Jane's* 1940 issue in particular.

The problem lay less in the raw material of information, rather more in its interpretation.

For example, a widespread criticism of Churchill's grasp of naval affairs in a Far Eastern perspective is how he was so obsessed with commerce protection. He tended to measure up Japanese naval potential largely in German terms. The famous example is his dispatch of the *Prince of Wales* and the *Repulse* (Force Z) to Singapore. Churchill had persuaded a reluctant Admiralty that the high-speed pair could deter Japanese aggression from threatening Indian Ocean commerce routes 'by roaring about', to cite his ever-ready rhetoric. He complained how all three of the first-built King George V-class battleships were tied down in home waters against the likelihood of the great German battleship *Tirpitz* rampaging into the North Atlantic and severing the island nation's lifeline. So why not pull a trick like that on Japan? Well, Japan had no lifeline in the Indian Ocean, only potentially in the South China Sea. One needed a lot more than Force Z to dispute it. Winston and his Admiralty advisors had underestimated Japanese naval aviation.

If, however, they had spun their office globe to the South China Sea, they would have found that the Japanese Empire's jugular hugged the coast of China, lying therefore within land-based air cover all the way north to Japan. In contrast, the broad Atlantic wastes could only be partly patrolled from the air. There was in actuality no parallel. A more credible threat to the jugular could have come from the very substantial American submarine fleet based in the Philippines, except they were armed with defective torpedoes. Only the handful of Dutch submarines ran up the few successes against the IJN in the months Japan rolled all before it in the conquest of South-East Asia. As for the Royal Navy, it contributed no submarines to the defence of the Malay Barrier. The British preferred to keep their large T-class submarine, that had been designed for the Far East, at home or in the Mediterranean.

Churchill, in his account of the Second World War, shows only a passing interest in what the Japanese might have been preparing in the form of new carriers. Roosevelt and the US Navy were far quicker than their allies in recognizing the marine aviation revolution in naval warfare after Pearl Harbor. Unfortunately, the president did not survive the war to write his memoirs.

As for the British Empire, within a generation it came to die for lack of the right aircraft carriers to fight in the big oceans and the right aircraft to fly from them in 1942. The Americans and Japanese excelled at carrier warfare because each of their navies had its own naval air force. Until the eve of war, the British had lost their original Fleet Air Arm to RAF control, which proved disastrous for the Royal Navy (a subject we return to in Chapter 6). It was worse still for the German navy, which had to rely on the Luftwaffe for aircraft. As a result, Hitler never had a single operating aircraft carrier.

Just when both air and surface arms in combination were so needed when Malaya was invaded, the RAF failed to provide modern land-based fighter cover for Force Z off the Malayan coast. Originally the Admiralty's plan had been to risk the Royal Navy's old and expendable R-class battleships made to operate in a coast defense mode protected by Hurricanes and Spitfires. But these had been allocated for shipment to Russia rather than to Singapore. So, the R-class were held back in the Indian Ocean. Instead Prince of Wales and Repulse were brought forward, to act as a deterrent against attack by Japan by 'roaring about'. Andrew Boyd's recent *The Royal Navy in Eastern Waters* prefers to blame the Admiralty rather than Churchill for the resulting debacle.

Let us now move on into the fog of the burgeoning Pacific War to see where Allied naval intelligence was or was not cognizant in the case of IJN aircraft carrier recruitment.

Phantoms False and Shadows Real

It was not until the Doolittle Raid of April 1942, five months after Pearl Harbor, that any hard information about Japanese carriers enlightened US admirals. Whereas this was primarily a raid on the Tokyo area, a lone bomber carried out an overflight of adjoining Osaka and Kobe, reporting two carriers being built, these presumably being the *Taiho* on the stocks and *Hiyo* fitting out. Among the planes bombing the area of Tokyo Bay, one attacked the light carrier *Ryuho* in Yokosuka Navy Yard, hitting it with one bomb and usefully toppling a gantry crane at work on it with another. But nobody thought wise to pass a bomber over Kure, Nagasaki or Sasebo to get a hawk's eye view of what was going on there. These were Army Air Force fliers after all, with different priorities written into their mission, even if borne to the scene by the US Navy aboard the carrier *Hornet*, from which they proved just capable of taking off but having to fly on to China as they were unable to land on a carrier deck.

Allied confusion on the carrier front was of a different order. The primary phenomenon was that phantoms were being seen where there were no phantoms, or at least of the Phantom Fleet variety in the meaning of the last chapter. It was as if in that fancied scenario of ours, the Japanese would have had no need to cover up a switch of production from battleships to carriers. The US Naval Intelligence foxhounds sniffing in the bushes had their paws pointing at new carriers whether they existed or not.

The irony is that if these non-existent new birds in the bush were to be miraculously included in the full IJN order of battle available during 1942, and that inclusive of the Treaty-era carriers and the Shadow Fleet, something very close to an air-sea armada of 1,000 planes would need to be reckoned with, although panic would have been mitigated by gross underestimates of the number of planes carried by Japanese flat tops. Nonetheless, this sense of a thunderstorm brewing in a cloud of unknowing no doubt intruded ulcerously for President Roosevelt

So, what were these non-existent carriers and how does the timing mesh with the claim above?

Starting with 1940, we find *Jane's* adding a third carrier to the Soryu-class. Called by them the *Koryu*, this is slated to have been laid down in 1937 (1941 edition) or 1939 (1940 edition). Either would make it operational well in time for 1942 wartime use. The January 1941 edition of *Flight Magazine* wrote: 'Japan has six carriers, and one, the *Koryu*, on the stocks.' Either this influenced American media mentions of *Koryu* in the early war period, or else the information came to *Jane's* originally from US sources. The 'boys in the basement' at Pearl Harbor gave credence in early 1942 to the phantom carrier in a daily intelligence briefing to Admiral Nimitz, reporting a carrier of that name active in the area between Saipan and Formosa.

On the basis of historical precedents, the notion of a third in the class does stand up conceptually at least. In the 1920s, the IJN's plans for a class of three aircraft carriers had been unsettled by the Washington Treaty, such that two battlecruisers then building were to be converted and plans for the trio set aside. On the basis that Japan had by now walked out of the treaties, it was reasonable to suppose that for its next class of carriers it would also want a trio. With warships, pairs make less practical sense than trios. With a trio, one can expect always to have a pair operational if one of them is being overhauled. Hence the merit in a third unit for any class of capital ship was well recognized (and better still a fourth or a fifth). An example was how Britain in recent times relied for over three decades on the three-ship Invincible-class of modest-sized aircraft carrier.

Koryu was and still is a name in use. Late in the war, a class of suicide midget submarines with a crew of five was named thus. A *Koryu* of the merchant marine sails the oceans of the early twenty-first century world as a large bulk carrier. There are several renderings in translation, of which 'Shining Dragon' seems the more apt in the sense of dragons being thought of as covered in scales, like fishes.

On the eve of the Pacific War in 1941, however, *Jane's* finds itself in doubt: 'Actual existence of *Koryu*, reports of her launch notwithstanding, cannot be guaranteed.' The so-called launching it attributes to Kure Navy Yard, where the seaplane carrier *Nisshin* and super-battleship *Yamato* were then in progress. This imagined launch of an aircraft carrier could have been confused with that of the *Nisshin* at the end of November 1939 or of *Yamato* in the first week of August 1940. Alternately, disinformation might have been leaked as cover for the launch of the latter. Acts of disinformation can be hard to make stick today. In the secretive conspiratorial climate of Japan during the countdown years to war, disinformation was more in surfeit than in short supply. All it needed was a few arrogant careerists in Washington, combined with the hard drinking of that era; a lot could be swallowed, particularly if it had a cherry on top!

Jane's 1940 edition correctly reports the next class of Japanese carrier, the Shokaku-class, as to timing and yards, but appears to have ingested the official announcement as to size, speed and plane capacity, which aspect we will come to with the 'pet shop deception' later in this chapter. What is important here is that the 1942 *Jane's* reports 'a third ship of the *Shokaku*-class, *Ryukaku*, has been lost. A fourth may exist.' In that case, why should there not exist a fourth ship of the Soryu-class, the serious student here pointing out how the IJN had for thirty years turned out its battleship and heavy cruiser classes in quartets, so why not carriers likewise?

The mistruth about the *Ryukaku* emerged in the basement quarters of the Pearl Harbor submarine base discreetly occupied by US Pacific Fleet intelligence codebreakers. There, an overriding priority was to figure out the enemy order of battle and its capability. Captured documents demonstrated a misreading of the carrier name mentioned in IJN radio traffic as *Ryukaku* when what was meant was *Shoho*, which as we have seen was a mere light carrier of the Shadow Fleet sunk at the Battle of the Coral Sea.

Suspicion must first have arisen from examination of the excellent photographs taken in the Coral Sea from attacking planes. The *Shoho* appeared as having a flush-deck, whereas the *Shokaku* when under attack next day was revealed as having an island superstructure forward on the starboard side. There is also the problem of the improbity of the name of the *Ryukaku*; its translation as 'dragon crane' seems an oxymoron.

The boys in the basement, however, were tight-lipped about what they knew, so much so that the phoniness of *Ryukaku* took a long time circulating further afield. The illusion of a third, even a fourth member of the vaunted Shokaku-class survived the shame of *Ryukaku*'s exposure as a wraith.

Yet there is no record of them being alarmed to learn how the 1943/1944 *Jane's* perpetuated the *Ryukaku* myth, nor of the mentions of this phantom in Allied media, notably for example in that wartime periodical produced for US servicemen called *Yank*, which reported in a 1943 edition the existence of 'the new Japanese carrier *Ryukaku*'. There should have been great perturbation because of the danger of a copy of the issue falling into Japanese hands, such as being found in the cockpit of a crash-landed American bomber damaged over Rabaul. The evidence of the mistransliteration of the Japanese symbols could have indicated to Japanese intelligence that the Americans were decrypting their radio traffic. Fortunately, the foresaid issue of *Yank* magazine was never enjoyed in the Japanese naval officers' mess in Rabaul.

This danger equally attached itself to the misreading of the names of those heroes of the Shadow Fleet, the *Junyo* and *Hiyo*. Their names got rendered as *Hayataka* and *Hitaka*. A Japanese prisoner interrogated after Midway revealed the existence of a new carrier, the characters for which can be rendered in two transliterations, *Hayataka* or *Junyo*. Both sets of names mean much the same translated into English. Could he have figured that by giving American intelligence the longer form, upon being picked up as such by Japanese intelligence it would have alerted the IJN that the Americans had broken their naval code?

Unexpectedly, the wrong names took a long time to die. For instance, when the celebrated US submarine *Trigger* torpedoed the *Hiyo* outside Tokyo Bay in June 1943, submariner Edward Beach – who became author of a post-war bestseller on US submarine achievements in the Pacific War – still knew the carrier as *Hitaka* years later. *Jane's* 1944/1945 edition addenda section correctly captions an immediate post-war photograph of its sister ship at anchor outside Sasebo as the *Junyo* (although the Japan Section report penned earlier persisted in heading its entry '*Hayataka*'). The confusion might have been cleared up faster, and the IJN aircraft carrier order of battle clarified, if the Japanese had not made changes in the wake of Midway to the naval code that the breakers back in Pearl Harbor had been reading so effectively. The months it took for them to rebuild penetration fatefully led to the duration of the Guadalcanal campaign, when good intelligence was needed more than ever

The reality of the three light fleet carriers of the Shadow Fleet such as the *Shoho* was for a very long time missed by both the US Office of Naval Intelligence and by *Jane's*, whereas Phantom Fleet carriers became an article of faith, as we have shown. The light carriers seem to have been accepted, if hesitantly, as keel-up units and not necessarily conversions. That implies how the Phantom Fleet's Zuiho-class light fleet carriers (as proposed in the last chapter) might not have stirred much alarm or excitement. After all, were not the Japanese always producing these under-sized flat tops, the ONI in Washington might expostulate.

Here we can move on to the strange case of the 'Pet Shop' carriers, an instance of a very successful outright deception on the part of Japan.

Low-balling Scam on Carriers

The reader will recall how in the Treaty Fleet chapter, we showed Japan officially low-balling the displacements of ships limited by the Washington and London naval treaties, albeit that in this it was not the only culprit and there were mitigating circumstances.

Therefore, releasing the tonnage of the medium fleet carriers *Soryu* and *Hiryu* at 10,050 tons, when actually they were 15,900 and 17,300, unsurprisingly saw them downgraded in Allied eyes to light fleet carrier status, or comparatively little to worry about. This was helped by cognizance of their predecessor the *Ryujo*, which was conceived as a 'pocket' aircraft carrier, although for good reason in that it was laid down before the London Treaty ended the clause excluding carriers of less than 10,000 tons. The *Soryu* deception had been occasioned by the need to keep up the pretence of Japan's overall Treaty quota for carriers of 81,000 tons not having been exceeded by the recruitment of the *Soryu* and *Hiryu*. There being only 20,100 tons of the quota left in hand, it was glibly released that the pair were assessed at 10,050 tons each.

Low-balling tonnages and other specifications continued even after Japan abrogated the Treaties. The two post-Treaty carriers, *Shokaku* and *Zuikaku*, were billed by *Jane's* 1940 edition at 14,000 tons, or somewhere between a light fleet and a medium fleet, when in actuality the 'Shockers' were 25,675 tons each. That classed them emphatically as large fleet carriers; some in the IJN even knowing them as 'super carriers'.

It was not until near the end of hostilities that the truth began to dawn, aided no doubt by the excellent combat photographs taken of the *Shokaku* at the Battle of the Coral Sea. Using a detail such as the width of a 5-inch AA battery common to many IJN warships, the length of the vessel could have been estimated, and from that most else that mattered. But what intelligence chief Layton's crew on behalf of Admiral Nimitz surmised did not necessarily filter through to the ONI in Washington.

Helpfully, the low-balling of displacement tonnages gave the impression that the IJN was somehow wedded to the notion of carriers dimensionally as cruisers rather than capital ships. Such confusion was possible because the lengths of the pre-war battleships, heavy cruisers, fast naval auxiliary converts plus medium and light carriers were all rather close to each other. There was not much actual difference between the length of the battleship *Nagato* and heavy cruiser *Ashigara*. The former's build was stout, the latter's slim.

This impression remained at large with the Office of Naval Intelligence in the serious matter of training US aviators, submariners and ship lookouts on how to identify Japanese warship types. The ONI produced a wartime manual (we quoted from the foreword to its post-war republication at the top of the chapter). For memory reinforcement purposes, the recognition guide included cartoons called 'Nip Notes'. The page on aircraft carriers shows the silhouettes of the pre-war carrier classes, with the recognition tip that 'if they have upper works at all the JAPs [carriers] are very small and bow or stern approach suggests a Nagasaki slum'. A couple of line drawing caricatures are included. One shows the inelegant backside of the *Kaga*, and the other has the *Soryu* on a dog's lead being exercised by a bow-legged Japanese sailor. Let us now take the reader to one case whither this nonsense was to lead.

At the Battle of Midway, both the *Kaga* and *Soryu* were set ablaze and sunk, in the former case by dive bombers from the *Enterprise* and in the latter case by those of the *Yorktown*. Both carriers wore their island superstructure well forward on the starboard side, unlike the *Akagi* and *Hiryu*, which sported them on the port side amidships. A flight leader of the *Yorktown* group of Dauntless dive bombers led his squadron's hawks in their stoop on the *Soryu*. Lieutenant (junior grade) Paul 'Lefty' Holmberg insisted that he and his fellow fliers had sunk the huge *Kaga* and not the smaller *Soryu*. He was still adamant thirty-five years later when interviewed for *Dauntless Victory*, an authoritative account of Midway by dive bomber historian Peter C. Smith. Perhaps to Pearl Harbor's intelligence chief he could well have expressed it like this: 'We hit *Kaga*, Layton, not one of your goddam dachshunds!'

'Blue Dragon' (a name for the Great Bear constellation) was no pet shop Pekinese exhibit; the *Soryu* was a Rottweiler. It and its dragon sister sank two aircraft carriers, two heavy cruisers and shared in the destruction at Pearl Harbor before going down in flames at Midway. The 'Dragons' were core members of the carrier striking force that revolutionized air-sea warfare. Caught on board the *Soryu* was the whole squadron of elite dive bomber aces led by Lieutenant Commander Egusa. Holmberg should have been well satisfied with the Egusa squadron's scalp and one of the six flight decks that had raided Pearl Harbor.

The irony is how in the last chapter we hypothesized two more Phantom *Shokaku*-size and four more Phantom *Soryu*-size carriers ready for battle by Pearl Harbor, without any shipyard in Japan actually having laid a single steel plate for any of them. Yet in 1942, it seemed at times that the US believed in four of the six. That this did not linger in the belief system for good was probably thanks to codebreaking and radio traffic analysis.

A further irony is that by officially low-balling tonnages, the IJN succeeded in fooling the ONI that its total carrier air fleet strength in late 1941 was 280 aircraft, when in fact it was closer to 500 and rising fast thanks to Shadow Fleet units coming on stream.

Call that the fruit of 'pet shop factor'. A close reading of Layton, aided by some digging around on the internet, suggests that at Pearl Harbor he had a good idea of how many carriers the Japanese could field by the end of 1941, but US Navy circles were overly influenced by a special report commissioned from a retired director of the ONI, Captain Puleston, an ex-boss of Layton's endearingly known to colleagues as 'Pulie'. His message was that the US had not much to worry about in the case of the Imperial Japanese Navy, and particularly not in the field of naval aviation.

The rating of the Japanese carrier fleet at only 280 operational aircraft was Pulie's.

The captain's estimate was based largely on taking at face value the low-balled carrier displacement tonnages specifications being released by Japan. That, along with so much else, cannot but have helped Washington's too-ready dismissal of any threat to Pearl Harbor from Japanese carriers – along with any alarm over the range of Zero fighters.

As we showed in Chapter 2, it was thanks to drop fuel tanks and fuel-saving innovations in flight that the already revolutionary range of the Zero was enhanced sufficiently that land-based bomber squadrons from Formosa were enabled to cover the opening moves on the Philippines with fighter escort (except against the large southern island of Mindanao, for which Yamamoto contributed the services of the light carrier *Ryujo*). The Zeros were now able to escort raids by land-based medium bombers whose long range had taken the Allies by surprise, although long warned of such by sources in China.

The IJN thereby could release all six of their attack carriers for the Pearl Harbor operation, the US base at the time being outside the range of any land-bound aircraft other than a handful of four-engined flying boats, and then only if refuelled en route by submarines. That was what was so revolutionary about the Hawaii operation: it introduced the era of the air-sea armada.

The 'carrier scare' in Washington that kicked off after Pearl Harbor would have come far too late for the industrial giant to match or cap a 1938–41 built Phantom Fleet. In reality, even the Shadow Fleet had stolen a slight march on that, which is worth repeating here.

Yamamoto would enjoy his eighteen-month window of opportunity, even to the excess we project in the next chapter. There, the Phantom Fleet goes operational on a 'two-ocean' front and the eighteen months extends into years.

The Unsinkable Aircraft Carrier Myth

The main fixation of US Naval Intelligence pre-war comes across less with the composition of the IJN and its aviation arm, and more with what was going on behind the scenes in the *Nanyo*, where the security blanket was even more overwhelming than in the home islands.

We shall now take a close look at the constellations of island chains out there in mid-ocean. *Japan's Islands of Mystery*, was how a travel writer entitled his book about them. The Canadian-born Willard Price and his vivacious American wife, Mary, had a great story to tell, for they almost alone pre-war penetrated the cloud of unknowing about 'the Mandates', as Americans called them, and lived to tell the tale. We will come to their revelations, but first a little background.

What was geographically identifiable to Europeans and Americans as Micronesia was an oceanic area of the Central Pacific almost the breadth of the United States land mass. It had three parts to it. To the west stretched the Mariana island chain, a north–south line skirting the western side of the Philippine Sea, which separated the chain from the Philippine island land masses. Their centre was Saipan. The island line continued diagonally south-west of the Marianas to Yap, and then to Palau. Breaking the line in the middle was American Guam, the US stepping stone to the Philippines.

In the centre of the Mandates were the Caroline Islands, with the Truk lagoon at their heart, and Ponape and Kusaie to the eastward. To the north and further east was all coral atolls, the Marshall Islands, which included one of the largest atolls in the world, Kwajalein. There was also Bikini, which played no significant part in the war but in 1946 became the venue for two atomic bomb tests against warships, Admiral Yamamoto's former flagship *Nagato* being placed in the centre of the fleet to be nuked as ground zero, except in the airborne test the bomb strayed over to the American battleship *Nevada*, which had already been sunk once, a victim of the Pearl Harbor raid. The sturdy *Nagato* survived, to everyone's great embarrassment. It even took a long time dying when the underwater test was tried next and the bomb placed as close as possible. There could be no greater tribute to its builders, the Kure Naval Arsenal, particularly as it was already pretty knocked about and almost sank on its way to Bikini. It had been on the *Nagato* that Yamamoto received the coded message 'Tora, Tora, Tora', signifying that surprise had been attained at Pearl Harbor. The movie of that title featured a monumental-size model of *Nagato* which was sold in 1970 at a Sotheby's sale in Los Angeles of 20th Century Fox film's props.

The foresaid island chains make up much of the Central Pacific, like a galaxy. Away to the north of it, beyond normal land-based air range, spreads the Hawaiian chain. Kwajalein was the point of the *Nanyo*'s sword, far away but the nearest point to Pearl Harbor. Today it is best known for having been the venue for the first big hydrogen bomb test.

On the Colonial-era maps of the globe, most of these island chains appeared as Spanish territories until the Spanish–American War, after which by obscure process they ended up as German. When in 1914 Japan joined with Britain and France in the war against Germany, the IJN made a very quick-off-the-mark bee-line for the islands, being rewarded after the war with the grant of a League of Nations mandate to administer them, provided Japan did nothing to fortify any islands and reported progress regularly to Geneva.

President Woodrow Wilson made an attempt to have Yap put under international control because it was the nexus for German undersea cables, but nothing ever came of that. The British and Japanese had already agreed to make the Equator the division line between a Japanese Mandate islands zone and a British Empire zone.

Whether or not, through the 1920s and 1930s, the Japanese Navy was building air and sea bases was not so important as that it was making its very best efforts to create that impression: foreign ships were not permitted to call; foreigners were refused passage on the single shipping line normally servicing the islands; and there was no civilian air service. Suspicions were rife when the IJN was put in charge of the islands in 1937.

In consequence, there came a 1938 order from Washington to the Tokyo embassy to make it a priority to find out if there were submarine bases, airstrips and seaplane facilities in the Mandates. Future Pacific Fleet intelligence chief Edwin T. Layton, then assistant naval attaché in Tokyo, was delegated to this task. But he could not book a passage there. The shipping agent was brutally frank: absolutely no foreigners were permitted in the *Nanyo*. Frustrated out of his mind, Layton was not to forget this episode when posted to Pearl Harbor as intelligence chief. He worked hard on radio call signs until he had located those for the main bases, such as Palau, Saipan, Truk, Ponape and Kwajalein. The density of traffic to these bases compared to other islands rather gave the game away as to which was military and which not. As the cipher continued to be broken down, it was found that addresses at these locations were such entities as defence force, garrison force, submarine base, landplane base and so on. The cloud of unknowing had been penetrated. New boy Layton received the vociferous congratulations of C-in-C Pacific Fleet Admiral James O. Richardson. His job remained secure through the terms of the admiral's two successors.

While serving in Tokyo as a naval attaché for three years, Layton could hardly have failed to come across Willard Price, who lived in Japan from 1933–38. During his writing career, Price came to visit over 100 different countries, often on behalf of the National Geographic Society, in the course of writing his *Adventure* series for children and travel books for adults. An obsession for him came to be a quest to tour these League of Nations mandated islands. Where no-one else went, that was where Willard and wife Mary most wanted to go.

They ran into all the usual problems, until suddenly one day what seemed a miracle happened. The shipping agent called to explain that Japan had been coming under very heavy criticism for its secretiveness in the South Seas. The Mandates Commission in Geneva had been asking unhelpful questions. Would the delightful young couple thus like to give the lie to all these false accusations, and go to see for themselves the absence of military facilities in the course of pursuing their work of documenting native customs and island flora? They duly booked passage on a small liner of the NYK line, but not before demanding a paper authorizing their landing on any island they wanted, which in practice was worthless as they needed the consent of the captain to disembark anywhere. Nevertheless, the document proved a disarming piece of paper to wave once they had sneaked off ship and found themselves confronted on these forbidden shores.

Whether Price was a spy for Layton is not known. All that needs acknowledging is that in the business of espionage, much is volunteered to the real spooks by the likes of journalists, not least travel writers, and all manner of professionals living overseas who happen to be close to what might be most interesting. Predecessors of whatever ilk who penetrated the *Nanyo* had come to sticky ends, however politely they might have been initially received.

The Prices' voyage took them first by fly-blown Saipan and Tinian and then to strange, hilly Yap, with its giant stone money which the Kanaka natives rolled to creditors by sticking a tree trunk through the hole in the centre, or if too big to roll, reregistered it at the 'All Men House', or council hall.

Next, to greater Japanese consternation, they moseyed around Palau, staying with a German missionary, through whom they met a reformed headhunting chief who explained his blood sport to them and showed off his collection of heads, apologizing there were so few, explaining that the Japanese were persistent seekers after souvenirs. The highlight of the trip came when their ship, turning east, headed for the great Truk lagoon in the Carolines. Resorting to their usual guile, they avoided the gaze of a busy ship's captain distracted by the business of arrival. An English-speaking native offered them a ride to shore in his outrigger canoe, suggesting they discreetly slip over the stern and duck under the sheets while he whisked them away. The ship returned a week later after a passage to Ponape and Kusaie. In the interim, they enjoyed a full week with this guide, paddling about what became known as 'Japan's Pearl Harbor'. Seldom absent was a police boat shadowing their progress from a distance, binoculars glued to their canoe.

Price was unable to pinpoint 'fortifications' as such, openly wondering whether Truk's natural topography was not more efficacious to the perceived needs of defence than masses of concrete emplacements. A perimeter reef of 35-mile diameter encircled the 243 islands inside the massive lagoon, these islands the eroded remains of a vast volcano that had long ago subsided. Each of the four entrances found itself overlooked from the commanding heights of one of the larger islands. A battle fleet would find the reef distancing its guns. Once it breached a passage through, it would come under fire from coastal defence guns located in caves on the overlooking heights.

Price then cites Admiral Suetsugu describing island bases like Truk as 'unsinkable aircraft carriers'. This is what had so entranced Yamamoto in the early 1930s when he called for a long-range medium naval bomber. Price sought signs of airfield development, and found it. He heard the roar of bulldozers at work on a small but flattish island, Eten. These were levelling and lengthening it for runways. There was always a ready explanation from the governor, hospitably so over a plate of *suki yaki* braced with frequent toasts of *sake*. Where did this brand-new, treble-width paved highway lead to, Price would ask. 'Nowhere,' came the reply, in a burst of amiable giggles. Or at least not at present; it was infrastructure for a colonist development-to-be. An airfield was explained away as being for the fishing fleet, with the planes to be equipped with new gear for locating fish shoals.

Parts of Samuel Eliot Morison's description of Truk in his history of US naval operations in the war read very close to Price's assessment. Either by reading his book or a proof prior to publication, Nimitz and his staff decided in early 1944 to leapfrog Truk from their new conquests in the Marshalls all the way to the Marianas Islands. They figured that massed carrier raids would neuter Truk's worth as a base and they could leave it to 'wither on the vine', much as had just been decided with Rabaul, thereby saving thousands of American lives. The next stop was to be Saipan.

There was to be no medal for Willard Price's revelations. However, he emerged from Truk alive, but only by dint of a very long swim. One day their guide took them shark fishing and the canoe capsized in mid-fight with a tiger shark. The guide later confessed that the police had asked for a repeat of the episode, but this time for him to leave the American in the water to drown. The guide promised the venturesome pair that this could be arranged close enough to shore that Price could be tipped into the brine and survive. This way, both the guide discreetly, and Willard energetically, might expect to preserve their lives.

The Prices' adventure continued. On Palau, an over-meticulous policeman interrogated them persistently. They were asked whom they might be planning to visit on the islands. Explaining his National Geographical Society credentials, Price answered 'nobody really'; they were just admiring flora and fauna. Before the questioning could become any more tricky, Mary burst into the room from the kitchen bearing oven-warm American-style doughnuts. The subject could now be changed.

Such is a flavour of an overlooked masterpiece of travel writing, much in need of reprint today. It documents the predicament of the indigenous Kanaka population under a Japanese colonial administration that subsidised the emigration of Japanese colonists to the islands. Despite an understandable mid-war bias on the part of the author, he is found ready to grant credit where it is due instead of just exposing colonialist exploitation. The Japanese approach to native management was very much 'nanny state'. The native chiefs were honoured, but found at their elbow the local policeman. These district policemen, however, were medically, educationally and economically trained. They were more like social workers than police. On the other hand, the Kanaka were denied futures to rise to; their place was as labourers and fishermen. Any ladders to opportunity and to middle-class status were removed where found, and certainly never supplied.

The *Nanyo* was seen by the Japanese as a colony for Japanese. They swarmed into the area between the wars, all the more so after the 1936 five-year plan was promulgated. In Japan, they could go to colonist school and learn how to get on in the South Seas. Once they found themselves on an island, they could check into bride's school, which operated rather like a dating agency, except the pairing up process was for marriage and not just for dating. In 1937, there were 15,000 Japanese in Palau, compared to just fifteen Germans when the IJN sailed into the lagoon in 1914.

This emigration was not confined to the *Nanyo* itself, but was also steered to strategic lands further south. A particular example was the large Philippine island of Mindanao. Price described its port city of Davao as a tropical Yokohama. While on Palau, his steamship agent told him that the fare to Menado on the Dutch East Indian island of Celebes (called Sulawesi by Indonesians today) was half-price. Why might this be so, he asked the captain, who replied that it was because in Japan they particularly wanted Japanese settling there. The captain said everything about the Celebes was excellent – the climate, the agricultural diversity, you name it; the Celebes was made in paradise. He even joined the Prices in a car trip when they reached Menado, no doubt the better to obtain for the region a good write-up in their forthcoming book.

The threat from mysterious Palau came alive on the very first day of the war, when Davao in the Philippines was the objective for a Japanese fleet based on Palau that was supported by the twenty-seven aircraft of the light fleet carrier *Ryujo*, Davao being outside the air range of the two-engine naval bombers stationed on Formosa. Palau was within range, but appears not to have had any twin-engine bomber squadrons stationed there, perhaps for lack of a bomber-length runway. Hence, limited carrier support was needed.

A little over a month later, with land-based bombers and fighters now in force at Davao, the same group crossed the Celebes Sea to seize Menado on the tip of the big island's trunk – Celebes looking on the map like a two-legged elephant, with three peninsulas united by a mountainous centre. With air support consolidated at Menado, the group struck on south to seize, with ground troops, Kendari on the island's eastern leg, seat of another Dutch airbase and with Staring Bay nearby, this the anchorage which the *Kido Butai* made its base for the rest of the 'drive south'. Thence the carriers set sail for the Indian Ocean Raid of April 1942. Centrally placed, Celebes and Davao were destined to serve as the strategic hub of the Greater East Asia Co-Prosperity Sphere. No wonder the pre-war interest in shipping as many Japanese into that area as could be persuaded to go.

Price prophesied that Japan 'will leave no stone unturned in their effort after the war to dominate Asia economically', even if totally defeated militarily. Japan's post-war 'economic miracle' ensured that the prophesy came partly true. Today, over 30,000 people of Japanese or part-Japanese descent reside in the former *Nanyo*.

The Prices' visit to the *Nanyo* was no doubt sanctioned because in the late 1930s there were as yet no garrisons stationed on the islands, no squadrons of warplanes, no naval port facilities, none of the panoply of war-making. There were only the seemingly over-ambitious 'civilian' infrastructure developments, such as the pier extending into very deep water, the three-vehicle-width roadway, the airfield for the bonito-spotting planes of the fisher folk and fuel tanks for islands that boasted only handfuls of motor vehicles.

However, within a year of the IJN's formal takeover of the *Nanyo*, the annual reports to Geneva tailed off, the security clampdown went viral and work on the bases no longer needed any fancy covers. A war had to be won, with Palau and Truk made fully receptive for the Combined Fleet.

By 1943, there lay in view two more mountainous islands to add to Truk lagoon's 243 isles: the super-battleships *Yamato* and *Musashi*. Arrayed by then on Truk's islands were airfields, submarine base, dry dock, radio station, tank farms, seaplane base and a substantial garrison force, well dug in and armed with coastal guns covering the four passes through the reef, as Price had predicted.

By way of contrast, much less was ever done militarily on Yap, Ponape and Kusaie, all of which were visited by the Prices. These islands were to give them least challenge and hassle. There, the nimble art of fancy footwork with the Japanese spin-doctors found itself largely untested.

Whatever was or was not the mischief going on in the Mandated islands, in the final weeks before hostilities all eyes at Pearl Harbor stared south to 'the Mandates', for that was the direction from which they could most expect trouble, if any. The fleet's long-range PBY flying boats were all deployed in a search arc facing the *Nanyo*. While there was the additional reconnaissance resource of the US Army's four-engine Flying Fortresses, these had to be hurried on their way to the Philippines. No-one thought fit to station a line of submarines as scouts to watch out for trouble from the stormy and neglected north.

Instead, Admiral Kimmel and his staff in Pearl Harbor were set on propelling the Pacific Fleet south to the Mandates as quickly as possible following the onset of war, battleships and all – the initial objective being the capture of Kwajalein. Thereby, Truk could come within range of the four-engine bombers and Wake be spared air attack from Kwajalein. This was to be a start to twenty-year-old plans that were constantly being updated for a surge across the Central Pacific to the succour of the Philippines, and from there to propel an advance by springboards for the defeat of the Japanese home islands.

The raid on Pearl Harbor killed off those plans for a Central Pacific offensive for two years. There simply was not the ability to project overwhelming mobile seaborne air power against Japanese naval aviation until the Essex Surge materialized operationally. Instead, the strategic focus moved to the South-West Pacific in order to maintain Australia and New Zealand as alternative springboards for future advance, and to preserve from Japanese tyranny the populations of two Anglo-Saxon nations.

In the South Pacific theatre, advances were very slow because each new landing had to be within supporting range of land-based air resources, for lack of aircraft carrier numbers. Here we can leave actual history and proceed to our next chapter, where we explore changed strategic perspectives and the possible denouements from unleashing against the Allies in the Pacific and Indian oceans our proposed great air-sea armada that we envisioned earlier in Chapter 4.

Chapter 6

Denouements

'From Africa eastwards through the Indian Ocean and Pacific we have lost command of the sea.'

(Field Marshal Sir Alan Brooke, Chief of the Imperial General Staff)

Thus confided to his diary the British Empire's senior wartime military chief (later ennobled as Lord Alanbrooke) on the day he heard of the sinking of the *Prince of Wales* and *Repulse* off Malaya, 10 December 1941. The loss of 'Force Z', as it was called, crashed into the world's consciousness three days after the loss of five American battleships at Pearl Harbor.

His is an interesting observation on a number of grounds, not least that it reveals how even in the knell of those naval disasters, a man often credited with having the sharpest mind of all the Allied leaders had not lost his sense of the battleship as king of the waves. He found no way to allay his gloom by thanking God no aircraft carriers had been sunk in either location. He had obviously not yet twigged that the aircraft carrier was king from 1942 on.

The carrier HMS *Indomitable* arrived in the theatre too late to provide air cover for Force Z. It had run aground off Kingston, Jamaica. The career of its captain was blighted thereafter, but the actual officer responsible got off scot-free, prompting cynics to wonder why he did not receive a medal for saving the *Indomitable* from the Japanese.

As for the three carriers of the Pacific Fleet, these were fortuitously absent from Pearl Harbor when the Japanese struck. The *Saratoga* was on the West Coast, *Lexington* was delivering Marine scout bombers to Midway Island air base to enhance its reconnaissance role and *Enterprise* was out ferrying Marine fighters to Wake, where the airstrip of this far-flung coral atoll in the western ocean was usefully staging batches of Flying Fortresses to the Philippines to reinforce General Douglas MacArthur's vaunted air force there.

It was feared that one outpost, Wake, was close enough to Japanese air bases, while the other, Midway, presented a ready target for marauding Japanese carriers. Given the political capital invested in what was a sort of strategic *force de frappe* as deterrent against Japanese aggression, heaven forbid that a single four-engine bomber be lost en route. That these bombers in ephemeral numbers proved to be pretty well useless as the war-winner they were promoted to be was as yet an unknown. In hindsight, they could have been better deployed as long-range reconnaissance for Hawaii.

As we found in the last chapter, the northern approaches to Pearl Harbor had been left unguarded, all the planes available invested in patrolling the southwards sector; naval intelligence perceiving any threat as most likely emanating from the *Nanyo*, not from the stormy, fogbound wastes of the North Pacific whence the *Kido Butai* pounced, despite this having been the direction of carrier air attack chosen in a US Pacific Fleet exercise back in 1938.

As for the big bombers in the Philippines, they were mostly destroyed on the ground on the first day of war, despite more-than-adequate warning, unlike Pearl Harbor was given by Washington, where intelligence was reading Japanese diplomatic and consular traffic.

The two carriers could also have been destroyed if chance had not kept them far enough away that they could neither interfere nor be attacked; that was owed to how no-one knew where the Japanese carriers were in the chaotic hours following the attack. Equally, Admiral Nagumo had no idea where any American carriers were, other than that none were in Pearl Harbor.

It could be said that servicing the unnecessary needs of General Douglas MacArthur through the course of the Pacific War often proved the most costly burden ever endured by the United States Navy. On this occasion at least, his needs ironically helped to preserve two carriers for great glory, as ably as did a reef off Kingston, Jamaica, allow HMS *Indomitable* to share in the final victory against Japan.

So much has been written about Pearl Harbor that it does not need much recycling here. The one thing about it that the reader might best hold in mind is how it seems that most on the US side had forgotten about the seven battleships sitting there at anchor and an eighth in dry dock. They were too slow to accompany the fast carriers to Wake and to Midway. The fleet's equally fast heavy cruisers could do that. As for Japanese battleships, any US carriers currently in the Pacific could outrun even the four souped-up Kongo-class ex-battlecruisers. So why squander fuel escorting carriers when their escort was not required? Battleships had become the white elephants in the room, holy cows ripe for putting out to pasture, added to which they drank far too much oil. That was the reason the US Pacific Fleet command kept them in harbour during the worrying days before the expected outbreak of war. The oil was needed for the anticipated move on the Mandates. That was to be the fleet's first and immediate operation if war broke out.

All anyone cared about in Washington in late 1941 was the Philippines and the need to stage those precious Army Air Force four-engined bombers through the chain of island bases to Big Mac in Manila. Officials only came to remember the Navy's great Pearl Harbor base and its out-of-date battlewagons, the ugly ducklings of world navies, when they woke up one morning to hear most of them had been sunk at their moorings.

Instead, it had been left to the Japanese to remember Pearl Harbor's battleships. They did not want them interfering with the 'drive south' into Indonesia by appearing on their highly exposed Philippine flank; ironically, a feat that in practice was not far short of miraculous given the incapacitating logistics that were current at that time.

Here again was this great and unfounded fear of the battleship and its mighty guns, even on the part of Admiral Yamamoto himself. How was this?

The Japanese were unaware that the previous commander-in-chief of the Pacific Fleet, Admiral Richardson, had with heartfelt persistence advised President Roosevelt of two unwelcome realities. Firstly, that the battle-line lacked the supply capability to go waddling across the Central Pacific in order to 'jump the Japs'. Congress had been diligent in this respect. How better to deny to the US Navy the means for doing anything so daftly warlike than by limiting funds for naval auxiliaries; the fleet would run out of oil and ice-cream before they could reach the halfway line. Secondly, was the President aware of how extremely unpopular with the Pacific Fleet had been the move in May 1940 from the west coast to Pearl Harbor? For the crews, there were so very few 'white women' to date in Hawaii (the main alternative, ironically, were chatty, keen-eared Japanese immigrant gals), while the married men were so far from home and family. For staff officers, there were continual logistical headaches in that Pearl Harbor was not possessed of the ample resources of San Diego. Everything had to be shipped there, which meant taking up valuable ships from trade.

The White House and State Department argued back that there had been many signs that Tokyo was being deterred by the Pacific Fleet moving to its forward base. Richardson's political riposte was that the IJN was far from being stupid; it was, in fact, a very bright service. By all means develop Pearl Harbor as a springboard base to act as a deterrent, but for goodness sake, he argued, take the battleships and carriers back to California, where they could be serviced properly and undergo training safely outside any discernible risk envelope. He argued that the Pacific Fleet stationed at San Diego was a more effective deterrent for Japan. Richardson had even foreseen the danger of an airborne raid on Pearl Harbor from aircraft carriers, although that was far from being his main reason for withdrawal. It was by expressing his fears that he stepped too far: in October 1940, he bluntly told the president that American foreign policy was provoking, indeed tempting, Japan into a war the US armed forces were not ready and able yet to fight; in other words, that he was warmongering.

As Pacific Fleet chief at Pearl Harbor, Richardson must have known it would require months of preparation before this mighty ironclad fleet could weigh anchor and sail off to glory in execution of Plan Orange – the plan to cross the Pacific and strike at Japan's cities – or whichever version of it attempted to match the logistical exigencies and the political temper of the day. Whatever the case, this involved first storming into the *Nanyo* en route to the Philippines, and thence to the Japanese home islands. In any version, cautionary or bombastic, there was the same inbuilt limitation – by the time they reached the Philippines, the Japanese goal of possessing Dutch oil would have been achieved. In Washington, this was indeed acknowledged secretly, following what is generally called the Eisenhower Report. 'Ike' had served as MacArthur's chief of staff in the Philippines, and on his return he was ordered to make an assessment of its defence needs. Ike determined that the Philippines were indefensible because they could not expect to be resupplied.

What those such as Eisenhower and Richardson surmised was lost on the normally perspicacious Yamamoto aboard the *Nagato* and on the

Japanese Naval General Staff in their big red brick building in Tokyo. All they saw at Pearl Harbor was a dagger pointed at Japan, without regard to the flabbiness and unpreparedness of the arm that wielded it.

The British, meanwhile, had been busy making their own assessment, consequent to which much pressure was applied to Washington in attempting to persuade America to move the Pacific Fleet to Singapore. This was politically indefensible due to the rising US tide of isolationism and anti-colonialism, as touched on in the first chapter. The best that Washington could come up with in compromise was to promise that if war indeed came, the US would immediately launch a naval offensive against the Marshall Islands in the upper centre tier of the *Nanyo* – the most obvious target being the atoll base of Kwajalein, such an operation being sustainable by the existing fleet train of supply auxiliaries. Thereby, they argued, the IJN might be tricked into creaming off key units from the 'drive south' in order to fend off a flank attack from the Central Pacific. This at least would take the pressure off the British, Dutch and Australians in South-East Asia. Glib and eager tongues in Washington and its embassies aspired to convince their allies accordingly.

So it was that the US Pacific Fleet stayed put at Pearl Harbor and did not return to the west coast.

Richardson had ruffled a lot of feathers and found himself moved on. Early in 1941, Admiral Husband E. Kimmel, a protégé of President Roosevelt, was appointed in his place. Within a year, Kimmel was gone, in order to be set up as scapegoat for the catastrophe that Richardson had prophesied. As so often in the American past, the White House drew upon a Texan in its hour of need. Enter Admiral Chester W. Nimitz as C-in-C Pacific Fleet. Staffers, like Intelligence head Edwin T. Layton, came to serve under three successive Pacific Commanders-in-Chief that year. The difference was that Nimitz was to be his boss for the duration of the war, by the end of which one could be tempted to say they were like a married couple, so closely did they gel.

We can now revert to Sir Alan Brooke's despair espoused at the outset of this chapter. Brooke was to be proved half-right. The Royal Navy did have to retreat all the way to the African coast for lack of a viable carrier force, but it was only the surviving battleships that America withdrew to California. Admiral Nimitz continued to base the three Pacific Fleet carriers at Pearl Harbor, these soon to number four when the *Yorktown* arrived from the Atlantic, then five when the brand-new *Hornet* was worked up enough to fight in the Pacific, and finally six when the *Wasp* could be released from Atlantic and Mediterranean duties. Once that had been accomplished, the US could enjoy fleet carrier parity with the IJN, any edge the Japanese subsequently enjoyed only being thanks to the four speedier Shadow Fleet units, equivalent in air power to a pair of large fleet carriers, given their lesser-sized air groups.

The US Pacific Fleet was therefore still in business after Pearl Harbor, and almost from the outset the available carriers were used to raid Japanese outposts, finally thrilling America with the bold Doolittle Raid on Tokyo. This operational activity might not amount to command of the seas, but at least America was contesting it. The President sought to assert command of Congress by the same token, while vows to allies were being honoured.

British carriers, in contrast, not being competent to fight Japanese carriers at that time, limited themselves to securing nearby African objectives, such as covering the invasion of the Vichy French colony of Madagascar, the vast island off the east coast of central Africa.

There was an analogous situation to Hawaii in the Indian Ocean, in that the considerable-sized island of Ceylon (modern Sri Lanka) lying off the southern extremity of India was for the Allies the strategic hub, Britain fielding two naval bases there at Colombo and Trincomalee.

The Indian Ocean can await its turn, while we complete assessing the strategic situation in the Pacific.

The Hawaii Question

Without Hawaii, America did not have the operational reach to venture wide in the Western Pacific. But while Hawaii was absolutely essential as an *offensive* springboard, it was vulnerable *defensively*, as Richardson had foreseen. To lose Hawaii would mean America being forced back to its west coast, from where an inconvenient geography would conspire to handicap efforts at Hawaii's recapture, for there were no islands in between to provide springboards – the oceanic gap between San Diego and Pearl Harbor being 2,600 miles. Submarines could attempt a blockade, except – as we keep reminding the reader – there was this embarrassing issue of defective torpedoes that was not diagnosed fully until mid-war. As for patrolling shipping lanes off the coast of China, attacking the lifeline of Japan's Greater East Asia Co-Prosperity Sphere would prove a case of 'fuel too far'. Those boats that reached the China Seas could expect ephemeral patrol times compared to marathon transit times the whole way across the world's broadest ocean.

It has often been asked why the Japanese did not invade the Hawaiian islands, instead of merely raiding Pearl Harbor? The conventional explanations have usually been that they lacked the resources, and that the US Army was vigorously opposed. That orthodoxy has remained mostly unchallenged, but for a little-noted study by a professor of history at the University of Hawaii (of which more later). Only recently has the 'Hawaii question' found itself reopened.

For us, the 'Hawaii question' properly falls into three parts:

- Firstly, how close in actuality were the Japanese to deciding whether or not to invade Hawaii in the face of so many competing needs at that time, and what went wrong to prevent it?
- Next, how much better might an invasion attempt fare and conquest subsequently be sustained given a more ample carrier force, to wit the Phantom Fleet?
- Finally, what was the likely outcome on the progress of the Pacific War if the IJN's arms procurement policies had been more logically inspired and ruthlessly pursued, such that Hawaii and Ceylon could become invasion objectives of easy achievement?

Hawaii in itself is a shorthand expression for an archipelago of modest-sized islands of volcanic origin, lying more than a third of the way across the Pacific from San Francisco to Shanghai. On their eastern end was the giant of the chain, Hawaii island itself (normally called 'Big Island'), with its celebrated volcanoes. In the middle of the chain nestled the island of Oahu, flanked on either side by the rather larger Maui to the east and Kauai to the west. Further westwards stretched nothing much but atolls and reefs for 1,500 miles, until an extremity was reached with the island base of Midway, the so-called sentinel for Hawaii. From Midway, it's 2,250 miles on to Tokyo.

On Oahu was based the might of America in the Central Pacific, the Pacific Fleet at Pearl Harbor and the burgeoning naval infrastructure needed to sustain it. Pearl Harbor brought America 40 per cent of the way across the world's largest ocean. While that might not be up to the Imperial Palace portals, at least it was muscle on display from one hell of a lot closer than California.

We will start now with the first of our three questions.

How close in actuality were the Japanese to deciding whether or not to invade Hawaii in the face of so many competing needs at that time, and what went wrong to prevent it?
This is a long one to answer.

If we start at the receiving end of the Japanese raid, those experiencing it, whether on hand or from afar, trembled in expectation of invasion – even that it might ensue in the hours that immediately followed the raid; and if not, for sure within the month. Admiral Stark, the professional head of the US Navy, feared a return of the Japanese carriers in support of landings in the general area of the Hawaiian islands and the seizure of 'sentinel' outposts such as Midway and Johnston Island as a preliminary to an assault on Pearl Harbor itself. Admiral Kimmel in Pearl Harbor nursed similar fears as he looked out on the devastation all around him.

Most of the United States' considerable air forces congregated there had been destroyed on the ground. The cream of the fleet lay mouldering in the harbour mud, while army ground forces amounted only to a division or so of unblooded fighting men. It could be expected that if the Japanese carriers lingered offshore, the two returning American carriers would be overwhelmed if they counter-attacked, and otherwise would wisely flee for California (if their attendant oilers could indeed fuel a run to the west coast). Further air raids could be expected, as only twenty-nine out of 411 Japanese carrier aircraft had been lost and few American fighter aircraft had been spared to oppose further onslaughts.

The issue of why there were no more raids on that terrible day, or on the following day, is a fraught one. Suffice it to emphasize that a rogue factor had arisen for Admiral Nagumo: where were the Pacific Fleet's three aircraft carriers? The Japanese did not know that the *Saratoga* was at San Diego and the other two returning after ferrying aircraft to distant Wake and Midway. These could prove to be nearby, as indeed was the *Enterprise*. In the course of further pounding of Pearl Harbor and air bases on Oahu, it could prove very embarrassing for Admiral Nagumo if 200 or so American planes from these three carriers approached out of the blue to attack his own vulnerable carriers (as later happened to him so disastrously at the Battle of Midway).

Neither Nagumo nor his chief of staff, Admiral Kusaka, had been stout-hearted when confronted with the Hawaii plan. Both had opposed Yamamoto on the project, expecting to lose a carrier or two. After the dreaded event, their force surprisingly intact and objectives achieved, why risk one's luck and the emperor's ships? Nagumo was a battleship believer and no kind of air admiral. Aboard the *Akagi*, he was a fish out of water, dependent upon the cautious advice of the brighter and air-experienced Kusaka. For Nagumo, it was sufficient to have sunk most of the battleships; 'damn the Yankee carriers, let no further risk be allowed to sully the IJN's triumph' is rather what seems to have prompted his mood.

In the event, it was ironic that this very absence of American carriers gave excuse to Nagumo's resolve to head his *Kido Butai* back home. The regular Pacific War reader may at this point care to reflect how in a way Pearl Harbor, rather than the Battle of the Coral Sea, was the first carrier-to-carrier battle of the war. For when we consider naval battles, we tend to think in terms of ships present and engaged. Yet ships can be absent from the scene of battle but still influence its outcome merely by existing. They act as the unseen presence on the game board.

We leap ahead rather here with the next statement, but will nonetheless make it: by more than doubling the number of Japanese fast fleet carriers, any skittishness on the part of Chuichi Nagumo would be blown off his flagship *Akagi*'s flight deck, such that an invasion scenario would have become obligatory, indeed the very orders with which he would be catapulted into enacting. But without that preponderance of carriers, there was clear vulnerability to a counter-stroke from possibly as many as three US carriers. Consequently, the fleet slewed around, headed into sheltering northern storms and sail back to the 'land of the rising sun'.

Right in the middle of the raid, carrier aircraft did clash with carrier aircraft when a squadron of dive bombers from the *Enterprise* actually flew from the carrier to arrive above Pearl Harbor. Six were shot down by Zero fighters and one by American anti-aircraft fire. Admiral Halsey's carrier was that close to its base. As such it was in deep peril, except he was directed by Pearl Harbor to charge off south like a bull into an empty china shop, instead of north into the arms of Nagumo.

As we shall shortly show, invasion was considered by bolder minds a sound scenario with just the six fast fleet flight decks then available. We will call this option the 'Genda Scenario', after Commander Minoru Genda, the planner of the Pearl Harbor raid and operational genius of Japanese naval aviation. He urged that on the outset of war against America, there must be invasion of Oahu, no mere raid.

Less promising might be rated plans for invasion slated for nine months later, but that is usually the more commonly cited option. We will call that the 'Watanabe Scenario', after Yasuji Watanabe, Yamamoto's staff officer charged with preparing the plan. This was dependent upon a decisive victory over the Pacific Fleet aircraft carriers at Midway. Planned to follow was an invasion by four army divisions of Oahu in August or September 1942, once the carriers had reinstated their air groups to full strength.

As a 'what if' sequence of events, the 'Watanabe scenario' was comprehensively demolished in a perspicacious appraisal by Anthony Tully on his CombinedFleet.com website. His main grounds for dismissal were logistical: the means to carry out such an operation against a vastly reinforced American base did not seem to him to succour any hope of ensuring a Japanese occupation of the Hawaiian islands. He also dismissed the 'Genda scenario', but on less solid grounds.

Since Tully's robust critique has come a revelatory article by Canadian historian Angelo N. Caravaggio in the prestigious *Naval War College Review*, entitled '"Winning" the Pacific War; the masterful strategy of Commander Minoru Genda', which is based upon a close reading of seventy-two interviews of Genda conducted post-war by a historian on General MacArthur's staff in Tokyo, Gordon Prange. Whereas it is well known that the idea for a Hawaii operation came from Yamamoto and that he invited the prominent 'air admiral' and planner, Rear Admiral Onishi, to examine its feasibility, it was to the IJN's operational naval air genius that Onishi turned for drawing up an actual plan. Genda's plan rejected Yamamoto's idea for a one-way raid outside land-based air range from Oahu; this had called for the air crews to be picked up by destroyers and submarines after ditching in the ocean. Genda felt that the decisive action of the war would be to deny the use of Oahu and its base at Pearl Harbor to the Americans as a springboard for operations into Japan's avowed sphere of influence, the Western Pacific and South-East Asia.

At risk of repetition, we remind the reader of the strategic geography that Genda was looking at. A glance at an atlas shows how holding Hawaii brought American muscle 2,600 miles, or 40 per cent of the way across the world's largest ocean from San Francisco. The remaining 60 per cent would bring it to Tokyo. Between the American west coast and Pearl Harbor lay nothing but empty sea. Thus, to lose Hawaii was to lose the whole Pacific, for lack of springboards between the west coast and Pearl Harbor. In contrast, the 'road' from Pearl Harbor westwards to Japan was conveniently littered with volcanic island chains and coral atolls, presenting a ladder for punching all the way up to the Japanese homeland's solar plexus – its highly flammable, mostly wood and paper-built coastal cities.

In dismissing the notion of a December 1941 invasion of Oahu, Tully presupposes Imperial Japanese Army opposition to the release of any more divisions than the eleven diverted from the Asiatic mainland and from homeland reserves for the 'drive south' on the Dutch East Indies, Malaya and the Philippines. He also rightly points out that for security reasons, the IJN sedulously avoided notifying the IJA of their intention to raid Pearl Harbor, so it was not as if they were about to ask for divisions in the first place.

From possibly not having waded through the totality of what Caravaggio terms the 'veritable treasure of unexamined transcripts of interviews' that historian Gordon Prange conducted in Japan after the war, Tully missed that the 'Genda Scenario' did not need to ask the IJA for more divisions, because for Genda the Hawaiian operation gained precedence over any plans for the Philippines. The latter could wait for a later invasion. Divisions and their shipping allotted for Philippines operations would more than suffice for Oahu, it being his insight that the Hawaiian islands were the prime objective in defeating America, not the Philippines, and that when Hawaii fell the Philippines would become indefensible and simply drop into Japan's lap. He correctly foresaw the Pacific War as one of seizing island air bases in order to project air power onwards, and avoiding large-scale army operations. Genda was what later in the Pacific War they liked to call a 'leapfrogger'; on an intellectual basis at least, the first of the leapfroggers.

Rejection of Tully's second criticism is sustainable on two grounds. The IJN could ask the IJA for a couple of good divisions without answering the question of exactly when and where the Hawaiian landing would take place. Such divisions could have included the crack 7th Division from Hokkaido, the northernmost of the main home islands of Japan. It was then in reserve. There could also have been the better of the two full divisions intended for the Philippine operation against the main island of Luzon. That early in the game, two experienced and battle-trained divisions should have proved more than ample for seizing Oahu. They could be shipped to a jump-off position in Saipan well in advance, in order to practise landings.

As for the Navy telling the Army General Staff when they would land and just where, the answer could be, 'To Saipan for amphibious training as soon as possible, thence depending on the intelligence picture and prospects for command of the air over the best prospective destination.'

Historians have made much over how the IJN and IJA detested each other, but this did not obviate dedicated co-operation in operations planning during the 'drive south'. It was maybe a symptom of 'victory disease' that led to relationships reverting to type afterwards.

It could have been plausibly explained to the generals how the main threat to the flank of Japan's 'drive south' could be eliminated without initially having actually to invade the Philippines. Actual events on 7 December 1941 saw the IJN's medium bombers from Formosa destroy most of MacArthur's air forces on the ground on the opening day of the war, without any carrier support. Following the main raids on airfields north of Manila, American forces in the Philippines found themselves left with no offensive capability worth the punch except for a lot of submarines with defective torpedoes.

Nor could there be any hope of reinforcing American war resources in the Philippines, as the IJN would command the sea between them and America, and completely so if Hawaii fell. Even without MacArthur's Flying Fortresses being destroyed or evacuated, both Japanese services were well aware of the shortcomings of high-level bombing as any kind of strategic weapon. Even if the Philippines force of four-engine bombers had reached the projected 100 aircraft, it was only raids of over 1,000 of them in 1945 that made any strategic impact.

Prior to Tully and to Caravaggio, we have John J. Stephan's *Hawaii Under the Rising Sun; Japan's Plans for Conquest After Pearl Harbor*, which meticulously examines Japanese sources. It reveals how after the Doolittle

Raid, the IJA swung around in favour of the 'Eastern Operation', as it was known. In May 1942, the 7th and 2nd divisions, and later the 53rd Division, were ordered to prepare for the operation. The operational orders for the three divisions to train for invasion of Hawaii surfaced among the Hattori Papers, thanks to an army staff officer of that name secreting away Army General Staff documents until after the occupation of Japan. As such, the Hattori Papers never fell into American hands. The Japanese Navy, in contrast, burnt almost everything. Nevertheless, post-war interrogations demonstrated how committed Navy elements were to the 'Eastern Operation'. There can thus be little doubt that if the Battle of Midway had gone the other way, the two services would have combined to invade the Hawaiian islands.

To have succeeded, Japan would not have needed to lose any flight decks beforehand and to have annihilated the US carrier force totally. Such a scenario could well have happened.

We shall now take a break to celebrate Minoru Genda, one of the most fascinating figures of the Second World War.

The Genda Factor

Japan's tragedy was that, before the Pacific War, Minoru Genda was ranked only a commander, not even a captain, least of all any level of flag officer. Yet no-one appreciated the naval development of the aerial dimension of war better than he. Historians such as Prange and later Norman Polmar noted how Genda finely combined the wisdom of strategy with the guile of tactics. In the IJN, Genda inspired respect among both his seniors and juniors, the crowning example being after the Midway debacle how one of Yamamoto's first concerns was whether Genda had survived. Indeed, once the surviving fleet came within air range of Japan, this living national treasure was flown on, so that no time would be lost in planning a regeneration of the *Kido Butai* such as best could take into account the lessons of the battle. The seeds of that were to blossom in Japanese victory at Santa Cruz almost four months later.

Genda was a brilliant manifestation of the Japanese managerial propensity for synchronizing 'bottom-up' with 'top-down' thinking.

He first sprang to fame as leader of an aerobatic team called Genda's Flying Circus that toured the country in a PR exercise for naval aviation.

In the China war, he proposed using advanced bases for fighters in order to be able to offer escort for longer-range bombers to their full extremity. He was posted to London in 1940 as an assistant naval attaché, instructed to learn as much as possible about the air war in Europe. He was there through most of the Battle of Britain and predicted the RAF victory on the strength of perceiving it to be flying better fighters than the Germans. How neither contestant had a dogfighting single-seater to match the IJN's Zero may have been premature for Genda to report, as the Japanese fighter only came into production in 1940, unless Genda had been among those who tested the prototype.

As we have described earlier, the Japanese Embassy in London was a hotbed of pro-British sentiment. On the way home, Genda rated his report to be so important that it never left his person. His departure preceded the Royal Navy' carrier raid on the Italian naval base of Taranto. Thereafter, naval attachés from the Berlin embassy went to Italy to obtain details for experts like Genda to study.

Genda told Prange how he got the idea for what became known as the 'Genda Box' on his return from London in October 1940 when he was visiting a newsreel cinema in Tokyo. The news footage showed a group of four American carriers in formation. It made him realize that massed carriers could act greater than the sum of their parts, both in offence and defence. The navies of the world had been content to operate their carriers individually, or in pairs. Not now Japan, where in early 1941 Yamamoto created the First Air Fleet, combining all the IJN's carriers under a single command. Genda was ordered to work out procedures and tactics for the force. The Genda Box was, however, highly vulnerable, depending upon two factors. The first of these was being able to marshal a preponderance of force in defence. The other factor was that upon completing strikes, the fleet was expected to spread out of the box in readiness for counter-strikes. At Midway, there was not the preponderance of force the Japanese had assumed, ambush had been discounted and the need to launch a second air strike fatally postponed dispersal.

Yet the concept of the Genda Box did not die. As the Essex Surge began, there was scope for many boxes, or task forces, thereby creating a balance between concentration and dispersal.

Genda's war ended in charge of fighter forces equipped with a new aircraft to compare with the US Navy's best, and manned by the last of the IJN's aces. These exacted a heavy toll of US carrier planes in the First Kure Raid in March 1945. The main targets were the remaining IJN carriers, which suffered little damage. Counter-strikes reduced the carrier *Franklin* to a burning and exploding wreck, and severely damaged other big fleet carriers. While not exactly a carrier-to-carrier battle in the 1942 sense, 'First Kure' was in a way the last carrier battle of the war, as carriers were hit on both sides.

Genda foresaw so much of how the Pacific War would unfold, particularly how it would be an island war, a war about bases as springboards, and less a land war. He was a Nimitz man before Nimitz. We don't know what he said about MacArthur, as the general was virtually the shogun in Japan during the period Gordon Prange was asking all his questions, and Prange was the general's man.

Norman Polmar, in writing his standard work on aircraft carriers, cited Minoru Genda as one of three collaborators. As for the post-war American interrogators, they deliciously found still alive the staff planner of the 'day that will live in infamy'. No wonder Genda was subjected to seventy-two separate interviews!

After the war, Genda rose to be a star of the Japanese Defence Forces. Little could his interrogators have guessed what a friend of the United States he was later to become, such that President Kennedy awarded him the US Legion of Merit.

A photograph of Genda taken in his hour of destiny enables us to take a candle to the man. In portraiture, the first rule is always look for the eyes. Genda's right eye beams iron-cold appraisal and self-confidence, while in the left seems to lurk a tell-tale gleam of daredevilry.

* * *

Genda's invasion plan for Hawaii never survived the scrutiny of his superiors. It went straight to Yamamoto via Admiral Onishi, who appended his own observations to it; the latter have not survived. Table-top games played in September 1941, however, revived interest in the plan, except Yamamoto chose to rework it using Watanabe, the staff officer closest to him and his regular partner at *shogi* (Japanese chess), which acted as his main relaxation.

The option to invade dropped by the wayside, mainly because Yamamoto as Commander of the Combined Fleet was having such a struggle forcing any Hawaii operation past the strident opposition of the Naval General Staff. The deadlock was only broken when he threatened to resign along with all his staff. But that threat was only good for a raid being approved.

Following the attack, however, a sharp sense grew at the top level of the Japanese armed forces of a great missed opportunity, of Genda having been right all along. He was, however, now with the *Kido Butai* at the side of Nagumo and Kusaka. So it was Watanabe again who was deputed to work on a plan for the 'Eastern Operation', as it came to be called. More army divisions were now called for, instead of just one-and-a-half, in recognition that Oahu would soon be vastly reinforced, particularly as the timing put the operation so far down the line. First, Singapore and the Dutch East Indies had to be won, the Philippines fully secured and Australia cut off. There could then ensue a move into the Central Pacific, such as might draw the American carriers into battle, but only once the *Kido Butai* had reconstituted its air groups. Once the US carriers had been 'annihilated', the invasion of Oahu would follow, calculatedly at least nine months after Pearl Harbor.

For preferred denouement, we have chosen Genda for the Phantom Scenario as there would so plainly be the number of carriers to ensure its success, and we feel that setting the invasion nine months away would have upped the odds against the army part of the operation succeeding, although an alternative history blog on the internet recommended an invasion of neighbouring Kauai island instead of Oahu, particularly as Kauai had airfields. If one could pummel Oahu from nearby air range, like Rabaul was later in the war, the base itself might become inactive. It might even be starved into submission, particularly if enveloped by a subsequent invasion of 'Big Island' at the eastern end of the chain.

An initial landing on Hawaii island had been the recommendation of Rear Admiral Tamon Yamaguchi, the aggressive commander of the 2nd Carrier Division, on account of its greater proximity to a pair of atoll outposts to the south of the Hawaii chain. Of these, Johnston Island was indeed considerably closer to Oahu than was Midway. Add to that how Big Island lies between Oahu and the American west coast. Airfields there would be ideally positioned. Yamaguchi wanted first to seize

Johnson and Palmyra atolls with their airstrips, and then land on the lightly defended Big Island using naval troops. Finally, having impressed the IJA, he would win sufficient divisions for the invasion of the strongly defended Oahu.

Oahu was by far the most populous of the Hawaiian islands. Like them all, its 400,000 population was more or less dependent on imported food. The islands themselves produced predominantly only fish and pineapples. Defence was almost wholly located on Oahu. Yamamoto himself had considered how useful holding half a million hostage Americans on the islands could be as a means of winning a peace settlement. There was also the attraction of the population including a very large Japanese minority as a resource for internal security and administration.

There is the additional problem with the Watanabe Scenario that obtaining four divisions from the Japanese Army might prove asking too much due to its obsession with the Soviet Union. A 'drive north' into the Soviet Far East on the part of its army in Manchuria was planned if Hitler's armies crossed the River Volga. Indeed, a September invasion of Oahu would have coincided with the arrival of Hitler's Sixth Army on the west bank of the Volga before Stalingrad. It was no good then the IJN protesting that the Phantom Fleet could guarantee those four divisions a safe passage and an easy campaign when they reached Hawaii; instead, the Army would quite emphatically need them to support the drive into the Soviet Far East, namely to Khabarovsk and Vladivostok. The IJA enjoyed the political assets to bounce that ball into the basket. A 'drive north' had always been its preference. Devouring a juicy chunk of Siberian steak was far more enticing than risking a ride across the Pacific to Hawaii atop the hated navy's seaborne saddles.

In answering our first big question at some length, we have shown that invasion was thrice contemplated and much debated, if finally rejected. In the third case, the defeat at Midway lobbed the Watanabe plan into the bamboo thickets. We have been dealing in actualities only so far, but next let us see how things could have changed given double the number of aircraft carriers available. We thus proceed now to the second question.

How much better might an invasion of Hawaii have fared and the conquest be sustained, given a more ample carrier force, to wit our Phantom Fleet?

This can invite a very brief answer. For the first step, we return to the end of Chapter 4, 'Phantom Fleet', to help us choose a carrier team for an invasion of Oahu as Japan's opening move of the Pacific War.

In the first table there are the carriers that Yamamoto could choose from for the actual famous raid, namely the six largest flight decks and at the same time the fastest of the ships. The light carriers and seaplane carriers, having shorter endurance and lesser speeds, were delegated to southern operations or to air crew training. The four seaplane carriers usefully housed a float plane version of the Zero fighter, which enhanced their air combat potential.

Turning to the second table, we can see that the Phantom Scenario doubles the number of fast fleet carriers. For pulverizing Pearl Harbor and as air cover for invasion of Oahu, that promises a massive ship-borne air force of over 750 operational strike aircraft, or about 900 inclusive of spares stowed on board and float planes carried on cruisers and battleships. That is well over double the 400 or so deployed on the historic raid.

As for the light carriers and the seaplane carriers, close to another 200 carrier planes would be available for the southern operations, again double the historic number.

*   *   *

Let us slip now into the immediacy of the present tense in order to narrate what could have been the hand dealt by fate.

With the size of air-sea armada being proposed, US air defences on Oahu will find themselves swamped. The IJN requires a consequently smaller need for surprise. Admiral Nagumo can even hold back a large reserve in case American carriers are absent but close enough to interfere. The first he will know, because American carriers being in port or out is being reported on a daily basis from the Japanese Consulate in Honolulu.

If absent from the base, they have to be out at sea somewhere, but exactly where is unknowable. In readiness for an intervention, Admiral Nagumo can hold one carrier division in reserve, armed with anti-ship weapons ready to strike, and with a seaplane carrier added to his force his scouting arm is reinforced. He uses the Jake float planes from the seaplane carrier and those of the escorting fast battleships and cruisers for scout patrols, in order not to deplete his bomber strength. Once the morning raids return, a second pair of carriers can join the anti-ship strike reserve. As land-based American air strength dwindles to near zero, over half the force can go into reserve in readiness for a carrier-to-carrier fight.

With such numbers of aircraft, Genda can expect to win consent to the three days he asks for standing off Oahu and pummelling it hard while the transports disgorge their troops. Invasion may then impel the American carriers to intervene, in which case they would go into the bag as well as the battleships in the harbour.

He can count on Yamamoto's gambling instincts to agree, the admiral being a believer in the sage old advice that without taking risks in war, little is ever gained. His passion for gambling constantly exercised his cold calculation of odds. Here, with all these carriers, the risks are now reduced to very little. We already know from his biographer how it amused him that capturing Oahu would round up as prisoners a large proportion of the brains in the US Navy – including no doubt some of his former poker game opponents from Washington days. His point as expressed to staff officers, according to his biographer, was that it took such a long time to train a navy officer and then for that officer to mature to senior rank. That was several times longer than it took to build a capital ship.

It is all very well seizing Oahu and the rest of the Hawaiian islands, but how long before they are wrested back by an armada sortieing from San Diego? To answer that we need to look at the chart at the end of this chapter, showing the production schedule of new aircraft carriers in the United States, and at the final charts at the end of Phantom Fleet chapter, which show the wartime production we calculate as possible in Japan.

We find that the Essex Surge has barely caught up with the Phantom Fleet by 1945, such that the Allies would until a year later lack anywhere close to the 60:40 preponderance in fleet carriers (and better than two-to-one in carrier aircraft) they enjoyed at the June 1944 Battle of the Philippine Sea. But first there comes a hard fight on the ground for Oahu. As we have found above, San Diego is about 2,600 miles from Oahu. From there, there is another 3,709 miles of Pacific to fly across before reaching Tinian in the Marianas Islands, whence flew the B-29 Superfortress *Enola Gay* to bomb Hiroshima.

Critics of invasion scenarios have been quick to point out the logistic problems in resupplying any Japanese base in the Hawaiian islands. We respond by reminding them that Rabaul is about 3,000 miles from Tokyo, and yet the IJN did a great job of supplying Rabaul for two years, and the Allies blenched from invading it, so strongly was it defended. So why could they not as adequately resupply Hawaii, particularly as Rabaul and other threatened Japanese bases would become irrelevances if Oahu was held? What had been pumped into Rabaul was equally capable in the case of the Phantom Scenario of being stacked up on Oahu.

In Phantom Scenario, we have no need to supply Rabaul, for an invasion of Hawaii would automatically sever Australia from the war, such that no campaign in the South-West Pacific would ever have taken place. MacArthur would not have had a war to fight. With Australia and New Zealand isolated in their rear, and with Pearl Harbor as a road block in the Central Pacific, the IJN could massively build up its land-based air forces and conserve aircrews, and not least fortify the island chain from Iwo Jima south to Saipan and Guam, Yap and Palau as an inner line of defence, or line of *ne plus ultra*. It was the actual South-West Pacific campaign that over two years wore out Japanese naval aviation. In the Phantom Scenario, there is no need for that to happen: there is no South-West Pacific campaign, no New Guinea campaigns, no Philippines liberation campaign and no MacArthur legend.

The Phantom Fleet scenario makes the Central Pacific approaches to Japan the only conceivable route for the Allies to take. That was eventually so in reality, except there was not initially a carrier fleet large enough to smother the land-based air resources that the IJN could flock into the *Nanyo*. There had also been the political problem of saving Australia, New Zealand and MacArthur's forces there. This was found eminently possible after Midway, as Japan now lacked the size of carrier fleet that could likewise overwhelm land-based aerial resources at the point of contact.

It will be apparent from the tables that any clear margin of superiority in fleet carriers on the part of US forces could not dawn until 1945. From that it is not hard to deduct that the reconquest of Hawaii might have been condemned to wait for three or four years. What during all that time would an aggressive Japanese Empire – uncharacteristically sitting on the defensive in the Pacific – have done with its air-sea armada?

One can squat like a spider in the centre of the *Nanyo*'s protective web, using as epicentre Truk's great lagoon, from where would come a quick pounce on any raiding force that tangled with its outlying air bases or posed an invasion threat to Hawaii. Meanwhile, the priority for logistical resources can be argued as the need to fortify the inner defence line west of the Philippine Sea and the Celebes, all the time waiting for America to surge back in full raging force.

In this cautious scenario, attacks against the American west coast are limited to submarine action, the submarines being based at Pearl Harbor, which would also become a hive for the big four-engine flying boats that the IJN was to use so effectively for long-range reconnaissance. If the political pressure to 'do something' grew too strong, then a nice little ploy might be a move on Alaska, the base on Unalaska island called Dutch Harbor the apt choice. In this scenario, Hawaii is seen as exerting a long delaying action on the US comeback but eventually to be lost by Japan, and likewise Dutch Harbor, but not forsaking the hope of trading them in a peace negotiation, as seems to have been the idea uppermost in Yamamoto's mind, according to Watanabe and others.

Whatever the strategy chosen after the invasion of Oahu by the Japanese, there will be for them much mopping up. The 'move south' into Indonesia and Malaya will require rapid completion and the Philippines to be secured. Without any army divisions available to invade Australia, it and New Zealand can be cut off by seizing island air bases between Australasia and the United States, such as those on Samoa, Fiji and New Caledonia.

More appealing to the IJN offensive temperament as a strategy might be raids on the Americas, particularly on naval base infrastructure in San Diego and repair facilities in the Seattle area, also destroying the Panama Canal locks at Gatun, thereby delaying the trans-Pacific comeback and rendering its logistics less sustainable. To indulge in such antics carried a risk – that of running into overwhelming American land-based air resources. An article of faith in carrier warfare was if not exactly to 'hit 'em where they mostly ain't', certainly never to enter the wasps' nest and risk all without being able to project overwhelming force, thereby smothering land-based air resources locally and intercepting reinforcements from further afield.

A third strategy beckons seductively, one that accepts the first strategy's staying put in the Pacific but seeks 'something to do' offensively by exploiting opportunities in the Indian Ocean. And so it is that we come to our third question.

Finally, what was the likely outcome on the progress of the Pacific War if the IJN's arms procurement policies had been more logically inspired and ruthlessly pursued, such that Hawaii and Ceylon could become invasion objectives of easy achievement?
We have already partly answered the Pacific aspects, albeit without taking the assessment forward to a late-war denouement.

Let us now turn to the Indian Ocean, which became a new frontier for the IJN following the conquest of Singapore and the Dutch East Indies. We have mentioned how the large island colony of Ceylon (today the nation of Sri Lanka) off the south-east tip of the Indian sub-continent was the strategic hub of the Indian Ocean, just as Hawaii was for the Pacific. We noted how the British had made naval and air bases out of Ceylon's two major ports, Colombo in the south-west and Trincomalee in the north-east.

In the event, all Japan actually ventured in the case of Ceylon was to unleash the *Kido Butai* to raid both bases, as the IJA had refused to supply divisions for an invasion. They were more interested in seizing Burma (modern Myanmar), in order to cut off supplies emanating via the Burma Road to Nationalist China from India. There was an IJN plan for invasion, just as there were plans for the invasion of Oahu, except this time it was not a Combined Fleet plan by Yamamoto henchmen but the plan of Captain Sadatoshi Tomioka, on the Naval General Staff in Tokyo. Perhaps if Genda had been behind the plan, Burma would have been 'leapfrogged' in favour of Ceylon. Just as he proposed postponing invasion of the Philippines until Oahu had fallen, so Burma's invasion could follow Ceylon's conquest.

Little in Burma would have been lost in the event, as Rangoon fell in March 1942 to two understrength but experienced Japanese divisions moving overland from Siam (modern Thailand). This opened up the port to speedy reinforcement by sea, including the crack 18th Division which had so distinguished itself in the Malaya campaign. The division was fed into Burma through the port of Rangoon just as the *Kido Butai* struck across the Bay of Bengal at Ceylon. If instead sent to Ceylon in its thirty-eight-ship convoy, it could land each side of Trincomalee. The meagre British forces were divided between defending Colombo and Trincomalee. Only 150 miles separated the bases on opposite sides of Ceylon. Two roads leading from Trincomalee to Colombo would have further divided any defence. There was little need in Burma for the 18th Division, because other Japanese forces were on the way by sea or overland to the region, where the British forces were already beaten and hard to reinforce over a mountain chain between them and India. Burma was doomed before the convoy with the 18th Division ever docked in Rangoon.

There could be two ways to go for Japanese strategy after Ceylon: the tame or the wild choice. The tame option limits further advance to setting up reconnaissance seaplane bases in the atoll chains in the middle of the ocean and sitting back while India implodes in unrest or open revolt against the British Raj. To help along the latter, why not send the light carriers on a raid between Bombay and Aden, or even commerce raiding in the South Atlantic? Cheek can win wars, as the Doolittle Raid showed: it provoked the fatal Japanese adventure against Midway.

An attractive option in the scenario is to seize Diego Suarez at the northern end of Madagascar as a submarine base. This had actually been planned as a project. Not the least of its appeal to the IJN was historical, in that Madagascar was where the Russian Baltic Fleet had sheltered, rested and tried to rendezvous with a reserve squadron before resuming its death ride to Tsushima. Madagascar was a Vichy French colony, and Vichy had not made a big fuss over the Japanese occupation of Indochina and had many bones to pick with Churchill.

The more ambitious course – one is tempted to call it the 'Wilder Shores of Araby' scenario – opens more wilfully to what strategists term the 'Orient' option and entertains the prospect of the Axis powers joining up. This would be done by seizing Aden and Oman at each end of the Arabian peninsula in order to interdict the resupply of the British Army in Egypt, cut off the flow of oil from the Persian Gulf, put a stop to the flow of Lend-Lease aid to the Soviets through Persia (modern Iran) and cork President Roosevelt's dreams of supplying China via the Indian Ocean and British India.

The Orient concept may be confusing to the modern reader. Pre-war, the celebrated passenger line serving the route from Britain to India was called P&O. The 'P' stood for 'Peninsula', by which was meant Arabia, and the 'O' for 'Orient', by which was meant all points eastward, in particular the Indian sub-continent.

This might well offer a worthwhile prospect of 'something to do' while waiting out the two or three years for America to come bouncing back across the Pacific. There could even have been a physical link-up with the Nazis in the Middle East, which had been advocated by Hitler's navy chief, Admiral Raeder.

Such a course of events might have had the roof fall in on Stalin and the Allies. For example, in the second half of 1942, 20,000 trucks were shipped from America around South Africa to be landed at Basra in Iraq, then driven through Persia to the Russian front in the Caucasus and to Saratov on the Volga. Those trucks helped roll into place the forces for the winter offensive that resulted in the famous pincer assault on the flanks of the Nazi Sixth Army when it was bogged down before Stalingrad, it thereby being surrounded and forced to surrender. The trucks also supplied the Stalingrad Front by trundling supplies and reinforcements down the Asiatic side of the Volga. It had often been the case that whenever Churchill pressed British tanks on him, Stalin asked for American trucks in preference. It was mainly trucks that America shipped to Persia, because to reach the Soviet armies they did not need rail transportation. Persia (as the Iranian plateau was called then in honour of the national language, Farsi) was the more important route for Lend-Lease supplies to the Soviets, less so the more-written-about Arctic route which became so dangerous in 1942.

Slipping back now into actual events, we have Churchill as witness to how such nightmares (even without the Phantom Fleet factor) caused the British Cabinet in Whitehall and the Viceroy of India more anguish and despair for the future of the British Empire than any other they had faced to date. President Roosevelt responded to their pleas for help by enabling the expedition to Madagascar that pre-empted any Japanese move on the Vichy French island. His Admiral King offered to shift two modern battleships and a carrier from his Atlantic Fleet to the British Home Fleet at Scapa Flow, in order to facilitate the transfer of an equivalent Royal Navy contingent to reinforce the British Eastern Fleet in the

Indian Ocean. This was less to save the future of the British Raj in India, and more to maintain the flow of supplies and fighting men around Africa to the Suez Canal, Persian Gulf and India, and of war materiel to Nationalist China. Winning back the Mediterranean became the initial part of the Allies' 'Europe First' strategy. Supplying the Russian fronts was also intrinsic to that strategy.

It was truly a world war; and nowhere more crucial than in the Indian Ocean did that all come together.

The paradox is that it never did come together. There never had been an Axis plan as such. Even if there had, an event was about to happen to kill it stone dead.

The American victory at the Battle of Midway blew away Allied fears of Japanese expansion into the Indian Ocean, as their remaining flight decks had now to be readied to oppose American offensives in the South Pacific.

As for Hitler, he was never too sure about the Japanese as a race. We can imagine him in his mountain redoubt high above Berchtesgaden at afternoon tea time, the hour which found him at his most affable and indiscreet. He passes around his guests the dainty Viennese cream pastries nestling in their twee paper doilies, amiably clucking away 'playing mother' with the neo-Gothic silver tea urns. He ruminates about their strange Axis allies – how they were there on the other side of the world, and by all appearances doing a good job for the Tripartite Alliance; but does one want to get in bed with them as well?

Hitler was forever egging on his Foreign Minister, Joachim Ribbentrop, to badger the Japanese into attacking the British at Singapore. Yet when the vaunted Far Eastern fortress actually fell, he was reported as being in an indignant froth about it, expostulating about how a race of 'yellow men' could have so defeated a fellow Aryan race.

Thanks to Hitler's fastidious prejudices, what historians have called the 'Orient' option could all have come together very nastily for the Allies in the context of the Phantom Fleet factor; just as it makes an invasion of Hawaii overwhelmingly persuasive, so too an invasion of Ceylon, similarly the strategic hub to an ocean.

Before actually going into battle with the Phantom Fleet in the Indian Ocean, let us set the scene for the reader in terms of actual events. Following the fall of Singapore and the Dutch East Indies, two IJN forces began girding their loins for a sally into the Indian Ocean. One

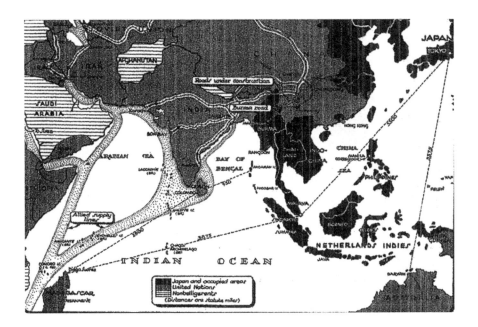

was the Malaya Force, that now faced west towards India. The other was Nagumo's *Kido Butai* of five carriers, now temporarily less the use of the sixth and largest: *Kaga* was being repaired after running aground. Nagumo's jumping-off point was Kendari in the Celebes.

Each fleet was awarded a separate mission. Admiral Jisaburo Ozawa, commander of Malaya Force on board his flagship the heavy cruiser *Chokai*, led four other heavies and the light carrier *Ryujo*. His mission was to undertake a commerce raid in the Bay of Bengal, that part of the Indian Ocean flanked by Ceylon, India, Burma and Malaya, while Admiral Nagumo raided the British bases on Ceylon off the southern point of India, in the hope of catching the British Eastern Fleet and destroying it. A submarine force was dispatched to the western side of India for more commerce raiding and to help locate the British fleet if absent from its bases.

However, Admiral Somerville, in command of the Eastern Fleet, had warning of the forthcoming raid thanks to the codebreakers. Consequently, he took the Eastern Fleet off to a secret anchorage in an obscure coral atoll. It was hoped the Japanese knew nothing of this Addu Atoll. The idea was that the fleet would be as good as off in the blue but within ambush range of the *Kido Butai*. Some idea of the odds Somerville faced was deductible from the codebreaks – his two big fleet

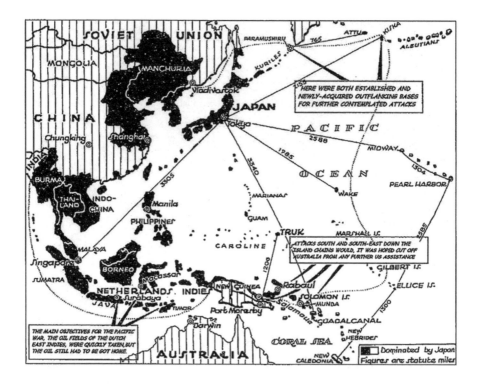

carriers versus five or six Japanese carriers. On the other hand, there lay the ardent hope that Nagumo could be ambushed while occupied in raiding the land bases, and there was a ready and able gambit for doing so without incurring the certainty of retaliation. This was to advance at the close of day to a good night-launching position before high-speeding out of range before daylight, using the rest of the night for cover. His torpedo bombers were only slow Albacore bi-planes, but they were radar-equipped and well-trained for night flying. At that time, the IJN lacked such carrier air capability, or at least the radar-assisted form of it. There was nonetheless a severe degree of risk if Japanese aerial reconnaissance was up to the mark. Fortunately, it was not; the limited search patterns typical then of Nagumo's force were directed towards Ceylon rather than westwards, where Somerville's ambush force lurked. As such, Nagumo first picked off two British heavy cruisers, the *Dorsetshire* and *Cornwall*, crossing his front, and on a subsequent occasion the light carrier *Hermes* off the coast of Ceylon. These were sunk by Val dive-bombing attack in what has been generally agreed the most astonishing feat of that art of the war. Hardly a bomb missed its target.

On the British side, reconnaissance was more effective, but its results were marred by communication lapses sufficient to deny Somerville his night attack. Meanwhile, the skippers of the sunken warships had been rescued and joined in a conference to help decide what next to do. Upon hearing their dread stories, the admiral found himself even more inclined to skedaddle as fast as his forces could steam, for they all now realized what they were up against. Japanese naval prowess with torpedo bombers was a given, but there had now come this demonstration of what the IJN was capable of against fast-moving warships using dive bombers. How many of them they could only guess – in fact well over 100, compared to less for all types of aircraft aboard the Royal Navy carriers. In addition, Nagumo started his campaign with about ninety Kate torpedo planes. His fighter strength alone outnumbered the total air strength of the British force. As for quality, it was like British doves fighting Japanese eagles.

How Somerville had dared risk the Eastern Fleet against such odds has its main explanation back in Chapter 5: Allied naval intelligence estimates had failed to discover how Japanese carriers could operate twice as many aircraft as the false official data indicated.

Somerville made a strategic decision to keep his fleet 'in being' by withdrawing it to the other side of the Indian Ocean, in the hope of reinforcement and above all being re-equipped with better aircraft. There, troop convoys to Suez could be protected – at least against raiders – for the good of the war against Hitler.

But what if American carriers had also been present off Ceylon alongside Somerville's *Indomitable* and *Formidable*? The Anglo-Saxon reader familiar with the outcome of the US ambush of Nagumo's fleet at the Battle of Midway will exult.

We are rather leaping ahead here, in more ways than one. Was it even possible for an American task force to have been operational in the Indian Ocean in April 1942? Well, it was just, because under the Phantom Scenario, US carriers had only that way to go as no credible challenge to the IJN could be put together in the Pacific at that time.

Meanwhile, the war with Hitler had to be won. Yet here was the lifeline to the Middle East under threat from Japan; the lifeline that must never be cut. As for the Japanese, why not present them with a 'two-ocean' problem with the Allies operating on interior lines by forming a

United Fleet that can switch in entirety from one ocean to the other via the Panama Canal?

We thus have Admiral King switching the three carriers of the Pacific Fleet to Simonstown in South Africa and leaving his Atlantic carriers in the Atlantic; the *Wasp* to help run convoys to Malta as it did, and the *Yorktown* with the *Ranger* to Scapa Flow to mark the *Tirpitz*, thereby allowing the British Home Fleet to switch three of its four Illustrious-class armoured deck carriers to Simonstown in South Africa to join the three Americans. Indeed, it was close to such dispositions that Admiral King actually agreed as cover to the Madagascar expedition, with the exception of the Pacific Fleet carriers going off in that direction. In the Phantom Scenario, it becomes the logical addition to a reconfiguration of Allied forces, such as was actively being discussed in reality between Washington and London in the post-Pearl Harbor timeframe.

Thus, present off Ceylon is a United Fleet of three American and three British aircraft carriers, with stowed on board 300 aircraft to fling at Nagumo, who fielded five carriers which had an operational strength of 318 aircraft aboard.

In the Phantom Scenario, we conjecture him being allotted an extra four fleet carriers for a total of 570 aircraft. These would be terrible odds against Somerville, except Nagumo would find himself tied down to supporting an invasion of Ceylon. Somerville would be in with a chance, having the lee gauge and the superior intelligence thanks to the codebreakers.

Here we shall have to disappoint Anglo-Saxon readers, as we don't feel that such a force could have reached Ceylon in time, and might not even have taken that direction. From a tactical point of view, the Hawaii invasion will have demonstrated the overwhelming might of IJN naval aviation. Looked at from the strategic stance, the primary need was to defend the Simonstown-to-Suez lifeline. Why risk throwing away the fleet in a vain and doomed defence of Ceylon? Instead, make the Japanese fight farther from home and burn up their dwindling reserves of oil. Another reason was logistical: supplies had first to be shifted down to the South Atlantic. A third reason was incompatibility, for at that time, the two navies lacked the ability to fight together as one. First and foremost, the British carriers needed to be stripped of their planes and American models provided instead (as indeed was done before the *Victorious* joined the American Pacific Fleet in the South-West Pacific in the late spring of 1943).

We shall not, however, deny the reader his battle, albeit in Phantom Scenario the location moves west and three or four months later. We now once again adopt our 'what if' mode by slipping back into the present tense.

Incredible Victory

Under the Phantom Scenario, we posit the first proper carrier-to-carrier battle of the war taking place in June 1942 off the Seychelles islands north-east of the northern tip of Madagascar. This is assuming that Tokyo adopts the 'Orient' strategy, in which it will need springboards to Aden and Oman on the Arabian peninsula as a first step towards linking up with the Nazis and Mussolini in the Middle East. Let us war game an outcome to the Battle of the Seychelles.

We propose a Japanese order of battle comprising four carrier divisions, each with two fleet carriers accompanied by one light fleet carrier for scouting and extra combat air patrol, giving a total air strength of about 600 aircraft. The two newer divisions are diverted north to raid the Red Sea and Persian Gulf approaches at Oman and Aden, while the two older divisions under Nagumo give cover to the invasion convoy. These arrive off Victoria in the Seychelles and the troops duly disembark to little opposition. The main body comprises the *Akagi* and *Kaga* with the *Ryujo* in support as one division, and the *Shokaku* and *Zuikaku* with the *Ryuho* in support as the other.

The two raiding divisions fall back to the Seychelles from the north in reinforcement. The Aden group arrives first (*Hiryu* and *Soryu* with *Shoho* in support), the Oman group commanded by Jisaburo Ozawa a day behind (*Unryu* and *Koryu* with *Zuiho* in support).

However, the Allies are already out at sea, thanks to a tip-off from the codebreakers. Flying off the three American flight decks, their ninety American Dauntless dive bombers catch Nagumo's carriers with their planes on board, and duly set alight the *Kaga*, *Akagi*, *Soryu* and light carrier *Shoho*. The *Zuikaku* and *Hiryu* retaliate by crippling the *Yorktown* and *Lexington*, only to be caught by a late-day attack by the dive bombers. The *Hiryu* is sunk, as is the light carrier *Ryujo*, but the *Zuikaku* dodges into a rain squall and survives, as does *Ryuho* (not to be confused with *Ryujo*), the light carrier accompanying its division. The *Shokaku* takes heavy bomb damage and is out of the fight, retiring home at high speed.

Overnight, the torpedo bombers on the British carriers finish off the cripples on the Japanese side to seal a great victory. There is, however, a reprise when Ozawa's raiding division joins up with the *Zuikaku* and *Ryuho*. The intact Allied carriers elude them, but the Japanese airmen finish off the *Lexington* and *Yorktown* and damage the *Enterprise*. IJN submarine *I 168* puts a torpedo into *Indomitable*, but not fatally. The Allies are left almost bereft of serviceable air groups and with just two carriers able to fly aircraft on and off, each of these British armoured deck carriers. It is the Allies who depart the battlefield after their ambush and the Japanese are able to secure the Seychelles, half their carriers surviving.

Does this sound too dramatic? Well, it only compresses into a single action the tactical outcomes of the first three carrier-to-carrier battles of the Pacific War, namely Coral Sea, Midway and Eastern Solomons. A common feature of these battles was how no prizes could be awarded to respective reconnaissance efforts. One side is to learn from the Seychelles, the other not, as we shall see in due course.

For the Allied newspapers, this all comes as an incredible victory, the 'Miracle at the Seychelles'.

British Admiral Somerville is thereupon ennobled as Lord Somerville of the Seychelles, while his American partner Admiral Halsey receives the Congressional Medal of Honor.

Tokyo's schedule for forward plans is delayed while the shock of this tactical defeat is absorbed. For the Allies, the interval helps them ship supplies and reinforcements into Egypt for the desert campaign against Rommel that in the autumn will see his defeat at El Alamein and the Allies landing in French North Africa. The July 1942 victory at the Seychelles will indirectly win the Mediterranean for the Allies.

'The Day of the Eagles'

As in reality, the Phantom Scenario Japanese are nothing if not persistent. Their next objective is the island of Socotra. This can be seen on the map as quite a large island – not as long as the much-fought-over island of Guadalcanal in late 1942, but not much less. It commands the sea routes to Suez and to the Persian Gulf, and is today owned by Yemen.

Two fresh carrier divisions are dispatched from the Pacific to Ceylon and the damaged division withdrawn from the Indian Ocean, leaving the intact 3rd Carrier Division (the *Unryu*, *Koryu* and *Zuiho*). Together, the three divisions are a force of two large fleet carriers, plus four medium and three light carriers. They are commanded now by Ozawa, who has some 440 aircraft aboard. Given an optimistic assessment of the Allied losses at the Seychelles, this is regarded as sufficient by Yamamoto.

Meanwhile, the Imperial Japanese Army is excited about unrest in India but worried by the tide turning against Hitler in Russia. The IJA suggests the Japanese Navy seize Socotra island off the Horn of Africa to cut off the supply to Stalin through Persia, and of Chiang Kai Shek through India. Well why not, replies the Navy; with the prospect of the Mediterranean falling to the Allies, the enemy could begin pouring fleets through the Suez Canal. The IJN must therefore cut off supplies to General Montgomery in Egypt and plug the Red Sea against aggression into the Indian Ocean. So, Socotra it must be.

In Admiral Somerville's flagship, the newly arrived and optimistically named *Victorious* (in replacement of the damaged *Indomitable*), there is much anxiety. The IJN has carried out one of its periodic code changes; Allied intelligence is blind for a time. Somerville is chosen by the Admiralty to lead the North African landings, following C-in-C Mediterranean, Admiral Cunningham, being seconded to Washington as British Naval Representative. It is time for Admiral Halsey to take command of the Eastern Fleet, or United Fleet as it is now called. The Joint Chiefs of Staff of the Allies have ordained that command of the United Fleet must rotate between the two allies.

Halsey can again survey from his bridge a force of three American carriers, the *Enterprise*, *Saratoga* and *Hornet*, and three British carriers, the *Victorious*, *Formidable* and *Illustrious*. They won't be his to command for much longer, as most if not all will be due for transfer to the Atlantic as cover for the North African landings, a risky enterprise for the Allies and therefore in need of overwhelming seaborne air power. Convoys to Suez can be discontinued for a while until objectives are seized and secured in North Africa, after which the United Fleet can come traipsing back, except by that time Lord Somerville may come back with them.

Nursing his medal in consolation, Halsey will have to crawl into the back seat again and defer to His Lordship.

Halsey badly needs a battle; just weeks are left before the fleet's return to the Atlantic.

One keen to oblige 'Bull' Halsey is Admiral Ozawa, a keen student of the American and British temperaments and of the track record of his opposite numbers. He will play toreador to the bull, he explains to his staff officers. His carriers will seek to exploit the longer range of their aircraft models by loitering far back from an advancing skirmish line of battleships, heavy cruisers and seaplane carriers. The forty to fifty float planes from the latter will reconnoitre – this five times the scouting disposition at the Battle of the Seychelles. The outer screen of big surface ships will be the cloak to wave at the 'Bull'. It will draw the Allies in, and they will waste much of their effort attacking the cloak elements and not the more distant toreador, if indeed the latter proves to be within range. To be more sure of tempting Halsey's fliers into attacking the advance guard, a staff officer interposes a suggestion; why not sacrifice a couple of light fleet carriers as additionally attractive bait? If any attackers penetrate this skirmish line, they will be reported by it to combat air patrol command, which will vector out fighters from the carrier groups for early interception. *Sake* is then called for, and toasts are drunk in anticipation of a glorious victory: '*Banzai, Banzai!*' they yell.

The defeat off the Seychelles has shaken Yamamoto to the soles of his boots. He commends Genda as Ozawa's air commander, hoping that between the two of them they can absorb the lessons of the battle and rethink carrier tactics. The plan being toasted is theirs. Morale is sky high. 'No more Nagumo', the airmen exult, for now the *Kido Butai* has a real carrier admiral, Ozawa. 'And welcome back Genda!'

This time, surprise is achieved thanks to a precautionary naval code change by the IJN following the Battle of the Seychelles. An army brigade is duly popped ashore at Socotra. Ozawa can now afford to stand off the island and await the counterattack unencumbered with calls for shore-side air support. Socotra is only lightly manned, victory at the Battle of the Seychelles having lulled the Allies into believing they have headed off an 'Orient' strategy. Ozawa moves forward, he moves back; his long feelers in the form of the forty or fifty Jake float planes catapulted off the seaplane carriers, battleships and cruisers of his advance guard all the time reaching out for the advancing prey.

Halsey has only one idea, archetypically of Halsey, and that is to tangle with the Japanese enemy. His partner, Admiral Vian, leading the Royal Navy carriers, is no objector. He is imbued with the tradition that the British fight whatever the odds, and fight to the death. The magic word for the Royal Navy was 'Coronel'. At the Battle of Coronel off the South American Pacific coast in November 1914, a very inferior squadron of British cruisers met a superior squadron of German cruisers and lost. Royal Navy tradition required a fight, even if against the odds, on the basis that any damage done to the raiding enemy could require retreat to the homeland for repairs or such a reduction in speed as to enable him to be caught by pursuers – anything to belay the impact of these raiders on the high seas. At Coronel, the victor was Admiral Graf von Spee. The pocket battleship named in his memory was in the opening months of the Second World War confronted by a Royal Navy cruiser force. In the resulting engagement, the *Graf Spee* was damaged enough to be forced to retreat to the neutral port of Montevideo, where its skipper scuttled his ship and then shot himself. The cruiser force, with a mix of pluck and guile, had put paid to the pocket battleship.

Sir Phillip Vian himself is a congenial companion for Halsey. He joins the fleet with a redoubtable reputation as a courageous naval antagonist, whose actions, particularly in the Mediterranean, epitomized this revered Royal Navy tradition. Once, with only a handful of light cruisers and destroyers, he held off an Italian force of a battleship, heavy cruisers and lighter ships, thereby allowing a Malta convoy to escape its clutches. In the halls of Etajima, the doctrine of engaging with the enemy on sight was hammered into the minds of its Japanese naval college students by the college's early British instructors.

Halsey has no plan in particular, just to sail for Socotra and fight. He has arranged for each of his three American carriers to exchange its torpedo bomber squadron for a third squadron of dive bombers, and there are extra fighters on board as all now have retractable wings. Vian has raised the strength of his radar-equipped night-attack torpedo bombers. They are now entirely the new and fast American Avengers. He also now carries more fighters, thanks to retractable wings and some adroit deck parking. The idea is that by day, Halsey leads the attack and Vian conducts the defence; by night, Vian continues with the attacks. There is confidence that they will be encountering an equal or lesser force.

Dawn searches by scouting planes sight each other's fleets early in the morning. A pair of Dauntless dive bomber scouts from the *Enterprise* plant bombs on the light carrier *Zuiho*'s fantail, which puts it out of action but able to retire home. Its air group is already aloft before the bomb hits, and its Kates are part of the search detail. Its fighters tear apart most of what constitutes the *Enterprise*'s strike. The stronger *Saratoga* group fails to locate the Japanese carriers, expending its efforts on the advanced force screen. Only the dive bombers from the *Hornet* wing their way through. They are heavily eroded in number, first by over-the-horizon fighter interceptions vectored in by float plane pickets, next by close-in combat air patrol.

The Japanese have learned much since the Seychelles about the importance of a well-directed defence. The seaplane carrier *Chitose* is allotted the mission of ringing the fleet with a far-flung picket line of seaplane scouts to warn of incoming attacks. As a result, damage is limited. The *Ryukaku* is hit by bombs but hightails for home, its engines unaffected and with fires eventually under control. Its sister the *Chukaku* is able to dodge into a rain squall and thereby evade attack.

The remarkable attack on the *Zuiho* in the very early hours of battle, however, has badly rattled Ozawa. Whereas the first deck loads have left his carriers to attack the American fleet, still on board fully fuelled and armed is his second strike – a shipboard combustion nightmare if any carrier is struck, as happened off the Seychelles. The *Zuiho* is lucky in that regard, its air group dispatched early. He orders his dive-bomber group and fighters up and away. This leaves the unready torpedo bomber squadron separated from the dive bombers, such that there is no prospect of a co-ordinated attack – as was the IJN specialty. This saves the British carriers, as the first strike is ordered to go for the American carriers with their wooden decks and greater number of aircraft. The second strike can then deal with the British carriers' armoured decks. Torpedoes from the killer Kates will finish them off, providing the dive bombers split the defence for enough torpedo bombers to reach good launch positions. In the event, these second-wave Kates fatefully coming into battle alone are massacred by Wildcat fighters.

The first wave strike is highly successful, however. The *Hornet* is overwhelmed in a brilliantly co-ordinated attack, and is abandoned.

The *Enterprise* escapes any torpedo hits, but falls out of the battle due to bomb hits. It can escape, as can the heavily damaged *Saratoga*, loyally protected by a vigorous radar-directed fighter defence from the British carriers. The latter are badly knocked about, but not being torpedoed and their armoured decks not penetrated by bombs, they can escape likewise, except there can be no hanging about until dark to execute the intended radar-guided night torpedo strike. It is time to flee.

There is no vigorous pursuit from Ozawa, who has the invasion fleet to defend behind him and his destroyers are down on fuel. In any case, overly optimistic reports from his fliers leave his staff convinced that all or most of the enemy major units have been sunk or scuttled in the retreat. There is much celebration, and back at home propaganda broadcasts proclaim 'The Day of the Eagles'.

In the aftermath, Halsey bows out for temporary health reasons and Sir Philip Vian – now Lord Vian of Socotra – assumes command. There is an urgent public relations twist to the award of Vian's honour, it being due to unrest in India – there is a need to proclaim victory. After all, only one Allied carrier is actually lost and three or four Japanese carriers are claimed as now being out of the order of battle. This was one way of looking at the rebuff. Vian's able handling of the British carriers, comparing well to Somerville's at the Seychelles, thereby acts as another consideration on the part of His Majesty's Honours Board.

In the aftermath of the battle, there is an unexpected reprise that heaps more glory on Vian. Unknown to the Japanese, there is an Allied army division at Aden ready to hop across to Socotra and supplant the rather weak Japanese force. A spy in Ceylon reports that Ozawa's fleet is now back there. Vian seizes this opportunity to use the more intact carriers to provide air cover for landing most of the division. Destroyers shuttle back and forth, bringing in the rest of it. Meanwhile, the damaged carriers are patched up in Simonstown and then sent back home to be repaired before Operation Torch, the landings in North Africa.

Vian follows a month later with the rest of the carriers. The Allies will not benefit from all the carriers they had hoped for in covering the North African landings, but more than they were in reality able to deploy, such that an extension of the landings eastwards into Tunisia gains more support from the planners.

In reality it was a great regret on the part of the Allies in not having pre-empted the Nazis moving into Tunis. The invasion of Sicily might then have followed far earlier than it did, and the landings in Italy made north of Rome instead of south of Naples, thanks to overwhelming carrier air support.

Yamamoto unknowingly has the Indian Ocean to himself, but Ozawa needs a month or two to recoup. Plane and pilot losses have been extremely heavy. One carrier division is sent off to Japan to train. Yamamoto ponders whether the Allied carriers are now back in the Atlantic and might soon be on their way to the Pacific. He wonders how advanced the US is with its new carriers and when the IJN can expect to confront them. How bold of them to 'do a United Fleet on him'; whereas one thought America had a 'two-ocean' naval problem, now Japan has one' Forget this 'Orient' thing of the Indian Ocean, the other two divisions are instead sent to Truk. And so the spider crawls back into the centre of Willard Price's *Islands of Mystery* that we visited in Chapter 5.

* * *

Readers familiar with the Pacific War will have recognized that our Battle of the Seychelles is inspired mainly by the Battle of Midway, albeit with reminders of the carrier battles of the Coral Sea and Eastern Solomons.

Nor, in its defence, is the Battle of Socotra so fanciful either. The location is transposed, but the actions are based on the Battle of Santa Cruz, which came at the crux of the six-month Guadalcanal campaign in the South-West Pacific.

In plotting a Phantom Scenario and casting the characters and order of battle, the strategic framwork may be entirely different, but the tactical parameters have been made to inhabit familiar ground.

Anyone wanting to be more creative can make a computer game of it! All we are attempting is the thinking man's aircraft carrier book. So the closer we stick to tactical reality the better, and we invent only in salute to strategic differences. That has been our guide.

Middle War Strategy

We will now return to strategy and consider how the two sides might have been most tempted to seek advantages over the other during 1943 and 1944, on the basis that superiority, let alone parity, in carriers would elude the Allies during that time.

For the Allies, there was to be found a convenient comfort in the unanimously agreed 'Germany First' policy, such that the Japanese war could be set aside for later. Consider how in Phantom Scenario, one of the most logical consequences would be the early isolation of Australasia from the war. In reality, the only departure from 'Germany First' had been the South-West Pacific campaign that American Naval Chief of Staff Admiral Ernest J. King foisted on the Allies as being justified by the peril to Australians and New Zealanders. But what the Allies did not know was how the Japanese Army had put its big flat foot down when the IJN asked for enough divisions to secure bases in northern Australia. They would be needed for seizing Vladivostok and securing an advance across the great River Amur to Khabarovsk (that is if Hitler had crossed the Volga, remember?).

An irony is that Australia's virtual line of defence was in effect the Amur, 4,000 or so miles away. But that, reader, is strategy for you.

For the great purpose of 'Germany First', the initial stage had to be securing the Mediterranean and the Atlantic coast of North Africa, followed by driving Italy out of the war. Such was set in motion during late 1942 but not consolidated until September 1943, due to the Allies not having sufficient carrier-borne air support to seize Tunisia in addition to Algeria and Morocco. Consequently, the Allies found themselves first having to defeat Rommel in Tunisia before they could land in Sicily and then Italy. The Allies' United Fleet of attack carriers had been needed for the first phase, and had duly left the Indian Ocean for that purpose. So where does it go next? There are three options beckoning.

The 'Orient' option is to go back to the Indian Ocean, but this time being able to use the shortcut of the Suez Canal. On the down side of that option is that the passage through the Mediterranean would be risky until Italy was out of the war and the Germans out of Crete.

A Pacific option in early 1943 appears premature, given that the second tranche of four improved Shokaku-class carriers, along with more of the Unryu-class, are now augmenting the IJN's order of battle (see Phantom Fleet Table 4), and this before the first stage of the Essex Surge is combat ready. Additions to the IJN order of battle will register with US naval intelligence thanks to fresh success at codebreaking. The call signs of the new carriers will begin appearing in the radio traffic, as will those of air groups associated with them and escort groups allotted to the carriers.

Any American lunge from California across the Eastern Pacific to retake Oahu in 1943 looks too risky. On the other hand, there are limited options available for low-risk hit-and-run raids, such as Admiral Nimitz actually directed early in the war, and for seizing or taking back outlying bases – Dutch Harbor in the Aleutians being a good Phantom Scenario example (or an atoll in the Maldives off southern India as an 'Orient' example). The risk of encountering the whole of Ozawa's fleet looks unlikely, and, if confronted with only part of it, then opportunity beckons for another victory such as that off the Seychelles. Either way, things do not look promising for 1943 Pacific initiatives.

Hence the third 1943 option, which is the one we adopt for the Phantom Scenario. That is for the United Fleet to stay put at Gibraltar and help advance the war in Europe, meaning that more resources can be supplied to the Japanese war faster but slightly later via the Suez Canal. The swifter the progress against Hitler and Mussolini, the more the press and public may for the time being take their mind off Tojo. And progress in the Mediterranean could have been very fast. The great Allied carrier fleet could have supplied the muscle to deliver Italy much earlier. It would not be needed for D-Day because Normandy was within England-based fighter and bomber range. But there was one good deed it could do before sailing off to Panama and into the Pacific. That would be making quite sure the German battleship *Tirpitz*, in its well-defended Norwegian fjord, would never sail again. To do that would enable the Allies to release all fleet carriers to the Pacific.

And so here we go again, the Allies inflicting a 'two-ocean' war on Japan by using a growing 'two-ocean' navy. In the short term, exploiting the 'Brit factor' is a way of closing disparity in carrier numbers, first in the Mediterranean using an impenetrable umbrella of air protection. A United Fleet enables a 'two-ocean' war.

And so it is that we find the United Fleet on the west coast of America ready to roll towards Tokyo in 1944. Well, not quite; the respective orders of battle are not yet propitious for that. It is still wise to exploit the 'two-ocean' factor in order to keep Tojo off-balance, and Yamamoto wondering how many task forces are facing him from both directions without realizing that the United Fleet is conceived as a single force that moves together wholly, or at least once the objective is Hawaii or Ceylon. Until ready for that, it can feint in both directions and confuse the enemy.

First we have them feint toward Hawaii, but instead take back Dutch Harbor in Alaska. Then comes the really sneaky thing. It is to avoid those canals altogether, because presumably they are watched by spies: a monocled Nazi padding around under a smelly kaftan can be imagined in the case of Suez, and we fancy some Argentine or Peruvian Japanese emigrant operating a tacky Chinese laundry or custom tailor business in Panama City.

To elude these snoops, we shift the Pacific Fleet's carriers around the Cape of Good Hope, passing by Simonstown in favour of a well-prepared atoll in the Indian Ocean, the only observers being a handful of natives speaking no known language. Together with any carriers already there, the United Fleet storms across to Ceylon in June 1944, covering an invasion fleet with three divisions aboard and using the landing craft historically used for Saipan at that time, and with massive land-based air support from southern India, from whence the transports can sail. Ceylon beckons as so much the easier feat than Hawaii, because land-based air support from India can be applied.

What other reasons are there to take back Ceylon before Hawaii? There are found by the Allied planners sound strategic reasons for invading Ceylon before Hawaii. For Nimitz, as commander of Pacific Fleet, needs to encourage the IJN into shifting its centre of gravity to a more central position the better to act in both directions, and thereby encourage it to divide, with one half in Truk and the other at Singapore, for example. This will aid the invading of Hawaii in late 1944 or early 1945. Nimitz will be aware that the Japanese are in a precarious position out there, two-thirds of the way across the Pacific. Even Truk is 3,034 nautical miles away from Hawaii. At 2,135 miles away from Pearl Harbor, Kwajalein is closer, but it is more of a perimeter base or advanced jumping-off point for Hawaii. Saipan is no closer at 3,224miles, and Tokyo slightly further at 3,355 miles. To mount a counter-attack, Ozawa would have to sail from one of those three points – Japan, Saipan or Truk – unless given warning, in which case advancing to Kwajalein from Truk or Saipan is the obvious first move. That would be Truk in practice, as the Marianas lack sizeable anchorages.

Why not base the Japanese carriers at Pearl Harbor? That is hardly likely after what transpired on 7 December 1941, it being exposed to attack from the north, and indeed from the east.

In contrast, Truk was ideal as a naval base because of the protective web of air and seaplane bases surrounding it. Counter-clockwise from east to west, Lae, Rabaul, Kavieng, Nauru, Tarawa, Mili, Kwajalein, Eniwetok, Wake, Saipan, Yap and Palau ringed the IJN's spider in its web. Even in the middle of the *Nanyo* there were bases such as Jaluit, Ponape and Kusaie. The US had first to break that ring before risking an assault on Truk. On the other hand, once that ring was broken, the spider perforce must flee from its web.

In reality, it did so soon after 4 February 1944, when a Liberator flew the 850 miles from Torokina, a base in the Solomon Islands. This was thanks to how the US had been climbing the 'Solomons Ladder' since the Guadalcanal landings in August 1942. By November 1943, Marines had their boots firmly rooted on Bougainville, and a month or two later its Torokina airstrip had been extended enough for four-engined bombers, thereby enabling the first snoop into Truk lagoon. In the meantime, Kwajalein in the Marshall Islands had fallen, and Eniwetok was shortly to follow. 'Seabee' construction crews would soon ready Kwajalein for bombers to reach Truk. It was time for the fleet to move west to Palau, as we saw in Chapter 4.

Progress in reality, however, had been made easy in the Central Pacific due to the struggle for the Solomons and siege of Rabaul shredding Japanese naval aviation. In the Phantom context, breaking the Truk ring could have proven a very tough nut to crack, particularly with an equal or superior carrier fleet at its centre and IJN land-based naval aviation more or less intact.

In any case, Hawaii first had to be won back.

We are now at the end of 1944. We propose that the invasion of Hawaii goes unchallenged by the IJN. It has no protective islands to act as sentinels on its northern and eastern sides. Its eventual return is foreseen anyway, as a trade-off for a Japanese sphere of influence in the Western Pacific. Holding it is seen as having delayed an American comeback, which eventually has to happen.

As explained earlier, Nimitz will need Pearl Harbor back as his springboard for any advance on Japan by the direct route across the Central Pacific. With Hawaii re-won, his first objectives will be Kwajalein and Eniwetok, both atolls being large enough to shelter fleets and to act as forward supply bases. The problem with Kwajalein for Nimitz is its proximity to Truk. From his central base, Ozawa can issue forth in counter-attack and bring on a great carrier battle while he still has overwhelming superiority in carrier numbers and a well-hoarded land-based supply of Betty medium bombers skilled in night torpedo attack. What is needed is a diversion that sends all the IJN carriers, or at least some of them, elsewhere on a wild goose chase.

In reality, progress had been made easy for Nimitz in the Central Pacific due to the struggle for the Solomons and siege of Rabaul decimating Japanese naval aviation of all kinds. But in Phantom Scenario, there is always the brutal factor of Japanese carrier superiority and the ongoing retention of veteran air groups, both carrier-borne and land-based. The only two useful palliatives are codebreaking and plucking from the pack that ever-ready joker card, the 'two-ocean' gambit. As in reality, Truk will certainly be bypassed in favour of a decisive leap to Saipan. But there is some ready way of moving the game on more quickly.

If in Phantom Scenario we invent Japanese carriers that never existed, in reaction it is surely only fair to allow an American response – such as greater Essex-class construction than actually happened? We demur on two counts. First, the shock of Pearl Harbor led to orders for all the carriers for which there were suitable yards. Secondly, the further shock of learning a year or two later of a follow-on quartet of Shokaku-class and in addition more medium carriers would have come a bit late for new orders if these extra Essex carriers were to be combat-ready by 1945.

On the other hand, we should not forget the humble 'jeep carriers' being produced by the score, such as the sixteen escort carriers that played such an unexpected and heroic role at the Battle of Leyte Gulf, as we encountered in Chapter 4. As the Battle of the Atlantic played itself out, and Hitler hunkered down in his Berlin bunker, finding themselves Pacific-bound would be many more escort carriers. We therefore add two more task force groups of eighteen each for a grand combat total of fifty-four escort carriers. Additionally, another one is broken up to supply plane ferries and to escort supply echelons and other support services.

Three years after the Seychelles, the United Fleet has caught up. It's finally a match for the enemy. In Phantom Scenario, the Pacific War can be won just before close of 1945; but will it? The game begins.

We have set the scene in other chapters (and earlier in this one) for the circumstances under which to anticipate a final denouement to the war in the Pacific. Readers will be reminded how it will be necessary in order to drop an atom bomb on Japan to first have possession of the Marianas Islands, and secondly to have extended existing runways or have built new ones long enough to fly off heavily laden four-engine B-29 Superfortress bombers. At 1,284 miles, there is no point nearer on the Central Pacific route to Tokyo. The alternative jump-off points for nuclear bombers were unthinkable. Who in their right minds would let the Soviets anywhere near this super-secret technology, and who would want to rely on flaky Chinese Nationalists?

The Marianas stood in the way of the Allies reaching China. So they had to be taken simply in order to get to China. But once the Marianas were in the bag, why get involved in a continental land war just in order to be able to nuke Japan, when it could be done at a trifling comparative cost from those self-same islands?

It did not need Tojo to know about the atom bomb for the Japanese to realize that the game was up once the Marianas were lost to them. They knew the range of the Superfortress, and thus they knew their cities could expect to be incinerated. Indeed, the firebombing of Tokyo by massed bombers caused as many casualties as either atom bomb. In reality, to oppose the initial landings in the Marianas on the island of Saipan, the entire Japanese fleet was committed to battle for the first time since 1942. Additionally, there was a land-based air fleet on which overly optimistic hopes had been set. Between the two of them, they expected to chew the US fleet to pieces and win revenge for Midway. It did not work out that way because there were not enough carriers, most of the aircraft models were obsolete and the pilots were grossly undertrained and inexperienced.

Let us next set the scene for a final naval–air battle to end all naval battles.

'Essex-Surge'

<u>*Essex*-class fleet carriers (CVs)</u>. While ordered in 1941 work went on around the clock after Pearl Harbor. The first group of eight (below) became combat operational at the decisive Battle of the Philippine Sea in the early summer of 1944, less two in repair. The next pair were combat-ready in time to participate in the Battle of Leyte Gulf in late October. The successive quartet became active in 1945 and therefore available for our 'mother of all carrier battles' in September 1945 (See Chapter 7). The final trio might also have made it into the US order of battle there given urgency and supreme effort. Against that, deduct battle losses earlier against largely land-based air while the IJN carrier fleet remained uncommitted.

Carrier Name (Navy Number)	Shipyard	Commissioned
ESSEX (CV-9)	Newport News Shipbuilding, Virginia	Dec 1942
LEXINGTON (CV-16)*	Fore River Shipyard, Massachusetts	Feb 1943
YORKTOWN (CV-10)*	Newport News Shipbuilding, Virginia	Apr 1943
BUNKER HILL (CV-17)	Fore River Shipyard, Massachusetts	May 1943
INTREPID (CV-11)	Newport News Shipbuilding, Virginia	Aug 1943
HORNET (CV-12)*	Newport News Shipbuilding, Virginia	Nov 1943
WASP (CV-18)*	Fore River Shipyard, Massachussetts	Nov 1943
FRANKLIN (CV-13)	Newport News Shipbuilding, Virginia	Jan 1944
HANCOCK (CV-19)	Fore River Shipyard, Massachusetts	Apr 1944
TICONDEROGA (CV-14)	Newport News Shipbuilding, Virginia	May 1944
BENNINGTON (CV-20	Brooklyn Navy Yard, New York	Aug 1944
SHANGRI LA (CV 38)	Norfolk Navy Yard, Virginia	Sep 1944
RANDOLPH (CV-15)	Newport News Shipbuilding, Virginia	Oct 1944
BONHOMME RICHARD (CV-31)	Brooklyn Navy Yard, New York	Nov 1944
ANTIETAM (CV-36)	Philadelphia Navy Yard, Pennsylvania	Jan 1945
BOXER (CV-21)	Newport News Shipbuilding, Virginia	April 1945
LAKE CHAMPLAIN (CV-39)	Norfolk Navy Yard, Virginia	Jun 1945

Independence-class light fleet carriers (CVLs) were allotted carrier numbers 22-30. They were to number nine. All were laid down, launched and commissioned evenly over the course of the year 1943 and all from the same shipyard, New York Shipbuilding, Camden, New Jersey. They joined the Pacific Fleet at a rate of close to one a month, thanks to being converted from cruiser hulls on the stocks, or a lot faster than new-build Essex-class. They could operate 33 aircraft compared to near 90 for the big carriers. In order of commissioning the light fleets were Independence, Princeton, Belleau Wood, Cowpens, Monterey, Langley, Cabot, Bataan, San Jacinto. All but the first fought in the Marianas at the Battle of the Philippine Sea.

* US carriers were named after either victories of the past such as Saratoga, Lexington, Yorktown or Ticonderoga, or famous ships of the past such as Hornet, Wasp, Bonhomme Richard, or Cabot. CV-16 had been allotted the latter name when news came of the sinking of the Lexington at Coral Sea. The name was changed accordingly to Lexington. The Cabot name became that of a light fleet carrier instead. The practice continued after Yorktown, Wasp and Hornet were sunk during 1942. The Japanese were left wondering what they had sunk or had not!

Further Essex-class were completed following the Pacific War. After 1943 light fleet carrier production ceased with the exception of two Wright-class vessels only to be completed after the end of the war. Light fleets were, as said, only a stopgap measure due to the time taken to build an Essex-class large fleet carrier. Their cruiser hulls and engines enabled them to work at fleet carrier speed.

Chapter 7

The Mother of All Carrier Battles

'The world has a way of undermining complex plans. This is particularly true in fast moving environments [which] can evolve more quickly than a complex plan can be adapted to it. By the time you have adapted, the target has changed.'
(General Carl von Clausewitz, *On the Theory of War*)

L et us then set the scene for a Phantom version of the Battle of the Philippine Sea, or rather the Battle of the Marianas Islands because, as we shall see, the action is unlikely to be limited to that body of water to the west alone. It is set at the earliest a year later, but only possible even then thanks to the infusion of massed escort carriers following the war in Europe.

Selected for the initial landing, as in 1944, is Saipan, thence, once more or less secured, further landings to follow on the adjacent Tinian and Guam to the south.

There are three directions from which the Allies can expect a Japanese response. One, obviously, is from the *Nanyo* to the south-east, although by the stage Nimitz is ready to invade the Marianas, Truk is no longer a safe anchorage for the Japanese carrier fleet. On the other hand, the *Nanyo*'s island bases are 'unsinkable aircraft carriers', such that the land-based air fleet could be vectored in from Palau, Yap and Truk, and in particular those squadrons of long-ranged two-engine Betty bombers trained in night torpedo tactics.

Further air attack can be expected from air groups staged in from Japan to jump-off points on the island bases of Chichi Jima and Iwo Jima. There could well also be a carrier fleet attack or diversion from this northern quarter.

As Admiral Nimitz and his staff peer at the charts and measure distances, it seems that the most likely axis for an IJN attack will be from the Philippines, either around the huge archipelago north or south or using a couple of straits through the islands. There is codebreaking intelligence that the IJN is split between its home waters and an obscure location fringing the Celebes Sea called Tawi Tawi – a position straddling the gap between the land masses of Borneo to the west and the Philippine Mindanao to the east.

This indeed had been the actual case in 1944. The reason for selecting the Tawi Tawi anchorage was to bring the Japanese carrier fleet closer to its oil sources, due to US submarines sinking so many tankers and navy oilers. In Phantom Scenario, that factor comes into play once Hawaii and Midway are regained by the US, so the US submarine fleet can move forward. We posit that the oil problem in 1945 Phantom time is not as severe as it actually was in 1944, but nonetheless a growing worry. The IJN carrier fleet is therefore found split. The older part is quartered at Tawi Tawi with the gas-guzzling converted battleships and heavy cruisers. The newer carriers are in home waters, where they can better train their air groups.

As victor of the Battle of Socotra – the much-applauded 'Day of the Eagles' in Japanese media lore – Ozawa can choose his options. For the commander of Japanese carriers, there seem to be two choices.

One is what he performed in historical actuality, which we will briefly narrate (using the past tense, as is our mode for reality). Adopted for the June 1944 Battle of the Philippine Sea was a strategy that eschewed the traditional Japanese gambit of dispersed forces, feints, diversions and 'end runs' (in American football terminology an 'end run' is an outflanking move). Instead, all forces met together at a rendezvous point in the Philippine Sea to fight as a single body, the better to exploit the far longer range of Japanese carrier aircraft over their American equivalents.

Ozawa had reckoned that the cautious Spruance would prioritize his mission, which was first and foremost to protect the Saipan invasion fleet; he would therefore resist the temptation to lunge out into the Philippine Sea to engage Japanese aircraft carriers, for fear of a secondary force making an outflanking move and whacking the transports and supply train. Ozawa's range advantage was further enhanced by the availability of Marianas air bases, whereat the carrier planes could refuel and rearm in order to make a second strike at the American carriers on their return flights. He could also expect to have the lee gauge, thanks to the prevailing trade wind being in his favour. Thereby he could launch strikes into the wind and at the same time keep on course towards the enemy, whereas Spruance, once in pursuit, would find himself speeding backwards to launch strikes, handicapping his chances of closing the range with the Japanese fleet.

Ozawa also had what he wrongly perceived to be his chief advantage: land-based air forces compensating his numerical disadvantage. The First Air Fleet under Admiral Kakuji Kakuta was a huge naval land-based air force distributed through the war zone. More of this anon, but for now it is sufficient to explain that Ozawa was counting on its raids whittling down the strength of the US fleet.

In reality in June 1944, all these advantages became a wasted hope due to the abysmal quality of the IJN aircrews – almost all ill-trained replacements – added to which the aircraft models were mostly now out of date and suffered from the congenital Japanese obsession with sacrificing protection for greater range.

Moreover, Spruance's fleet was superbly equipped with on-board radar-savvy combat command centres, the precursors of the computer room warfare of today. Perceiving it to be rash to attack, Spruance's air commander, Admiral Mitscher, in tactical command of the American carriers, was obliged by Spruance to husband his fighters in defence. The result was 'The Great Marianas Turkey Shoot', as the battle went down in history. No US carrier was hit and the vast majority of Japanese attackers were shot down.

Now that Ozawa's sting had been drawn, only next day did Spruance surge out into the Philippine Sea and unleash his carriers in pursuit of the Japanese fleet. The result was only a limited success, due to the strike being dispatched so late in the day that the planes had to return in the dark, occasioning severe losses from so many crews having to ditch in the sea, albeit most were rescued. The decisiveness of the battle owed more to the work of the fighters in defending the fleet and to the submarines *Albacore* and *Cavalla* sinking the Japanese flagship *Taiho* and Pearl Harbor veteran *Shokaku*.

It had been the first confrontation between the rival sides' carriers in twenty months, and there was much frustration in many American quarters with the cautiousness of Spruance. There were those who longed for the return of 'Bull' Halsey, not least his fans in the press.

Halsey did indeed return to command the fast fleet carriers, but this only due to a rotation system. Nimitz had one admiral and his staff participating in current war plans and then executing them as the Third Fleet (Halsey), while the other admiral and his staff helped plan the future moves in the Pacific War in preparation for performing those as the Fifth Fleet (Spruance). The Japanese were aware of this alternating fleet number/fleet commander rotation, and it was said to influence their plans. Be that as it may, their next plan for winning 'decisive battle' reverted to dispersion, feints and 'end runs' – an entirely apt strategy for confronting 'Bull' Halsey, as it so happened, when as Operation Sho it was put to the test against the naval idol of America in the great Battle of Leyte Gulf in October 1944.

But before moving on to the Battle of Leyte Gulf, there must be a brief break to allow political ground to intrude because its outcome decided strategy. The Battle of the Philippine Sea secured the capture of bases in the Marianas Islands on the east side of that sea, in order for the Superfortresses to bombard Japanese cities. Despite this strategic necessity having been gained and the Japanese islands having at last come within air range, General MacArthur managed to persuade the president to let him first liberate the Philippines archipelago on the west side of the sea. Nimitz was baulked from bypassing the Philippines and crossing the Philippine Sea to the north, then more decisively severing the jugular between Japan and its resources by invading Okinawa.

Such a move could have been far more effective and much quicker, and at far less cost in American lives. Instead, Okinawa came nine months later and at terrible additional cost. The Japanese had made good use of those months in fortifying the island. Only from Okinawa could an actual invasion of Japan be launched and initially sustained. So why this aberration and the diversion to the Philippine archipelago? Why was that not leapfrogged?

The explanation is that it was an election year. General MacArthur was a political general. He dazzled the mighty, including Winston Churchill. At his behest were more newspapers than the Pope had cardinals. In contrast, Nimitz belonged to the 'Silent Service'; he was a naval gentleman. He was the man who bit his tongue rather than risk rupture with the Army over their absurd claim that Army fliers had sunk all the Japanese carriers at Midway when all four had in truth been torched by dive bombers flying off his Navy carriers.

When President Roosevelt invited the two of them to meet him at Pearl Harbor, it was Nimitz's naïve expectation that MacArthur would conduct himself like a gentleman and as a good strategist. Instead, Big Mac flew in from the South Pacific like a hero out of Hollywood, playing tall and acting loyal to his growing legend. Everyone was gobsmacked, including an indulgent Roosevelt. Who could refuse this big man in his iconic leather flying jacket, puffing on his famous corn cob pipe, this great American hero? How dare anyone let down his poor Filipinos? Let 'Dug-Out Doug' fulfil that now-famous vow of his upon leaving the beleaguered Philippines back in 1942: 'I shall return!' And so the general did, becoming the American Caesar, and soon to be the shogun of Japan.

He waded ashore at Leyte with his retinue of staff officers, Filipino politicians and media cronies. No doubt the pictures were distributed before the sun had set.

This landing right in the middle of the Philippines had been anticipated by Japanese intelligence, and a plan was ready. It called for the entire Imperial Japanese Navy to disrupt the landings. It was a case of 'banzai or bust', as the Allied move threatened to cut off the IJN from its oil supplies and thus render the fleet redundant. In the wake of the Battle of the Philippine Sea, however, the carrier force was a spent entity. It was stationed in home waters the better to train new air groups, but these were far from ready. Consequently, the ploy became to use the carriers as decoys to lure Halsey – now back in the fast carrier driving seat – into the Philippine Sea in pursuit, while the battleships and cruisers, stationed near Singapore to be close to oil supplies, executed a pincer movement from the south using the two straits that intersect the archipelago, thereby entrapping the American invasion fleet inside Leyte Gulf.

The plan worked in essence, but not in timing. American reconnaissance failed to spot Ozawa's carriers early enough in the game, thereby exposing Admiral Kurita's Centre Force to heavy air attack from Halsey's carrier groups. The resulting delays upset co-ordination with the Southern Force. Convinced he had kyboshed Kurita, Halsey hared off overnight after Ozawa's carriers. The San Bernardino Strait was thus left unwatched, even by a single destroyer. Halsey had scooted off to engorge the bait. Kurita gratefully slipped through the open door.

The anti-climax that was the strange outcome was covered in Chapter 4.

* * *

So much for what actually transpired. But how might fare a more evenly matched contest a year or so later? What would be the Phantom Scenario denouement?

The reader may well anticipate that the IJN will face a choice between a full-force straight punch, as Ozawa delivered at the Battle of the Philippine Sea, and a dispersal strategy, as practised at the Battle of Leyte Gulf. As for the US Navy acting in the defensive role to protect the landings on Saipan, the Japanese reaction will surely depend on which American admiral is on watch. In the timeframe we are considering – late summer 1945 – in reality that was a Halsey period in command.

In contrast, we can serve a Spruance scenario if that is the preference, but what about its predictability? It's the 'Wagram' option, if one was offered the Napoleonic choice between a Wagram and an Austerlitz; the eponymous Clausewitzian bloodbath of a victory by attrition versus a victory won by superb manoeuvring. Given the circumstances of the Phantom Scenario, the great contest will wear much of the apparel of the 'Turkey Shoot', but with important differences that will make it less decisive. There will be important carrier losses on the American side, for one example. As another, the IJN carrier fleet will remain in being.

So it is that in Phantom time, it is with Halsey that we gallantly sail into the Battle of the Philippine Sea in early August 1945, leaving Spruance at Pearl Harbor with Nimitz to plan the next round of conquest in the race to Japan.

We continue now in the Phantom Scenario's present tense for our grand climax to the Pacific War.

The Japanese Muster

At the Navy Ministry in Tokyo, they gather in front of the charts. They all concur how of course the Allies will bypass Truk and move on to the Marianas; the war has become a Central Pacific game, after all. They agree that the Allies have no closer springboard for long-distance bombing of Japan. To the south, there is no threat from Australia and the South Pacific.

The IJN will have two-and-a-half years to fortify the Marianas. The carriers must be preserved until the islands are invaded, for everything depends upon the outcome of the naval battle – it's a second Tsushima or bust!

If America and its allies are to be thwarted, an equivalent 'battle of annihilation' is what will win the war. The need is to refight Tsushima at Saipan, but with Navy eagles rather than Navy guns.

On the war games table, they play the scenarios. There are those who favour the straight punch, others who prefer feint and dispersion. Genda then speaks out and proposes 'envelopment'. 'Envelopment', they cry, 'what is this?'

Genda explains that it is to surround the Yankees from three or four sides and thus make victory decisive. It is that or their nation dies. The odds are against them in a long war; the elders of the Japanese Navy were always correct on that. The nation needs an annihilating naval victory.

Genda's plan particularly focuses on the southern and eastern approaches to Saipan. In reality, these were covered by long-range Liberator reconnaissance planes from bases captured by MacArthur's forces during the Rabaul and New Guinea campaign, in particular the island of Manus. Such reconnaissance could be projected as far as Palau and Yap. But with the MacArthur factor ruled out, the IJN has a reconnaissance-free approach zone to the Marianas from the south – this a special advantage in the Phantom Scenario. Big ocean spaces are needed in which to deploy, thereby reducing the risk of US submarine patrols spotting fleet approaches. That all invites the main thrust to come from the south. Thence the veteran carrier divisions bearing the elite of carrier-borne air crews will sneak up on Saipan from the south-west, sheltered by land-based air cover on Palau and Yap. As this approach promises the best chance of surprise, two other approaches to Saipan are considered as diversions and feints, in order to draw off American opposition to the north-east and to the west. The objective of Southern Force is to smash the invasion fleet and its supply train after Halsey's carriers have mostly sped off in pursuit of other IJN carriers making their presence felt earlier in the west and the north-east.

This envelopment strategy can hopefully aspire to a Tsushima scale of victory. Genda argues that nothing less can thwart the will of America. He wins the argument.

In command of Southern Force is Ozawa with all eight of the large fleet carriers in four attack divisions, each with two large and one medium fleet carrier. The aircrews are trained in night operations and have radar. Ozawa's aerial forces are some 800 strong. There is a preponderance of bombers on the big attack carriers, and of fighters and scouts on the medium carriers. All carriers and their escorts are capable of 34 knots or better. Escorting forces are light because Ozawa will strike from afar, exploiting the far greater range of his aircraft compared to the American carrier planes. Should he nonetheless be engaged in fending off strikes, he can rely on the high speed and manoeuvrability of his carriers.

Based in Formosa is Western Force, comprising more expendable vessels. These include all eight light fleet carriers, a mere two medium carriers and no large carriers. The surprise element is five battleships that have been in part converted into carriers. That amounts to fifteen flight decks in all, to which can be added two of the IJN's seaplane carriers. Genda's idea is to give the illusion that Western Force is the main body. After much debate, it is decided to include all the heavy cruisers as further signature to that. He begs Yamamoto himself to lead Western Force. Yamamoto runs up his flag on the *Nagato*, his battleship flagship from Pearl Harbor days. He will have three roles.

The first is to project saturation reconnaissance over the American fleet, in which task he will be able to deploy the fifty float planes of the heavy cruisers and a further forty on the pair of seaplane carriers. At all times he will need to know exactly where Halsey's carrier groups are, both for his own purposes but also on behalf of the forces of Kakuta, Ozawa and Genda.

Secondly, he will tempt Halsey away from Saipan by lingering far out in the Philippine Sea. The approach will take the central route through the Philippines by passing through the narrow San Bernardino Strait, in the expectation that the force will be spotted by US submarines as it debouches into the said sea. Western Force fields 530 aircraft in all, heavily proportioned in favour of fighters. The carriers will hurl at the US carriers full deck strikes out of the sunset, land on Marianas airstrips and return reloaded for a dawn strike on the way back to their carriers.

Yamamoto's speed will conform to that of five converted battleships. These have had the rear turrets removed and flight decks superimposed on their quarterdecks. The other eight big guns and the pagoda masts remain. Twenty-two bombers can be catapulted off each, the survivors alighting on conventional carriers. Well protected by armour, these 'hermaphrodites' can be expected to absorb a lot of punishment.

As for his light fleet carriers, these are very agile. He hopes the Americans will encounter a hard time in retaliating against his force, not least due to the heavy proportions of fighter aircraft aboard.

Once his main shot has been expended, Yamamoto will break radio silence in order to co-ordinate the movements of the other forces and begin to turn tail; anything to impel Halsey out of his corner and into the centre of the ring.

Thirdly, Yamamoto will use the cover of night and their high speed to hurl the heavy cruisers at the invasion forces in order to occupy the attention of air defences after dawn, when the strikes of Ozawa and Genda will hit Halsey along with the remnants of his own air groups.

Northern Force will be commanded by Genda himself, now promoted to rear admiral. It comprises the newest carriers, all twelve being medium-size Unryu-class grouped in four divisions of three apiece. This fleet is sheltered in home waters. In the Inland Sea, it can train the newer air groups safe from submarine attack. Their air strength is 680, but the quality is nowhere up to the standards of Southern Force. Their speed is also a little less. The newer carriers are mostly powered by pairs of large destroyer engines, due to shortages of cruiser-size engines. Their escorts are a mixed bag.

Genda will feint from the north and then veer eastwards before continuing his advance southwards. This will position him in air range of intersecting the line connecting the American invasion fleet with its bases, both a further temptation for Halsey and a danger to the supply line. Genda will be positioned so that if Halsey tries to cut off his retreat to Japan, Genda and Ozawa can move in on a less-contested Saipan. If Genda does get jumped by Halsey, then his carriers can disperse eastwards in order to perpetuate the threat to the supply line, eventually harbouring at Truk for fresh fuel and shelter. Helping them to reach Truk will be the new Tamano-class fast fleet oilers with replenishment aircraft aboard.

An effect of this strategy might well be that the Americans cream off some escort carrier divisions from Saipan in order to provide air cover to incoming supply convoys, and maybe even a task force or two of fast fleet carriers. Genda is prepared to give his all in the cause of helping Ozawa land the killer blow.

The inveterate fault of dispersal tactics lies in the difficulty of co-ordinating attacks, particularly if radio silence is to be observed. All three carrier forces are therefore given a date and a time when all are to attack in full force, unless redirected by Yamamoto. The contingency is in the event of Halsey playing a cautious Spruance-like defence by hunkering down off Saipan. In the event, though, that he charges north-east or west at Yamamoto or Genda, or indeed at both, then the killer attack on the invasion forces will be primarily that of Ozawa's Southern Force and the land-based squadrons.

A word now about the land-based aerial forces. We posit IJN land-based air fleets at 1,500 aircraft to be distributed as follows: 150 each are quartered at Chichi Jima, the Marianas (Saipan, Guam and Rota), Yap, Palau and Truk; ready to be staged forward to Chichi Jima are 450 at Yokosuka and 300 on Mindanao for staging through Yap. In command is Admiral Kakuji Kakuta, just as in the actual Battle of the Philippine Sea.

Thus, the IJN will have some 3,500 naval aircraft to pit against Admiral Halsey off Saipan. Unlike the actual case of the year before, these planes are mostly new models and the aircrew far better trained. There is also fuel still for everybody thanks to the American submarine offensive being so long delayed, although now started; this having been the fruit from Japan occupying Pearl Harbor and Midway for so long.

Now we turn to assess what Nimitz can muster in defence.

The Allied Armada

We have already awarded three times the number of escort carriers that fought in the actual Battle of Leyte Gulf in late 1944 to a Battle of the Philippine Sea fought over a year later. That is worth a minimum of 1,350 aircraft. The slow speed of the 'jeep carriers' need be no handicap in the event of a Spruance-style defence. In the mother of all carrier battles to come, their role will be interior defence. They don't have the speed to pursue. Their guarding presence, on the other hand, increases the temptation for Halsey to charge east or west with his fast fleet carriers, for with that swarm of aircraft aboard the American escort carriers, any Japanese massed attack on Saipan shipping can expect at best a Pyrrhic victory, if victory at all.

Here in Phantom time, August 1945, Halsey has chosen as his flagship the brand-new battleship *Missouri*, the president's home state, for by this time Franklin Delano Roosevelt is dead and Vice-President Harry S. Truman has assumed FDR's mantle. Halsey's long-time air chief,

Admiral Marc Mitscher, houses himself and his staff on board the Essex-class carrier *Shangri La*. And therein lies a story. When asked at a press conference whence General Jimmy Doolittle's bombers had flown for their April 1942 raid on Tokyo, President Roosevelt was constrained for security reasons from answering that they embarked from United States Navy aircraft carriers. He had, however, enjoyed reading James Hilton's *Lost Horizons*. The plot of that bestselling novel was about a mystery Tibetan monastery. The president's response was 'from Shangri La', for so the monastery was called. This carrier actually performed as Admiral McCain's flagship in the First Kure Raid in March 1945, close to three years after the Doolittle Raid. General Doolittle's wife was chosen to break the bottle at the launch and naming ceremony.

We permit to join the order of battle eleven of the fourteen Essex-class carriers that were combat available by August 1945. Three others are excluded on grounds of attrition in the course of operations in the Mandates, in particular the big raid on Truk, because both the *Lexington II* and *Intrepid* had missed the actual Battle of the Philippine Sea due to torpedo damage. Given rougher passage in Phantom time, we add the *Bunker Hill*. In reality, the IJN did not expose its fast fleet carriers until the Philippine Sea, so that is also assumed for Phantom time, and consequently there is no interim damage to them.

In addition, there remain in play the two survivors from the pre-war fleet, the *Saratoga* and *Enterprise*, which we have permitted to come through the Seychelles and Socotra.

Add also twelve light fleet carriers. Of these, eight are Independence-class conversions from light cruiser hulls, the ninth being the name ship of the class also damaged in the Mandates. The other four are Wright-class conversions from heavy cruiser hulls on the stocks. In reality, two of these became available after the war ended. We fast-forward four of the class as a response to the US becoming aware of the pace of Japanese construction. A conversion could be ready within a year, whereas a large fleet carrier took far longer. We see six carrier task forces fielding 250 aircraft each, or 1,500 in all.

Add then Britain's contribution of six armoured flight deck carriers of much the same size as the Essex-class for another 300 planes. We don't add any of their light fleet carriers, as none of these had reached the combat zone by August 1945.

In toto, Halsey and Mitscher, his tactical commander of carriers, will have under their orders 3,150 combat aircraft. Whereas this is close to what the IJN can muster between their carrier fleet and naval land-based aerial forces for the mother of all air battles, there are qualitative advantages on the American side. One, importantly, is concentration. For another, their aircraft models are better at this stage of the war. Vitally, American radar and combat control centres prove far superior to anything the Japanese can deploy. Anti-aircraft guns, always superior to those of the enemy, are armed now with deadly close-proximity-fuse ammunition. They will have consequently a greater advantage overall in defence. The American carriers are also far more difficult to sink or knock out compared to the Japanese.

The compulsion now in Washington is to demand of the Pacific Fleet that it brings on the big fight before the patience of the public evaporates. The timing may not be perfect in terms of superiority, but the need is political. Hitler is dead and the Soviets about to come into the war against Japan. And the atom bomb indeed is ready. Aboard the invasion fleet are fifty bulldozers, ready to lengthen airstrips for the Superfortresses. Earmarked in particular is the flatter island of Tinian, from which the four-engined *Enola Gay*, the quaintly named raptor of the nuclear age, historically took off for Hiroshima.

The sailors aboard the Phantom Fleet may not suspect it, but they will have to triumph in the Battle of the Marianas or Japan will lose the war. Their leaders realize that only too well, which is why the whole IJN is committed to battle.

But before we lead the Phantom Fleet into its final battle, let us consider that the outcome will depend as much upon the play of three special factors as on plans for attack and defence and weight of numbers.

The Rogue Factors

The reader will have become aware in the course of his reading of this book how in the new air-sea warfare between carrier fleets, the best-laid plans found themselves exposed to rogue factors that proved their undoing. In theory they could be anticipated and provided for in planning, but in practice all too often inadequately so and all too much susceptible to circumstance. Our rogue factors are examples of what were famously described by Clausewitz as the 'frictions' of war, his best-remembered example of friction in the case of the land armies of his Napoleonic era being simply mud. For the Pacific War naval context, flag reconnaissance, intelligence and oil supply. We shall assess them one by one.

The Japanese attributed their catastrophic defeat at Midway to many things, but for Genda it was principally the failure to mount an effective dawn search towards the arc within which the American ambush force lurked. The lesson of the Battle of the Coral Sea had not been absorbed; there, both sides lamentably failed to pass the 'recce test'. What seems so astonishing about deficiencies in reconnaissance is how pre-war opinion assumed that the side which sighted the enemy without a reciprocal sighting could expect to wipe out the opposing carriers at no cost to themselves, given how extremely vulnerable aircraft carriers were. Midway was the supreme example in confirmation of the theory. As at Coral Sea, on the first day of battle there came a close call for Admiral Fletcher.

The Japanese learnt from these experiences, the Americans far less so, such that in the great Battle of the Philippine Sea two years after Midway, there was failure in the decisive early stage to pinpoint where Admiral Ozawa's Mobile Fleet lay out there to the west. In contrast, Ozawa's scout planes found each end of Admiral Spruance's 40-mile-wide box. It might have helped had there been a carrier-to-carrier battle between the time of Santa Cruz and the Phillippine Sea. At Santa Cruz, American reconnaissance performed quite well, as did Japanese. The result was a ding-dong, both sides sighting and attacking each other simultaneously. But for the IJN, there remained the nightmare of Midway.

We weight therefore the art of reconnaissance as an IJN advantage in the Battle of the Marianas that in Phantom time is to come.

Our next rogue factor is intelligence. There is a twist here. Whereas the Japanese never broke naval codes, like all navies they practised radio traffic analysis and they were rather good at it. In traffic analysis, you gather the volume of radio transmissions and plot their patterns, in order to gain warning of trouble brewing. Previously recorded patterns resulted in known outcomes. From those outcomes can be predicted the possible or probable outcome of the volume pattern incoming at the present.

The Japanese never woke up to the fact that their codes were being read. On the other hand, there was the problem that the Yanks appeared to be rather too adept at traffic analysis for comfort. So how could the Japanese deny them access? By using the telephone instead was the simple answer. This could only be at one location, the fleet anchorages in home waters, namely inside the safe zone of the Inland Sea and with ships at anchor. Without radio traffic from the Inland Sea bases, the US codebreakers in Oahu would be denied traffic analysis and the call signs of the new carrier divisions training their air crews there.

The practice then was to use land bases for training. Planes and carriers only came together for brief periods in order to practise landings and take-offs when radio disciplines could be observed. The result, predictably, will be that US naval intelligence underestimates total IJN carrier strength in Phantom time August 1945, and in particular will underplay any threat from the north, where Genda's own forces cunningly muster.

Weight the arts of intelligence as a US Navy advantage in the contest to come, but with a rogue Japanese twist in hand.

The next rogue factor is oil supply and delivery. We might be criticized for not citing logistics as a whole, rather than just oil. The masterpiece on US logistics for the Pacific War is the delightfully entitled *Beans, Bullets and Black Oil* by W.R. Carter. Supply of these three commodities so brilliantly to the US Navy and the Marines was what won the war as much as raising the flag on Iwo Jima and sinking almost the entire Japanese Navy. Supply of bullets and beans are plannables, as notionally in black oil. However, in the tight frame of carrier battles, the circumstances of replenishing oil fuel to the carriers and their escorts proved influential on tactical outcomes.

Here we remind readers of Von Moltke's celebrated caveat that the best-laid plans seldom survive first contact with the enemy. If you know the enemy plans and they know your plans, then rogue factors are in abeyance. But what happens when both sides are bound in the fog of war? Much of the time, fuel surely is not going to be in the right place at the right time and when most needed.

The reader will already have an appreciation of the importance of reconnaissance and intelligence to tactical outcomes in the Pacific War, but we have only dropped hints in the case of oil supply as a rogue factor. We need a digression. First, how was oil supplied and how was it delivered?

In reality, for the Leyte Gulf landings in the Philippines the US mustered a massive fleet of navy oilers and mercantile tankers. Obsolete tankers were anchored at Ulithi atoll. Five months before this, the locations had been further down the line of advance at Kwajalein and Eniwetok atolls as floating oil tanks. Their total capacity varied around half a million barrels.

Once the war moved on, the tankers could advance with it to the next supply anchorage up the line. Sending a mobile oil well along in the trail of the combat fleet was far faster and handier than building tank farms ashore. To sustain operations during the Leyte campaign, thirty-four fleet oilers grouped in ten or twelve task units were concentrated in order to fuel the fleet in echelons. Within easy distance of the fleet was grouped a forward force of nine to twelve tankers as a central rendezvous point; in other words, about a third of the whole fleet oiler strength sat upfront. Trundling back and forth from the floating oil tanks at Ulithi was a shuttle of resupply echelons, usually of three fully loaded navy oilers at a time. Emptied oilers joined the escort back to Ulithi for a fill-up.

Here we come to a blind spot in IJN planning: they never twigged how it might be more decisive to go for the oilers as a way of disabling carrier and invasion fleet operations. The first great missed chance had been the failure to set ablaze the oil tank farms at Pearl Harbor. As the war unfolded, the IJN's target priority after carriers was always transports. It could far better have been oilers and tankers. Imagine if the Japanese carriers pounced on that forward fleet of navy oilers, and if submarines straddled the resupply line to it.

Morison, in his classic history of the Pacific War, put a finger on this in his volume on the Marianas. He cited how almost the only success of Japanese land-based attack during the Battle of the Philippine Sea occurred when just five Japanese bombers hit all three of a slow-moving navy oiler echelon 40 miles south-east of Mount Tapotchau on Saipan. The IJN raiders had been looking to the south-east of the island for the US carriers, which were actually west of Saipan. To the south-east they happened upon this refuelling echelon sheltering inadequately from exposure to battle. As a result, in subsequent campaigns, refuelling was conducted outside Japanese air range, albeit that this entailed greater to-and-fro time for refuelling combat units. That was a measure of the shock when the oilers *Saranac*, *Neshanic* and *Saugatuck* were attacked.

Consider how a dagger had crossed the jugular. Imagine if the greatest armada in history ran out of gas and was left high and dry at Saipan. In Phantom time, that will become Genda's goal.

Thus, weight the art of oil supply logistics as a US Navy advantage, but reckon that by 1945 the IJN might see the light in terms of having a potential new target, even a new strategy.

* * *

The reader has now been presented with everything they may need for gaming their own Battle of the Marianas for possible outcomes. They have the ships, the planes, the admirals and their men, they know the geography and some strategy, have learnt the tactical gambits, and finally we have apprised them of the upset factors.

We propose one final denouement, albeit with variations. Let us start with the approach phase.

The line of approach of the American armada to the Marianas will be the wide corridor between Japanese bases at Truk and at Marcus atoll to the north. From each, long-range four-engine Emily flying boats – by now equipped with radar – can hardly miss the massive forces on the move west from the forward anchorages at Eniwetok and Kwajalein. Sure, these American forces may fork south-west for Yap or Woleai, but why go for less when you can go for more, for those islands are mere staging posts to the Marianas. So Saipan in the Marianas it will be; the Marianas are in Superfortress range of Tokyo.

Thanks to air reconnaissance, there will be no American surprise; the Japanese thereby gain a day or two for mustering their forces.

On the other hand, almost as soon as their forces sail forth from their various anchorages, some are detected by scouting US submarines. Halsey knows he can now expect the mother of all carrier battles.

Ozawa's Southern Force is spotted debouching from Tawi Tawi by submarine USS *Harder*. Yamamoto's Western Force is spotted by USS *Flying Fish* filing out through the San Bernardino Strait into the Philippine Sea somewhat later.

In Japanese home waters, Genda's Eastern Force makes a quick start but is also spotted, which he realizes from picking up the nearby radio transmission of USS *Archerfish*. He orders his Plan B to be followed.

Instead of his whole fleet working its way south and then to the east in order to cut off the invasion forces from their supply chain, a carrier division called Northern Force under Rear Admiral Obayashi is peeled off for an approach southward and then with a cut to the west.

Genda swings his other three divisions wide towards Marcus Island, keeping well outside American long-range air reconnaissance. He hopes to achieve surprise this way while tempting Halsey to slew off fast carrier forces in pursuit of Obayashi instead. Obayashi's instructions are to join up with Yamamoto in the Philippine Sea, in order to add further allure to its decoy role while also augmenting its hitting power. By taking the long way around to the east, hopefully unobserved, Genda gives more time for Halsey to be tempted into a lunge west into the Philippine Sea to bag Yamamoto. The plan depends upon fooling the American into believing Western Force is the main force and that Obayashi is the sole threat from the homeland quarter.

Ozawa's southerly approach will be to skirt Yap to the east initially, before altering course to a point south-east of Guam. This is well outside American air reconnaissance range from Eniwetok. Should the Americans move flying boats up to Saipan, such scouts will expose themselves to fighters based on Yap. In any case, most will be ranging out west into the Philippine Sea seeking Yamamoto.

Yamamoto has chosen to lead Western Force in order to exercise overall control of all forces, those at sea being constrained to observe radio silence, with the exception of his Western Force which needs to give its position away if it is to decoy fast carrier covering forces away from the American invasion shipping.

He reckons one such transmission will be to the other Japanese carrier forces and to land-based air groups to stage a joint counter-strike on Saipan. In practice, this is recognized as giving a cue in particular for Ozawa to move in closer and attack the American fleet carriers with his elite air groups.

Genda has asked for more leeway. He likens his role to that of Jeb Stuart, the Confederate cavalry general in the American Civil War, who rode around the rear of the Union's Army of the Potomac on many occasions, wrecking their supply lines. His less experienced air groups may find themselves challenged attacking American carrier forces, but may find easier meat east of Saipan, and even locate and sink much of the oiler fleet.

In that event, both the invasion fleet and much of the carrier support forces may find themselves 'out of gas' and barely able to evacuate.

On the Allied side, Halsey has every intention of lunging out at the Japanese carriers. His plan is to rely on his fifty-four escort carriers and the British carrier task force for his close-in defence of the beachhead and his shore defences-bombarding battleships. Either one of two things can happen. If the Japanese plan succeeds, only Western Force will initially betray its line of approach and be pinpointed ready for attack. If it goes awry, Halsey will see himself beset by up to four forces approaching from four different directions. Will he hunker down around Saipan or sally forth? And which of the four will he sally forth against?

During the early Japanese approach stage in the actual Battle of the Philippine Sea, Admiral Spruance found time to push two task forces north to raid Chichi Jima, the staging point for land-based air reinforcements from the homeland, before pulling them back in time to meet the Japanese carrier fleet. He had not the resources on hand to intercept land-based air forces from the south, as the feed lines were many and the staging posts were under constant attack from US Army Air Force bombers from southern air bases anyway. These could not reach Chichi Jima. We propose that Halsey does now have sufficient force on hand to at least blanket both Chichi Jima and Yap with carrier air strikes. He allots two carrier task groups north and south to each, holding the remaining two to the west of Saipan.

Thus, in the late approach stage, Halsey is already well strung out, but wisely pulls his horns in on receiving news of the submarine sightings of Japanese fleets on their way to him. Many Japanese planes are caught on the ground at both staging locations, but not the groups to be staged in from further afield. These are ordered to remain out of harm's way until the signal comes from Yamamoto for general attack.

Aware that the Americans are concentrating again, Yamamoto sees his cue here for baiting Halsey by mounting a morning raid against his fleet carriers in front of Saipan in the hope of drawing him into the wastes of the Philippine Sea, in order to give Ozawa and Genda a clear run on the invasion shipping. Genda has already begun to harry shipping on the east side of Saipan, for it is here that he expects to uncover oiler echelon rendezvous positions and catch incoming refresher echelons.

Halsey now has a new temptation; a second toreador has entered the ring, and this one threatens his lifeline to the rear. His aggression is being drawn two ways at once. Meanwhile, yet to reveal itself is Ozawa's force with the elite of Japanese naval aviation aboard the most experienced set of carriers.

The reader might say that for Japan the battle has been won in the approach stage, the rest a foregone conclusion; the Phantom Fleet will have proved worthwhile. It is the case we have been attempting to make, after all.

On the other hand, there is much that can still go right for the Allies. So let us consider a number of outcome options following on from the approach stage.

We begin with the most perfect scenario for Yamamoto and his fleet commanders.

Variant A: 'A Bonfire of the Vanities'

'Bull' Halsey does what he is supposed to do, that of course being circumstantial.

He splits his fast carrier forces east and west, sallying forth against both Yamamoto in the west and Genda to the north-east, leaving just the escort carrier groups and the Royal Navy task force at Saipan in defence. Ozawa then strikes them from the south-east. Genda finds the oiler rendezvous location. When he comes under attack from Halsey, he breaks radio silence to give the land bases the co-ordinates for the oilers. Meanwhile, he retreats east within range of the US oil resupply echelons before breaking off for Truk.

The other half of Halsey's forces blunt their sword against Yamamoto's superior range differential and sturdy defence. The oil supply crisis then takes charge; which ships should be kept going, which put out to anchor? Finally, there is Saipan itself. It was a tough enough nut for US troops to crack in June and July 1944, yet so much more so over a year later, with the mountainous island now as fortified as Okinawa. The supply problem could come as the final straw and the Marines and GIs have to be evacuated.

This Japanese naval victory coincides with Russia entering the war and invading Manchuria. In Japan, the IJN has triumphed, while the IJA has been defeated and is discredited. Yamamoto becomes prime minister with a mission to negotiate peace. Always the realist, he is prepared to give back all that has been taken in exchange for a Greater East Asia trade zone and a year or two for orderly accomplishment.

In return, Korea, Formosa, Okinawa, the Marianas (less Guam), Yap and Palau stay Japanese, excluding anything east of the Mandates, but all at the price of three years more in China on a stabilizing basis, the withdrawal being arranged in liaison with America.

This is all well and good for the emperor, we aver, except that the reader will recall Clausewitz knocking on the door with his quote at the outset of the chapter. Fate and the unexpected indeed have been ignored. Thus, our alternate outcome, as follows.

Variant B: 'A Close-Run Thing'

Fate can usually expect to put in its ironic appearances, frequently in the most likely forms.

Thus, what if defective American reconnaissance modes play true to form, and neither Yamamoto's larger decoy Western Force nor Obayashi's smaller decoy Northern Force are sighted from the air?

Whilst it is known that a substantial fleet has entered the Philippine Sea from the west, thanks to the submarine sighting as it debouched from the San Bernardino Strait, it is difficult afterwards – at the extreme range of American air reconnaissance and from spotty submarine reconnaissance – to locate exactly where on that vast body of water it will roam. Also to be considered is how that enlarged the arc of threat in the special circumstances of the Phantom Scenario; that is now a full circle, 360 degrees, given how the IJN fleets will be approaching from four directions.

There are delays, therefore, in attacking Yamamoto. Next comes awareness of a Japanese fleet threatening the other flank when Genda raids shipping to the east of Saipan. Once happy that Yamamoto's raid on his own carriers has been more or less massacred and the threat from the west thereby neutered, Halsey hares off east in pursuit of Genda in order to clear the line of supply. Ozawa, of course, will then strike the invasion shipping but fall afoul of all the escort carriers and the British fleet. Halsey, after chasing away Genda, will still have the strength meantime for a counter-strike against Ozawa.

It will have been a tough fight, and therefore a victory that the Duke of Wellington would have termed 'a close-run thing', but nonetheless a Waterloo for Halsey and the birth date for a *Pax Americana* on the world's oceans.

Afterword

The Ironies of Mars

The gods of antiquity were renowned in myth for their capriciousness. It was warned how those the gods wish to destroy they first turn proud, in some renditions driving them bananas. The god of war was no exception to the rule. To be tempted into playing with Mars is to be played with by Mars. Warmongers can well heed the dread message screeched at Julius Caesar by an Etruscan soothsayer in the Roman forum: 'Beware the Ides of March!'

In our account of the countdown to war for the mastery of the Pacific, it seems often that irony is heaped upon irony like mountains upon each other, Pelion piled upon Ossa as the Greek analogy goes.

The supreme irony is how the Pearl Harbor raid woke a sleeping giant and turned an isolationist nation into the global superpower it is today. While militarily the raid can be claimed to have been something of a waste of time, politically it was one of the decisive events of a tumultuous century.

The corollary to this irony is how America could never have become this superpower without the Imperial Japanese Navy's existence and consequent challenge. Almost totally wiped out by the end of the war, Japan then became a contender for the largest merchant fleet in the world, largely because slipways and construction docks were freed for building the super tankers that transformed post-war oil transport.

The lesser irony is how the world in the countdown to war was striving to forge a new generation of battleships, while aircraft carriers were an afterthought in comparison. None of the new US battleships were ready yet for the Pacific, and the new Essex-class carriers not until deep into 1943.

Mercifully for Roosevelt, the existing Pacific Fleet carriers were absent on aircraft-ferrying missions on 7 December 1941. What Pearl Harbor did was force both sides to fight with aircraft carriers. For each at first there was in reality only enough fuel for the cavalry, not for the heavy infantry. And that is what the ocean war became, the naval equivalent of a cavalry war.

The only battleship engagements of note in the Pacific War saw a pair of brand-new American battleships sink a First World War-era Japanese battlecruiser re-tread off Guadalcanal, and five Pearl Harbor re-treads – albeit with the help of destroyers – sink the two oldest of Japan's battleships at Leyte Gulf. The vaunted Japanese super-battleships were never to fire on any American battleship.

There were also ironies at the tactical level, supremely so at the Battle of Midway, where the Japanese innovation of mass co-ordinated strikes of dive bombers and torpedo attack planes well escorted by fighters should have won the battle for the IJN. Instead, it was won by a tragically unco-ordinated American strike which in its final moments haphazardly came together and won the day. Its success also prevented a mass co-ordinated strike by the IJN carriers, three being knocked out and the fourth thereby lacking another carrier's torpedo planes to accompany its dive bombers. The reader should enjoy for further ironies *Shattered Sword*, the splendid eye-opener on Midway by Jonathan Parshall and Anthony Tully.

In Orwell's *1984*, the world becomes divided into three warring superpowers: Eurasia, East Asia and Oceania. Orwell lived through the pre-war period, and of course the Second World War, when geographical 'new orders' of nations were the rage. There were antecedents of a sort, such as America's Monroe Doctrine, which sought a protective hegemony over the whole Western Hemisphere – Orwell's Oceania when bits of Britannia are added. The late nineteenth century's American credo, 'Manifest Destiny', inspired the notion of the new order. Thus, Matsuoka and Prince Konoye's Greater East Asia Co-Prosperity Sphere was to be guided by Japanese manifest destiny.

Vague as that prosperity sphere was defined, it could be adapted, on the hoof as it were, and not necessarily from Tokyo. Post-war events conspired to bring its hypocritical anti-colonialism credentials to fruition thanks to the break-up of the European empires and the post-war Japanese economic miracle.

In the course of writing I was reminded of the opening of the Book of Ecclesiastes: 'Vanity of vanities, saith the Preacher, all is vanities.' Thus, irony of ironies, all is ironies.

Index